Santa Fe

Lite & Spicy
Recipe

Lighter, healthier recipes from Santa Fe's renowned chefs

by
Joan Stromquist

Tierra Publications

Tierra Publications
2801 Rodeo Road
Suite B-612
Santa Fe, New Mexico 87505
(505) 983-6300

Other books in this series by Joan Stromquist:
Santa Fe Recipe
Taos Recipe
Southern California Beach Recipe

Additional copies may be obtained by contacting Tierra Publications. For your convenience, order forms are included in the back of the book.

Cover design by James Finnell
Chama Graphics
Santa Fe, New Mexico

Drawings by Larry Caldwell
Albuquerque, New Mexico

Library of Congress Catalog Card Number:
91-67972

ISBN: 0-9622807-2-0

Printed in the United States of America

Author's Notes

The making of this book required the creative energies of many talented people. In particular I wish to thank James Finnell for his vibrant cover painting, and La Fonda Hotel for allowing him to use their beautiful patio restaurant, La Terraza, as his inspiration. Also, I am indebted to Larry Caldwell for his innovative line drawings that delightfully capture the flavor of the Southwest.

But my most special thanks go to the chefs of Santa Fe who so generously provided me with these outstanding recipes. Their creativity, intelligence, and good humor made writing this book a pleasure.

These recipes are SPICY! That is, they are full of strong, zesty flavors, which does not always mean chile pepper "hot". The chefs' comments often include information on the "heat" of a dish, and how to increase or decrease it.

Each recipe is designed to be as healthy as possible, without sacrificing the integrity of the dish. Although this is not a health food cookbook, you will find the majority of recipes to be low in saturated fats, cholesterol, salt, and sugar. In many cases the chefs' comments suggest substitutions and changes in the recipe to make it even "lighter". You, the reader, are also encouraged to use healthy substitutions as you see fit.

However, I do confess that there are a few recipes, particularly in the dessert section, that are fairly rich and cannot be called "light". These are included in the book for two reasons. First, they are delicious! Second, the chefs and I reasoned that each serving is very small, so the total amount of "bad" ingredients consumed is minimal. I hope that the readers will forgive this slight deviation from the theme of the book and view these recipes as scrumptious "splurges".

For those of you who do not have access to many of the Southwestern ingredients called for in the recipes, several mail order soruces are listed under Supplemental Information on page 328.

Joan Stromquist

Restaurant Addresses

Adobo Catering
807 2nd Street
Santa Fe, NM 87501
(505) 989-7674

Alfredo's Restaurant
High Mesa Inn
3347 Cerrillos Road
Santa Fe, NM 87501
(505) 473-9515

Bishop's Lodge
Bishop's Lodge Road
Santa Fe, NM 87501
(505) 983-6377

Cafe Pasqual's
121 Don Gaspar
Santa Fe, NM 87501
(505) 983-9340

Casa Sena
125 E. Palace
Santa Fe, NM 87501
(505) 988-9232

Celebrations
613 Canyon Road
Santa Fe, NM 87501
(505) 989-8904

Chez What
213 W. Alameda
Santa Fe, NM 87501
(505) 982-0099

ek mas
319 Guadalupe
Santa Fe, NM 87501
(505) 989-7121

El Farol
808 Canyon Road
Santa Fe, NM 87501
(505) 983-9912

The Evergreen
Hyde Park Road
Santa Fe, NM 87501
(505) 984-8190

423
423 W. San Francisco
Santa Fe, NM 87501
(505) 982-1552

Francisco's
St. Francis Hotel
210 Don Gaspar
Santa Fe, NM 87501
(505) 982-8787

Galisteo Inn
HC 75, Box 4
Galisteo, NM 87540
(505) 982-1506

Garfield Grill
322 Garfield
Santa Fe, NM 87501
(505) 988-9562

Geronimo Lodge
724 Canyon Road
Santa Fe, NM 87501
(505) 982-1500

Grant Corner Inn
122 Grant
Santa Fe, NM 87501
(505) 983-6678

Guadalupe Cafe
313 Guadalupe
Santa Fe, NM 87501
(505) 982-9762

India Palace
227 Don Gaspar
Santa Fe, NM 87501
(505) 986-5859

Inn at Loretto
211 Old Santa Fe Trail
Santa Fe, NM 87501
(505) 988-5531

Inn of the Anasazi
113 Washington
Santa Fe, NM 87501
(505) 988-3030

Julian's
221 Shelby
Santa Fe, NM 87501
(505) 988-2355

La Traviata
95 W. Marcy Street
Santa Fe, NM 87501
(505) 984-1091

The Natural Cafe
1494 Cerrillos Road
Santa Fe, NM 87501
(505) 983-1411

Ogelvies
150 Washington
Santa Fe, NM 87501
(505) 988-3855

Old House
309 W. San Francisco
Santa Fe, NM 87501
(505) 988-4455

Old Mexico Grill
2434 Cerrillos Road
Santa Fe, NM 87501
(505) 473-0338

Ore House
50 Lincoln Avenue
Santa Fe, NM 87501
(505) 983-8687

The Palace
142 W. Palace
Santa Fe, NM 87501
(505) 982-9892

Paul's Restaurant of Santa Fe
72 W. Marcy Street
Santa Fe, NM 87501
(505) 982-8738

Peppers Restaurant
2239 Old Pecos Trail
Santa Fe, NM 87505
(505) 984-2272

Piñon Grill
100 Sandoval
Santa Fe, NM 87501
(505) 988-2811

Pontchartrain
319 Guadalupe
Santa Fe, NM 87501
(505) 983-0626

Pranzo Italian Grill
540 Montezuma
Santa Fe, NM 87501
(505) 984-2645

Rancho Encantado
Route 4, Box 57C
Santa Fe, NM 87501
(505) 982-3537

Santa Fe School of Cooking
116 W. San Francisco
Santa Fe, NM 87501
(505) 983-4511

Santacafe
231 Washington
Santa Fe, NM 87501
(505) 984-1788

Steaksmith
Old Las Vegas Highway
Santa Fe, NM 87505
(505) 988-3333

Swiss Bakery
320 Guadalupe
Santa Fe, NM 87501
(505) 988-3737

Wild Oats Market
1090 S. St. Francis Drive
Santa Fe, NM 87501
(505) 983-5333

Zia Diner
326 Guadalupe
Santa Fe, NM 87501
(505) 988-7008

Table of Contents

Food Categories

Appetizers

Soups

Salads

Salad Dressings

Sauces, Dips, & Condiments

Eggs, Cheese, & Vegetarian

10

Pasta

Fish & Shellfish

Potpourri

Desserts

Restaurant Table of Contents

Santa Fe
Lite & Spicy
Recipe

Appetizers

Spicy Shrimp Cocktail with Chipotle Chile Vinaigrette 22
Southwestern Chicken Filo Triangles 23
Lime Garlic Shrimp with Mango Mint Salsa 24
Tuna Ceviche in Lettuce Wrappers 25
Lamb Quesadillas with Pico de Gallo 26
Grilled Chicken and Roasted Pepper Pizza 27
Moroccan Eggplant with Cilantro Pesto 28
Sautéed Wild Mushrooms and Polenta 30
Oaxacan Mango with Citrus Salsa 31
Sea Scallop Sauté in Herbed Olive Oil 32
Marinated Oriental Chicken Strips 33
Broiled Sea Scallops with Sun-Dried Tomato Basil and Grand Marnier Cilantro Sauces 34
Blue Crab with Mustard Greens and Cucumbers, with Gazpacho Dressing 36
Grilled Mozzarella and Roma Tomatoes with Arugula Pesto 37
Black Bean Terrine with Pesto Pumpkin Seed Vinaigrette 38
Peruvian Skewered Beef 39
Tuna Yakatori 40
Shrimp Rémoulade 41
Southwestern Smoked Salmon Sushi with Refried Black Bean Paste and Roasted Tomato Sauce . . 42
Eggplant Caviar with Chipotle Oil 44
Roast Peppers and Fresh Mozzarella Cheese 45
Duck and Red Chile Won Tons with Ginger Soy Dipping Sauce 46
Sausage and White Bean Pizza 47

Spicy Shrimp Cocktail with Chipotle Chile Vinaigrette

Spicy Shrimp Cocktail

2   cups water
2   cups beer
1   lemon, halved
1   lime, halved
1   teaspoon fennel seeds
1   teaspoon chile pequin (hot red chile flakes)
1   tablespoon garlic powder
1   teaspoon salt
30   jumbo shrimp, shelled and deveined
     Chipotle Chile Vinaigrette (recipe follows)

In a large pot place all of the ingredients (except for the shrimp and Chipotle Chile Vinaigrette). Bring the liquid to a boil on high heat. Add the shrimp and bring the liquid to a boil again. Remove the shrimp with a slotted spoon.

On each of 6 individual serving plates spread on the Chipotle Chile Vinaigrette. Artfully arrange the shrimp on top.

serves 6

Chipotle Chile Vinaigrette

4   cloves garlic
1   small can chipotle chile peppers in adobo sauce
1   cup tomatoes, diced
2   tablespoons fresh oregano
1   teaspoon fresh mint leaves
1   tablespoon Dijon mustard
2   cups red wine vinegar
1   teaspoon salt
½   teaspoon black pepper
3   cups olive oil

In a food processor place all of the ingredients (except for the olive oil) and purée them together. With the food processor still running, slowly dribble in the olive oil.

makes approximately 1½ quarts

Southwestern Chicken Filo Triangles

"A lot of people are intimidated by filo dough, but it is not as scary to work with as you think. If you follow this recipe (which, by the way, tastes fantastic!), you will be pleasantly surprised by how well it works. It's better if two people work together to make this dish, but one person can do it as well. Once the filo triangles are made you should put them on a plate, cover them with a damp paper towel, and store them in the refrigerator until you are ready to use them. Or, you can freeze them, which is great, because then they can be made way ahead of time. One word of warning.....if you get frustrated while working with the filo dough, don't fall to temptation and stand there eating all of the chicken filling by yourself!"

"This is a really scrumptious hors d'oeuvre. If you want to serve it as an entrée, then cut the filo dough into 4 sections so that the triangles will be larger. Make 4 or 5 of them per serving."

Sylvia Johnson
Celebrations

2	whole chicken breasts, cooked, skin and bones removed, shredded, and chopped
½	cup Monterey Jack cheese, grated
1	red bell pepper, seeded and finely chopped
4	Roma tomatoes, peeled, seeded, and chopped
1	small can Ortega green chile peppers (hot), diced
1	tablespoon fresh cilantro, finely minced
1	16-ounce package filo dough, thawed in the refrigerator, and cut crosswise into 5 equal sections
1	cup butter (or as needed), melted
	Corn Relish (recipe on page 113)
	Guacamole (recipe on page 171)

In a medium bowl place the chicken, cheese, red bell peppers, Roma tomatoes, green chile peppers, and cilantro. Mix the ingredients together well.

Preheat the oven to 400°.

For each section of the filo dough (cover the other sections with a slightly damp cloth and keep them in the refrigerator), separate the pieces and lay them out flat on a large surface (work quickly). Brush all of the pieces with the melted butter. Turn them over and brush the other side.

Place a teaspoon of the chicken mixture at one end of each piece of dough. Fold the bottom left corner over the filling so that the bottom edge lines up with the side edge. Continue to fold the dough up in this manner (as you would fold a flag), so that a multi-folded triangle is formed. Keep the completed triangles under a damp cloth.

On an oiled baking sheet, place the filo triangles and bake them for 20 minutes, or until they are a golden brown.

Serve the triangles with the Corn Relish and Guacamole on the side.

makes 70 triangles

Lime Garlic Shrimp with Mango Mint Salsa

Lime Garlic Shrimp

1	lime, juiced
2	cloves garlic, crushed
1	teaspoon Chinese hot oil
½	teaspoon coarse grain salt
¼	teaspoon white pepper
12	large shrimp, shelled and deveined
	Mango Mint Salsa *(recipe follows)*

In a medium bowl place the lime juice, garlic, Chinese hot oil, salt, and white pepper. Mix the ingredients together. Add the shrimp and let them marinate for 45 minutes.

Grill the shrimp for 2 minutes on each side, or until they are just done. Serve the shrimp with the Mango Mint Salsa.

serves 4

Mango Mint Salsa

2	cups mango, diced
¾	cup red onions, finely minced
1	red bell pepper, seeded and diced
2	jalapeño chile peppers, seeded and diced
1	bunch fresh mint, chopped
1	lime, juiced

In a medium bowl place all of the ingredients. Chill the salsa in the refrigerator for 1 hour before serving it.

makes approximately 4 cups

"The marinade for this shrimp is really nice. The garlic, lime juice, and hot oil make the shrimp taste even more wonderful than they would by themselves, and the salsa adds the perfect touch."

"This salsa is really refreshing stuff. I would make a beverage out of it, like a mango-mint smoothie. Just imagine that rich, exotic mango flavor with the vibrancy of mint added to it.....it's truly wonderful! The addition of the onion and peppers change it from a sweet dish to a savory dish. Definitely pick a really ripe mango, because you want it to be nice and sweet so that the contrast against the other tastes is very strong. Other fruits can be used with this recipe. Pineapple is especially good."

"When I go to the supermarket I feel like my father when he goes to the hardware store. We both love to walk around and look at all of the great items for sale."

"To me, there are two approaches to cooking. One way is you read a recipe and then go out and buy the ingredients. The other way is to go out shopping, see what is available, and create the recipe from that. This is how I like to cook."

Robert Goodfriend
ek mas

Tuna Ceviche in Lettuce Wrappers

1	**pound tuna, cut into ½" cubes**
½	**cup lime juice, freshly squeezed**
1	**tablespoon orange juice, freshly squeezed**
1	**tablespoon lemon juice, freshly squeezed**
2	**tablespoons olive oil**
2	**serrano chile peppers, minced**
1	**small red onion, finely diced**
1	**medium tomato, finely diced**
½	**red bell pepper, seeded and finely diced**
½	**yellow bell pepper, seeded and finely diced**
½	**bunch fresh cilantro, chopped**
	salt *(to taste)*
4	**leaves red leaf lettuce, washed and dried**

In a medium bowl place the tuna, lime juice, orange juice, and lemon juice. Toss the ingredients together and then place them in the refrigerator. Let the tuna chill for 4 hours, or until it is opaque.

In another medium bowl place the olive oil, serrano chile peppers, red onions, tomatoes, red and yellow bell peppers, cilantro, and salt. Toss the ingredients together.

Add the mixture to the chilled tuna and toss the ingredients together.

On each of 4 individual salad plates place a red lettuce leaf. Spoon on the tuna ceviche and then carefully wrap it up in the lettuce.

serves 4

Lamb Quesadillas with Pico de Gallo

Lamb Quesadillas

⅔   cup smoked mozzarella cheese, grated
8   flour tortillas
20   ounces lamb loin, well trimmed, cooked medium rare, and
       cut into very thin strips
⅔   cup cheddar cheese, grated
⅔   cup Monterey Jack cheese, grated
6   ounces Ortega green chile strips
4   whole bulbs garlic, roasted *(see chef's comments on this page)*
       Pico de Gallo *(recipe on next page)*

For each quesadilla sprinkle the smoked mozzarella cheese on one flour tortilla. Place the strips of lamb on top. Sprinkle the cheddar cheese and Monterey Jack cheese on another tortilla. Place the green chile strips on top.

Heat a medium skillet on medium high. One at a time, place the two cheese-topped tortillas in the skillet, and heat them for 1 to 2 minutes, or until the cheese is melted.

Place the 2 tortillas on top of each other with the cheese sides facing in *(so that a "sandwich" is made)*. Repeat the process for the rest of the tortillas.

Cut the quesadillas into 6 wedges. Serve them with a roasted garlic bulb and some Pico de Gallo on the side.

serves 4

"Here is something very basic and simple to make, and if you like lamb, you will love this dish. It is so ordinary that I wonder how it can taste so good. I often am amazed when the simplest of dishes is more popular than complex recipes. When you heat the tortilla you don't want to use any oil, because it will get crispy and burn before the cheese melts."

"To roast the garlic you take the whole bulb, cut off the very top, pour on a little olive oil, and roast it in the oven for 30 minutes at 350°. The bulb spreads apart and you can pick out the little cloves with a fork, or pop them out with your fingers."

Frank Peña
Ogelvies

"This is one of our most popular appetizers. A whole bulb of roasted garlic comes out with each order. I have a lot of fun with the people who don't know what it is, and say, 'What the heck is this?' The garlic flavor is not raw and sharp.....rather, it is mellow and rich. You can play with it on your plate, because there still is skin on the individual cloves, and you have to pinch them out.....kind of how you get the meat out of crawfish."

Eric Sanders
Ogelvies

Pico de Gallo

1/8	**cup yellow onions, diced**
1/8	**cup scallions, diced**
1	**cup tomatoes, diced**
2	**jalapeño chile peppers, seeded and diced**
2	**teaspoons fresh garlic, minced**
1	**teaspoon fresh cilantro, chopped**
1	**tablespoon chile caribe** *(crushed red chile peppers)*
1	**lime, juiced**
	salt *(to taste)*

In a small bowl place all of the ingredients and mix them together well.

makes approximately 1 1/2 cups

Grilled Chicken and Roasted Pepper Pizza

2	**tablespoons olive oil**
1	**12" pizza dough round** *(recipe on page 299)*
1	**red bell pepper, roasted, seeded, and cut into thin strips** *(see chef's comments on page 159)*
6	**ounces chicken, skin and bones removed, grilled and sliced**
4	**ounces Fontina cheese, thinly sliced**

Preheat the oven to 450°.

Brush the olive oil on top of the pizza dough round. Lay on the roasted red bell pepper strips and the chicken slices. Lay the cheese slices on top.

Place the pizza on a flat sheet and bake it for 15 to 18 minutes, or until the cheese is hot and bubbly. Cut the pizza into 8 wedges.

serves 4

Moroccan Eggplant with Cilantro Pesto

Moroccan Eggplant

2   small eggplants
1   teaspoon vegetable oil
1   red bell pepper, roasted, peeled, seeded, and cut into thin strips *(see chef's comments on page 159)*
2   teaspoons fresh Italian parsley, chopped
¼   cup olive oil
    Cilantro Pesto *(recipe on next page)*
16   calamata olives

Preheat the oven to 375°.

Liberally pierce the eggplants with a fork. Place the vegetable oil on your hands and rub it all over the eggplants.

Place the eggplants on a baking sheet and roast them for 45 minutes. Turn them over with tongs, and cook them for 20 to 30 minutes more, or until they are soft but not dried up or burnt. Remove them from the oven and let them cool.

Peel the eggplants and remove most of the seeds with a fork *(without sacrificing the good meat)*. Chop the eggplants up into bite size pieces.

On each of 6 individual small serving plates place the eggplant. Place the roasted red bell pepper strips on top. Sprinkle on the parsley. Drizzle on the olive oil and place some of the Cilantro Pesto on top. Garnish the dish with the calamata olives.

serves 6 to 8

"This is a very tasty, easy to prepare Mediterranean appetizer. You want to oil the eggplants, just like they were going to get a suntan. Cook them long enough so that they are nice and soft and squishy. When you remove the seeds be careful that you don't ruin all of the flesh. This is good served with pita bread."

Ned Laventall
El Farol

Cilantro Pesto

1	**large bunch fresh cilantro, washed and thick stems removed**
¼	**cup lemon juice, freshly squeezed**
½	**cup olive oil**
½	**teaspoon ground cumin**
	salt *(to taste)*

In a food processor place the cilantro and purée it.

With the processor running, gradually add the lemon juice and olive oil so that a smooth paste is formed.

Add the cumin and salt, and mix them in.

makes 1½ to 2 cups

"If you have some fresh herbs, but you don't know how to use them all up before they go bad, then make them into a pesto, which is a method for preserving fresh herbs. We mix this pesto with some mayonnaise and sour cream, and toss it with cold pasta. It's also good just by itself with hot pasta and Parmesan cheese. Another good idea is to put a dollop in different soups that you make.....it's especially delicious in tomato soup."

Ned Laventall
El Farol

Sautéed Wild Mushrooms and Polenta

3	**cups chicken stock** *(recipe on page 295)*
1	**cup polenta**
1	**teaspoon salt**
1	**tablespoon red chile powder** *(hot)*
1	**tablespoon jalapeño cheese, grated**
2	**tablespoons butter**
2	**tablespoons olive oil**
2	**cups wild mushrooms, tough stems removed, wiped clean and sliced**
2	**tablespoons good dry sherry**
	salt *(to taste)*
1	**tablespoon olive oil** *(or as needed)*

In a medium saucepan place the chicken stock and bring it to a boil. Add the polenta and the 1 teaspoon of salt. Lower the heat and cook the polenta for 10 minutes *(stir it occasionally)*, or until it is stiff.

Add the red chile powder, jalapeño cheese, and butter, and stir them in. Let the polenta sit for 5 minutes.

Place the polenta on a flat surface and roll it out so that it is ¼" thick. Let it cool for 30 minutes.

Cut the polenta into shapes *(see chef's comments on this page)*. Place a smooth towel on top of a flat sheet. Place the polenta pieces on top of the towel, upside down. Chill the polenta in the refrigerator for 1 hour.

In a medium large sauté pan place the 2 tablespoons of olive oil and heat it on high until it is hot. Add the mushrooms and sauté them for 1 minute. Add the sherry. Reduce the heat to medium and sauté them for 2 minutes, or until they are tender, yet firm. Season the mushrooms with the salt.

In a large sauté pan place the 1 tablespoon of olive oil and heat it on medium high until it is hot. Add the pieces of polenta and sauté them for 5 minutes on each side, or until the outer edges are slightly brown.

On each of 4 individual plates place the pieces of polenta. Surround them with the sautéed mushrooms.

serves 4

"I have a cookie cutter that is shaped like a coyote, and I use it to cut out the pieces of polenta. The dough has an orange look because of the chile powder in it. Then, I use another cookie cutter to cut out a moon shape, and this dough has no red chile powder in it, so it's a yellow color. The coyote is difficult to turn over without breaking it.....it's best to use a flat griddle. You can cut the polenta into any shapes that you want, but I really like the Southwest look of this presentation."

"People in New Mexico seem to know a lot about wild mushrooms. They pick them wild and prepare them in many delicious ways. When you clean the mushrooms wipe them off with a damp paper towel. Don't wash them with water, because then they won't soak up the olive oil and sherry. If you use different kinds of mushrooms, then cut each kind into a different shape."

Tom Wright
Galisteo Inn

Oaxacan Mango with Citrus Salsa

Oaxacan Mango

4   ripe mangos
1   lime, cut into 4 wedges
4   sprigs fresh mint
    Citrus Salsa *(recipe follows)*

Set each mango on its end *(stem up)*, with the narrow side facing you. Slice off the two sides of the mango *(½" thick)*.

With a small, sharp knife score the flesh of each mango half in a grid pattern *(score the flesh as deeply as you can without piercing the skin)*. Hold the scored mango in your hand with the skin side down. Use your fingers to push up on the skin side so that the mango is turned inside out.

On each of 4 individual serving plates place two of the mango halves. Garnish the dish with a lime wedge and sprig of the mint. Serve the Citrus Salsa on the side.

serves 4

Citrus Salsa

6   tablespoons orange juice, freshly squeezed
2   tablespoons lime juice, freshly squeezed
1   teaspoon tabasco sauce
1   teaspoon kosher salt

In a small bowl place all of the ingredients and mix them together.

serves 4

"I got the idea for this recipe when I was in Mexico, where vendors sell fancily cut mangos that are impaled on a stick. You can buy one and stroll away eating it like a popsicle. This can be served for breakfast, as an appetizer, or for dessert. In the latter case I would omit the salsa and serve it with 2 lime wedges."

"Once I read that talent is the desire to express yourself. Food is a wonderful thing to express ourselves with, because it is an intimate part of our lives.....we are with it every day. Unfortunately, with so many convenience foods these days, and the popularity of microwave cooking, many people are forgetting the creative side of preparing food."

"I am a self-taught cook and my desire to learn is what drove me to be good. My mother was a fabulous cook, and when I was growing up she and my father had countless dinner parties. I remember by the age of 8, I had the official job of being the pantry chef."

Katharine Kagel
Cafe Pasqual's

Sea Scallop Sauté
in Herbed Olive Oil

Sea Scallop Sauté

12	medium sea scallops, washed, drained, and tough muscle removed
	salt *(to taste)*
	black pepper *(to taste)*
2	tablespoons olive oil
15	oyster mushrooms, finely chopped
3	shallots, finely chopped
2	tablespoons fresh parsley, finely chopped
6	large Roma tomatoes, skin removed, cut in half lengthwise, and seeds removed
	Herbed Olive Oil *(recipe on next page)*, **heated**
	salt *(to taste)*
	black pepper *(to taste)*
4	sprigs fresh basil
4	pieces crusty bread

Sprinkle the scallops with the salt and black pepper, and set them aside on paper towels.

In a medium sauté pan place the olive oil and heat it on medium until it is hot. Add the mushrooms, shallots, and parsley. Sauté the ingredients for 15 minutes, or until most of the moisture is gone. Set the pan aside so that the ingredients cool.

Fill the Roma tomato caps half full with the mushroom mixture.

In a large sauté pan place ¼ cup of the Herbed Olive Oil and heat it on medium high until it is hot. Add the scallops *(flat side down)*, and cover each one with a stuffed tomato cap *(stuffed side down)*. Sprinkle on the salt and black pepper. Cover the pan and cook the scallops for 3 to 4 minutes, or until they are done.

On each of 4 small, individual serving plates place 3 of the scallops topped with the tomato caps in a triangular pattern. Place a basil sprig in the center of the formation. Drizzle on some of the heated Herbed Olive Oil. Place a piece of crusty bread on the side.

serves 4

"Scallops are my favorite seafood dish, no matter how they are prepared. Once, over a period of several months, I had a friend over for dinner about 10 different times, and I always made a variation of this recipe. I would alter the ingredients slightly, until finally I came up with this version, which I think tastes best. I like the surprise element that you get from the presentation. At first, all you see are the tomato caps, which are swimming in olive oil with herbs. Then, when you cut into one, you see all of these other ingredients that you don't expect."

"When I was 3 years old my grandmother taught me about colors with M&Ms (it took me a long time to learn what blue, purple, and pink were because M&Ms don't come in those colors). She loved makeup, but wasn't allowed to wear it because of her religion. Still, I remember many times when, after my grandfather left for work, she would go upstairs to her dresser and pull out this little drawer that was full of different kinds of makeup. I would help her pick out the colors and she would make up her face, just for herself."

Jonathan Horst
Adobo Catering

Herbed Olive Oil

1	large garlic clove, pressed
24	fresh basil leaves, cut crosswise into ⅛" wide strips
½	cup olive oil

In a small saucepan place all of the ingredients. Heat them on low until they are warm.

makes approximately ⅔ cup

"I love to sop this herbed olive oil up with French bread. If you have any that is left over, you can use it to make a salad dressing. Also, it's delicious drizzled over grilled fish."

Jonathan Horst
Adobo Catering

Marinated Oriental Chicken Strips

4	whole chicken breasts, skin and bones removed, and cut into 1" wide strips
½	cup cornstarch
2	tablespoons canola oil
2	bunches fresh cilantro, chopped
2	bunches scallions, thinly sliced
1	tablespoon fresh ginger root, peeled and finely chopped
1	teaspoon chile pequin (hot red chile flakes)
1½	cups tamari
1	cup apple cider vinegar
¼	cup black sesame seeds

In a medium bowl place the chicken strips and cornstarch. Toss the chicken so that it is well coated.

In a large sauté pan place the canola oil and heat it on medium high until it is hot. Add the coated chicken strips and sauté them for 1 to 2 minutes, or until they are done.

In a medium large bowl place the sautéed chicken, cilantro, scallions, ginger root, chile pequin, tamari, and apple cider vinegar. Place the bowl in the refrigerator for ½ hour. Remove the chicken and strain it.

Toss the chicken with the black sesame seeds.

serves 6 to 8

"This is a great dish because it tastes wonderful and it couldn't be simpler to make. The combination of the tamari, cilantro, ginger, and red chile flakes is delicious. We flash-fry the chicken in canola oil, but you can bake it if you prefer. The taste won't change, but you will lose that delicious crispy, crunchy texture."

Lisa Sivé
Wild Oats Market

Broiled Sea Scallops with Sun-Dried Tomato Basil and Grand Marnier Cilantro Sauces

Broiled Sea Scallops

1   **teaspoon walnut oil** *(or as needed)*
1   **pound large sea scallops, cleaned**
      Sun-Dried Tomato Basil Sauce *(recipe on next page)*
      Grand Marnier Cilantro Sauce *(recipe on next page)*
4   **orange sections, membranes and seeds removed**
8   **leaves fresh cilantro**

In a small baking dish place the walnut oil. Spread it around so that the bottom is lightly coated. Place the sea scallops in the dish.

On ½ of the scallops brush on the Sun-Dried Tomato Basil Sauce. On the other half of the scallops brush on the Grand Marnier Cilantro Sauce.

Broil the scallops for 2 minutes. Turn them over and brush them again with the 2 sauces *(use the same sauce on this side as you did on the other side)*. Broil them for 2 minutes more, or until they are just done. Serve the scallops with the sauces poured on top *(make sure that you pour on the same sauce that you brushed on)*.

Garnish each serving with an orange segment and 2 cilantro leaves.

serves 4

"*Every week I have to come up with ideas for the specials on our menu and for our raw seafood bar..... and this is one of those creations. The two sauces really complement each other well and they both are delicious with the scallops. The flavors seep into the scallops and keep them moist. When you place the sauces on the plate they are next to each other, but when you eat them they tend to mix up together. This is a rather exotic appearing appetizer that is very easy to make. It's perfect to serve at a nice dinner party.*"

Jonathan Coady
Piñon Grill

Sun-Dried Tomato Basil Sauce

2	teaspoons olive oil
1	small clove garlic, minced
4	sun-dried tomatoes, reconstituted and chopped
⅓	cup red wine
4	large fresh basil leaves, chopped
1	teaspoon balsamic vinegar

In a small saucepan place the olive oil and heat it on medium until it is hot. Add the garlic and sun-dried tomatoes. Sauté them for 3 minutes, or until the garlic just starts to turn brown.

Add the red wine and cook it for 2 minutes, or until the liquid is reduced by ½.

Add the basil and balsamic vinegar, and cook the sauce for 1 minute more. Keep the sauce warm.

makes approximately ½ cup

Grand Marnier Cilantro Sauce

2	teaspoons olive oil
1	sweet shallot, minced
¼	cup Grand Marnier
½	cup orange juice, freshly squeezed
½	teaspoon red chile powder
2	sprigs fresh cilantro, roughly chopped

In a small saucepan place the olive oil and heat it on medium until it is hot. Add the shallots and sauté them for 2 minutes.

Add the Grand Marnier and flambé it *(see chef's comments on this page for instructions)*.

Add the orange juice and cook it for 2 minutes, or until it is reduced by ½.

Reduce the heat to low. Add the red chile powder and cilantro, and stir them in. Keep the sauce warm.

makes approximately ½ cup

Blue Crab with Mustard Greens and Cucumbers, with Gazpacho Dressing

Blue Crab with Mustard Greens and Cucumbers

¾   pound Blue Crab meat, cleaned
20   medium mustard leaves, washed and torn
½   pound cucumbers, peeled, seeded, and finely diced
2   limes, juiced
¼   cup walnut oil
    salt *(to taste)*
    black pepper *(to taste),* freshly ground
    Gazpacho Dressing *(recipe follows)*

In a medium bowl place the crab meat, mustard leaves, cucumbers, lime juice, walnut oil, salt, and black pepper. Let the ingredients marinate for 5 minutes.

In the center of each of 4 individual salad plates place the mustard greens and cucumbers. Sprinkle the crab mixture around the outside of the greens. Dribble the Gazpacho Dressing on top.

serves 4

Gazpacho Dressing

1   medium tomato, diced
½   cucumber, peeled, seeded, and diced
2   tablespoons fresh corn
2   tablespoons zucchini, finely diced
2   tablespoons yellow squash, finely diced
2   tablespoons jicama, peeled and finely diced
1   tablespoon yellow bell pepper, finely diced
¼   cup fresh cilantro, chopped
2   tablespoons champagne vinegar
¼   cup walnut oil
¼   cup catsup
    salt and black pepper *(to taste)*

In a medium bowl place all of the ingredients and mix them together. Chill the dressing in the refrigerator.

makes approximately 3 cups

Appetizers

"Another way to serve this crab is to pack it in a cup and then turn it upside down on top of the greens, so that the crab is in a mold shape. This is quick and easy to make, and it makes an elegant luncheon dish."

"I was born and raised in Mexico City, where my parents owned a restaurant. I used to help in the kitchen and I remember being fascinated by how many ingredients went into the Mexican sauces. If you have ever tried to make a mole sauce you will know what I mean, because there are about a thousand things that go into it. I like to use my background of classical Mexican cooking together with the influences from northern New Mexican cuisine. When I go back to Mexico City to visit my parents I always enjoy cooking for them.....both the traditional Mexican dishes and also some of my own creations that I have developed in this country. They love whatever I make!"

Martin Rios
Old House

Grilled Mozzarella and Roma Tomatoes with Arugula Pesto

"This makes a wonderful appetizer that you can put together in minutes. Don't let the cheese get too hot, or else it will melt and fall through the grill. All you want to do is to warm the cheese and tomatoes."

"Arugula is a green that has a spicy, peppery flavor. The pesto is best if it is made a day in advance, so the flavors will marry. It's wonderful with pasta and goat cheese, or with crostinis, which are small pieces of bread that are fried in olive oil. If you have a dinner party, it's fun to serve the pesto with the crostinis, along with roasted garlic, capers, sun-dried tomatoes, and goat cheese.....then your guests can build their own appetizers."

"When you roast the garlic, use the whole bulbs, with the skin on. Cut part of the tip off so that the cloves are somewhat exposed. Drizzle in some olive oil and bake the garlic at 350° for 30 to 45 minutes. It's done when the top starts to brown, the skins get golden, and the garlic feels soft. Let the bulbs cool for 5 minutes, and then the cloves will squeeze right out."

Steven Lemon
Pranzo Italian Grill

Grilled Mozzarella and Roma Tomatoes

8   firm, ripe Roma tomatoes, each one cut into 4 wedges
6   4-ounce balls fresh milk mozzarella cheese, quartered
2   tablespoons butter, melted and clarified
    salt *(to taste)*
    black pepper *(to taste)*, freshly ground
1   cup Arugula Pesto *(recipe follows)*

On each of eight 6" long bamboo skewers *(that are first soaked in water)* place, in an alternating manner, 4 tomato wedges and 3 mozzarella pieces. Brush on the clarified butter. Sprinkle on the salt and black pepper.

Grill the skewered tomatoes and cheese for 30 to 45 seconds on each side, or until the tomatoes and cheese are warmed through.

On each of 4 small individual serving plates place ¼ cup of the Arugula Pesto. Place two skewers on top.

serves 4

Arugula Pesto

¼   pound arugula *(green, small to medium leaves)*, washed and dried
10 cloves garlic, roasted *(see chef's comments on this page)*
2½ cups extra virgin olive oil

In a food processor place all of the ingredients and purée them until the pesto is smooth *(add more oil if it is too thick)*.

Store the pesto in the refrigerator *(it will keep for up to 2 weeks)*.

makes 3 cups

Black Bean Terrine with Pesto Pumpkin Seed Vinaigrette

Black Bean Terrine

1	tablespoon olive oil
1	red onion, chopped
1	stalk celery, diced
2	carrots, diced
2	jalapeño chile peppers, diced
1	pound black beans, cooked *(recipe on page 285, and see chef's comments on this page)* **and drained** *(reserve the cooking liquid)*
2	bunches fresh cilantro, chopped
1	tablespoon ground cumin
1	tablespoon ground coriander
2	eggs, lightly beaten
2	cups cream
	Hot Desert Seasonings Mix *(recipe on page 297), (to taste)*
	Pesto Pumpkin Seed Vinaigrette *(recipe on next page)*

Preheat the oven to 375°.

In a large stockpot place the olive oil and heat it on medium high until it is hot. Add the onions, celery, carrots, and jalapeño chile peppers. Sauté the ingredients for 8 to 10 minutes, or until they are tender.

Add the cooked black beans, cilantro, cumin, and coriander, and stir them in.

Reserve 2 cups of the bean mixture. Place the rest in a food processor and purée it. Add the reserved cooking liquid as it is needed, so that a thick paste is achieved.

Add the eggs, cream, and reserved bean mixture, and fold them in. Season the mixture with the Hot Desert Seasonings Mix.

Place the bean mixture in a buttered terrine. Place the terrine in a baking pan that is half filled with water. Bake the terrine in the water bath for 25 to 30 minutes, or until it is slightly firm.

Let the bean terrine cool, and then chill it in the refrigerator for 1 hour. Slice it into ¼" thick pieces and lay them flat on a serving platter. Drizzle on the Pesto Pumpkin Seed Vinaigrette.

serves 8 to 10

"I like vegetarian dishes that are boldly seasoned, and yet are light and healthy. In this recipe you should flavor the beans with vegetables (carrots, onions, celery, etc.) and spices (coriander, cumin, pepper, etc.), or else cook them in a vegetable stock."

"I highly recommend that you purchase a spice mill or coffee grinder so that you can grind up your own spice seeds and peppercorns. The flavors will be much fresher and more intense, and the quality of your cooking will be just that much better."

Pete Zimmer
Inn of the Anasazi

"If you can say one thing about my cooking, it is that I cook with gusto! If I am using garlic, then I want to be able to taste it. At the same time, I want all of the flavors to be balanced so that nothing is hidden."

Dolly Nevada Hand
Inn of the Anasazi

Pesto Pumpkin Seed Vinaigrette

1   bunch fresh cilantro, coarsely chopped
1   bunch fresh parsley, coarsely chopped
4   cloves garlic
1   cup pumpkin seeds, roasted *(see chef's comments on this page)*
1   lemon, juiced
1   teaspoon Hot Desert Seasonings Mix *(recipe on page 297)*
2   cups olive oil

In a food processor place all of the ingredients *(except for the olive oil)* and purée them together. With the food processor still running, slowly add the olive oil.

makes 1 quart

> *"The easiest way to roast the pumpkin seeds is in a dry pan on top of the stove, or in the oven on a flat sheet (300° for 5 to 7 minutes). Watch them very carefully because they will burn quickly. By roasting seeds the flavor becomes twice as strong. Just think of the difference between a blanched peanut and one that is roasted.....the flavor difference is incredible!"*
>
> Pete Zimmer
> Inn of the Anasazi

Peruvian Skewered Beef

1   teaspoon fresh garlic, minced
1/3 cup red wine vinegar
2/3 cup salad oil
1/2 teaspoon ground cumin
1   tablespoon chile pequin *(hot red chile flakes)*
1/2 teaspoon salt
1/2 teaspoon black pepper, freshly ground
2   bay leaves
1   pound top sirloin, fat removed, and cut into ½" cubes

In a medium bowl place all of the ingredients *(except for the bay leaves and the beef)*. Whisk them together well. Add the bay leaves and the beef, and toss them in so that the beef is well coated with the marinade. Refrigerate the beef for 12 hours.

Place the beef cubes on bamboo skewers. Grill them for 3 to 4 minutes *(turn the skewers so that all sides are cooked)*, or until they are done.

serves 4

> *"This skewered beef is a typical Peruvian dish that is both delicious and simple to make. In Lima you can buy the brochettes from ladies with their pushcarts on street corners, or in tiny specialty restaurants. Traditionally they are made with beef heart, which I love. The heart is the leanest part of the body, and it is very good for you. Every so often I get what I call a 'heart' craving!"*
>
> Alfredo Miranda
> Alfredo's Restaurant

Tuna Yakatori

1   cup soy sauce
1   cup orange juice
¼   cup catsup
½   cup fresh parsley, minced
1   teaspoon fresh oregano
4   cloves garlic, minced
4   lemons, juiced
1   pound yellow fin tuna, cut into ⅓" cubes
2   green bell peppers, seeded and cut into ½" squares
1   red bell pepper, seeded and cut into ½" squares
4   cherry tomatoes, caps removed, and hollowed out
2   tablespoons dry mustard, mixed with 2 tablespoons water to make a paste
1   teaspoon fresh chives, finely minced

In a medium bowl place the soy sauce, orange juice, catsup, parsley, oregano, garlic, and lemon juice. Add the tuna cubes and let them marinate in the refrigerator for 30 minutes. Remove the tuna and reserve the marinade.

On each of eight 6" long bamboo skewers, in this order, place a piece of the tuna, green bell pepper, tuna, red bell pepper, tuna, green bell pepper, and tuna. Grill the tuna and vegetables for 3 minutes on each side, or until the tuna is barely done.

Fill the hollowed-out cherry tomatoes with the mustard paste. Sprinkle the chives on top.

On each of 4 small, individual serving plates place 2 of the grilled, skewered tuna brochettes. Serve them with a stuffed cherry tomato and a small bowl of the reserved marinade.

serves 4

"Years ago I had a dish similar to this one in San Francisco, only it was made with chicken. Yakatori means 'skewered', usually with small bamboo sticks. This particular version is not spicy until you add the hot mustard paste to the marinade that is served on the side. Make sure that the tuna is very fresh, and cook it so that it is just medium rare. Some people insist upon cooking it more, but in my opinion that ruins the fish. Tuna is best when it is under-cooked."

"This is one of our best selling appetizers in the restaurant. It's easy to make, nonfattening, and tastes wonderful. You can increase the serving size and have it for an entrée."

Herb Cohen
Steaksmith

Shrimp Rémoulade

1	**pound medium shrimp**
2	**bags crab boil** *(preferably Zatarain's)*
½	**cup prepared horseradish**
1	**cup Creole mustard**
6	**cloves garlic**
1	**large onion, cut into eighths**
8	**celery leaves**
½	**cup salad oil**
¼	**cup Worcestershire sauce**
¼	**cup paprika**
⅛	**cup salt** *(or to taste)*
¼	**cup black pepper**
6	**lettuce leaves, washed and dried**
1	**lemon, cut into 6 wedges**

In a large pot of boiling water place the shrimp and the crab boil. Cook the shrimp for 2 to 3 minutes, or until they have turned pink. Drain the shrimp and let them cool slightly.

Peel and devein the shrimp. Refrigerate them for 1 hour, or until they are thoroughly chilled.

In a food processor place the horseradish, Creole mustard, garlic, onions, celery leaves, salad oil, Worcestershire sauce, paprika, salt, and black pepper. Blend the ingredients for 2 minutes, or until the mixture is smooth.

On each of 6 small, individual plates place a lettuce leaf. Place the shrimp on top and spoon on the sauce. Garnish each dish with a lemon wedge.

serves 6

"This recipe is a traditional southern Louisiana Creole dish. What distinguishes it from other rémoulade sauces is that it has a Creole mustard base instead of a mayonnaise base. You may use any kind of coarse-grain mustard that you have."

"Creole food by its nature is not very light, but it definitely is spicy! The horseradish in this dish really gives you a hot feeling in your nose and makes your eyes teary. If you are sensitive to this degree of heat, then reduce the amount."

"One trick is to pour a bunch of ice into the pot after the shrimp are done, and then let the shrimp seep in the spicy liquid for 30 minutes or so. This way they will absorb more of the flavor without cooking further."

Skip Kirkland
Pontchartrain

Southwestern Smoked Salmon Sushi with Refried Black Bean Paste and Roasted Tomato Sauce

Southwestern Smoked Salmon Sushi

6   flour tortillas *(thin)*
      Refried Black Bean Paste *(recipe follows)*
      Roasted Tomato Sauce *(recipe on next page)*
2   pounds smoked salmon, thinly sliced
1   cup jicama, peeled and julienned
1   cup red bell peppers, seeded and julienned

On each of the flour tortillas spread a thin layer of the Refried Black Bean Paste. Spread on a thin layer of the Roasted Tomato Sauce.

Cover the tortilla with slices of the smoked salmon.

Lightly sprinkle on the jicama and red bell pepper pieces.

Roll the tortilla up tight and round. Trim off the ends. Slice the roll into 2" long pieces.

serves 6 to 8

Refried Black Bean Paste

1½   cups black beans *(raw)*
2   jalapeño chile peppers, seeds removed
1   small yellow onion, roughly chopped
½   cup fresh cilantro
4   cups water *(or as needed)*
3   tablespoons olive oil

In a medium large stockpot place all of the ingredients *(except for the olive oil)*. Bring the liquid to a boil over high heat. Reduce the heat to low and simmer the ingredients for 1½ hours, or until the beans are tender *(add more water if necessary so that the beans don't scorch)*.

(continued on next page)

"This recipe was developed for a Share Our Strength benefit in Santa Fe. I wanted something that was unique, flavorful, with Southwestern flavors, and that could be made in small portions. The result was so beautiful that we ended up serving it at the restaurant. There are a variety of textures and colors.....white, black, red, and pink. When you roll up the tortilla some of the filling will squish out. Wipe it off and trim off any excess, so that you end up with a clean, pretty roll."

"Be careful not to burn the beans when you are frying them. You have to continually stir them or else they will scorch.....and there is nothing worse than burnt beans! You can make this into a soup by thinning it out with some water and then adding a couple of shots of tequila before you serve it. This also is good with huevos rancheros, or you can add some sour cream to it and serve it as a dip for chips."

Karen Woods
Rancho Encantado

Pour the beans In a strainer and drain off the liquid. Place the beans in a food processor and purée them so that a smooth paste is formed.

In a large sauté pan place the olive oil and heat it on medium until it is very hot and starts to smoke. Add the bean purée. While stirring constantly, fry the beans for 10 to 15 minutes, or until they are dry. Chill the paste in the refrigerator.

makes 2 cups

Roasted Tomato Sauce

½   cup olive oil
2   dozen Roma tomatoes
1   large white onion, peeled and cut in half
2   red bell peppers, seeds removed
2   poblano chile peppers, seeds removed
1   whole bulb garlic, broken up
¼   cup balsamic vinegar

Preheat the oven to 400°.

In a roasting pan place the olive oil. Add the remainder of the ingredients *(except for the balsamic vinegar)* and toss them around so that they are well coated with the oil.

Roast the ingredients for 1 hour, or until the tomatoes are brownish-black *(stir occasionally)*.

Push the ingredients through a fine sieve so that the seeds and skins don't go through.

Add the balsamic vinegar to the mixture and stir it in.

In a large sauté pan place the sauce. While stirring constantly, cook the sauce on medium heat for 10 to 15 minutes, or until it is dry and forms a paste. Chill the sauce in the refrigerator.

makes approximately 2 cups

Eggplant Caviar with Chipotle Oil

Eggplant Caviar

3	pounds eggplant
2	tablespoons lemon juice, freshly squeezed
6	tablespoons white onions, grated
1	cup olive oil
1	teaspoon red wine vinegar
¾	teaspoon dried oregano, toasted *(see chef's comments on this page)*
	salt *(to taste)*
3	small tomatoes, peeled, seeded, and chopped
½	bunch fresh cilantro, chopped
1	pita bread, cut into 8 pieces
	Chipotle Oil *(recipe on next page)*

Preheat the oven to 350°.

Place the eggplants on a flat sheet and bake them for 1 hour, or until the skin is shriveled and the flesh is soft. Let the eggplants cool.

Scoop out the flesh and place it in a food processor. Add the lemon juice and white onions, and purée them.

With the food processor running, slowly dribble in the olive oil and the red wine vinegar.

Place the mixture in a medium bowl. Add the toasted oregano and salt, and stir them in.

Place the mixture in the refrigerator so that it chills.

Just before serving add the tomatoes and cilantro, and fold them in.

Spread the mixture on the pieces of pita bread. Dribble a small amount of the Chipotle Oil on top of each serving.

serves 8

"This is a really tasty appetizer that has its origins in the Middle East. The main flavors are eggplant and olive oil, and it is very good for you."

"The recipe is very simple to make. The main thing is that the eggplant must cook long enough so that the flesh is completely soft. The skin gets crispy and shriveled, and the whole inside collapses. If the eggplant looks like it has been outside in the sun all day, then it is ready!"

"To toast the oregano you should put it in a small, cold pan. Put the pan on high heat, shake it around, and when the aroma from the oregano is released it is ready."

Don Fortel
Francisco's

Chipotle Oil

1	**pint olive oil**
6	**dried chipotle peppers, finely chopped**

In a medium saucepan place the olive oil and dried chipotle peppers. Simmer the ingredients on medium low heat for 5 minutes.

Remove the saucepan from the heat and let the oil cool. Store the oil in the refrigerator.

makes 1 pint

"This oil is really hot! It can be used in Chinese dishes that call for hot oil, or you can add a small amount to your salsa to give it more bite. It also makes a fabulous marinade, although you must use it sparingly. The dried chipotle peppers have a wonderful smoky flavor. They come in plastic bags and should be available in most stores."

Don Fortel
Francisco's

Roast Peppers and Fresh Mozzarella Cheese

2	**red bell peppers, roasted, peeled, seeded, and cut into thin strips** *(see chef's comments on page 159)*
2	**4-ounce balls mozzarella cheese, sliced into 8 pieces** *(total)*
4	**fresh basil florets**
¼	**cup capers, drained**
¼	**cup extra virgin olive oil**
	black pepper *(to taste)*, **freshly ground**

On each of 4 small, individual serving plates place the roasted red bell pepper strips. Place the mozzarella cheese slices on top. Add a basil floret and sprinkle on the capers. Dribble on the olive oil and grind on the black pepper.

serves 4

"This is an adaptation of an Italian caprese salad, except that I added the roasted bell peppers. I like the way the mozzarella cheese and peppers combine with the piquancy of the capers and the freshness of the basil. It is a very simple, basic dish, but it tastes exquisite."

Ken Calascione
La Traviata

Duck and Red Chile Won Tons with Ginger Soy Dipping Sauce

Duck and Red Chile Won Tons

2	**tablespoons peanut oil**
1	**whole roasted duck** *(350° oven for 45 minutes),* **cooled, skin and bones removed, and coarsely chopped**
1	**medium onion, coarsely chopped**
¼	**cup New Mexican red chile powder** *(medium hot)*
¼	**teaspoon salt**
¼	**teaspoon black pepper, freshly ground**
20	**won ton wrappers**
2	**eggs** *(or as needed),* **lightly beaten**
2	**cups light soy oil** *(or as needed)*
	Ginger Soy Dipping Sauce *(recipe on next page)*

In a large sauté pan place the peanut oil and heat it on medium high until it is hot. Add the chopped duck, onions, red chile powder, salt, and black pepper. Sauté the ingredients for 5 minutes, or until the duck is hot and the onions are tender.

Place the mixture in a food processor and purée it. Let the duck purée cool.

On a flat surface lay out 10 of the won ton wrappers. Brush them with some of the beaten eggs. In the center of each wrapper place a portion of the duck purée.

Lay out the remaining 10 wrappers and brush them with the rest of the beaten eggs. Place these wrappers, egg-brushed side down, on top of the duck purée-filled wrappers. Seal the edges tightly with your fingers. Cut the corners so that a round shape is formed.

In a wok or medium saucepan place the vegetable oil and heat it on high until it is hot. Add the duck won tons and deep fry them for 1 to 2 minutes, or until they are golden brown. Drain them on paper towels.

Serve the won tons with the Ginger Soy Dipping Sauce.

serves 4 to 6

"This dish is not low calorie because it is deep-fried, but the flavor is so fantastic that I wanted to include it. We use a light soy oil, and the won ton wrappers seal very quickly. If you serve this as an appetizer, then people can eat just a few. They can enjoy the taste and texture without consuming too much fat."

Paul Hunsicker
Paul's Restaurant of Santa Fe

"I am not a duck person, but I really love this dish! It's hard to describe the flavor, except to say that it is very different. The won ton is crispy and the filling is smooth. The hotness of the chile is toned down by the duck, and the gaminess of the duck is toned down by the chile. So the two ingredients really complement each other well."

Carol Moberg
Paul's Restaurant of Santa Fe

Ginger Soy Dipping Sauce

2	**scallions, finely chopped**
2	**teaspoons fresh ginger root, peeled and finely chopped**
1	**cup light soy sauce**
½	**cup dry white wine**
1	**tablespoon toasted sesame oil**

In a medium saucepan place all of the ingredients. Boil them for 5 minutes. Let the sauce cool.

makes 1½ cups

Sausage and White Bean Pizza

¼	**cup pizza sauce** *(recipe on page 116 or 117)*
1	**12" pizza round** *(recipe on page 299)*
¼	**cup cooked white beans**
2½	**ounces hot Italian sausage, sliced or crumbled**
4	**ounces mozzarella cheese, grated**

Preheat the oven to 450°.

Spread the pizza sauce on top of the pizza round. Add, in this order, the cooked white beans, hot Italian sausage, and mozzarella cheese.

Place the pizza on a flat sheet and bake it for 15 to 18 minutes, or until the cheese is bubbly and everything is hot. Cut the pizza into 8 wedges.

serves 4

LP CALDWELL

Soups

Spicy Beef and Black Bean Soup

2	cups black beans, sorted and rinsed
1	tablespoon olive oil
1	medium red onion, diced
2	cloves garlic, finely chopped
2	cups beef, trimmed of fat, chilled in freezer *(not frozen)*, and diced small
16	ounces tomato purée
8	green chile peppers, roasted, peeled, seeded, and diced *(see chef's comments on page 159)*
½	bunch fresh cilantro, finely chopped
2	tablespoons honey
2	tablespoons beef base *(or 2 quarts beef broth, reduced to ½ cup)*
1	teaspoon ground cumin
1	teaspoon ground coriander
½	teaspoon ground cloves
	salt *(to taste)*
	black pepper *(to taste)*
½	cup jalapeño cheese, grated
8	small dried chile peppers, washed

In a large stockpot place the black beans. Cover them with water, bring them to a boil, and then simmer them for 2 hours, or until the beans are tender *(skim off the foam from the top)*. Remove 1 cup of the cooked beans, purée them, and return them to the pot.

In a large sauté pan place the olive oil and heat it on medium until it is hot. Add the onions and garlic, and gently sauté them for 5 minutes, or until the onions are translucent. Add the diced beef and sauté it for 2 to 3 minutes, or until it turns an ash color. Add the mixture to the beans.

Add the tomato purée, green chile peppers, cilantro, honey, beef base, cumin, coriander, cloves, salt, and black pepper. Stir the ingredients together and simmer the soup for 30 minutes.

In each of 8 individual soup bowls place the soup. Sprinkle on the jalapeño cheese and place a dried chile pepper on top.

serves 8

"There are certain kinds of recipes for stews and meat loaves, where it is pretty hard to make a mistake, and this is one of those recipes. Also, it's one of those dishes that gets better as time goes on, maybe up to two weeks. If you have some leftover pot roast or roast beef, you could use it instead of the diced meat. There is a kick to this because of the chile peppers, but I don't think that hard core New Mexicans will judge this as being really spicy."

"When I first moved to Santa Fe I saw all of these bins around town in the fall that were roasting the new crop of Hatch green chiles. I didn't really focus on it too much. Later on, I realized that it was almost a ritual in this part of New Mexico. Everybody buys huge bags of roasted green chiles and then freezes them in zip lock bags. So, finally I did the same thing, and now my freezer is full of roasted green chiles. They have an amazing, delicious flavor, and I'm glad that I finally got with the program!"

Tom Wright
Galisteo Inn

Tortilla Chip Soup

1	pound chicken, skin and bones removed, grilled and diced
2	pounds tomatoes, diced
½	green bell pepper, seeded and diced
½	pound green chile peppers, roasted, peeled, seeded, and diced *(see chef's comments on page 159)*
½	large onion, diced
½	bunch fresh cilantro, chopped
1	quart chicken stock *(recipe on page 295)*
2	tablespoons lime juice, freshly squeezed
½	teaspoon ground cumin
¼	teaspoon black pepper
2	cups tortilla chips, crumbled with your hands
1	cup Monterey Jack cheese, grated

In a large stockpot place all of the ingredients *(except for the tortilla chips and cheese)*. Simmer them for 20 minutes.

In each of 6 individual serving bowls place the tortilla chips. Sprinkle on some of the cheese. Ladle in the soup. Garnish the soup with more cheese.

serves 6

"I don't sauté the vegetables first, because the soup tastes great without doing it, and this way it is just that much healthier. The recipe is fast and easy to throw together, and you can change it in any way you want. Put in jalapeño peppers for heat, use pork or beef instead of chicken, or add different vegetables. The lime and cilantro flavors come through, and they give the soup a perky, slightly tart flavor. This soup really brings you to attention!"

"When I cook I try to make the food so that it tastes good to me. It's okay to ask other people their opinions, but in the last analysis I go with my own taste. Some people have strange palates, and what they think tastes good does not taste good to other people. To be a successful cook your palate must be in sync with that of your customers."

Dan Kelley
Peppers Restaurant

"Dan is a very modest chef, and he says this tortilla soup tastes like no one else's in town. I have tasted it, and I believe him! The flavor is excellent, and it takes no time at all to make."

Patricia Helmick
Peppers Restaurant

White Gazpacho with Jicama and Red Onion

1   cup whole blanched almonds
3   cloves garlic, chopped
1   tablespoon salt
¾   cup water *(or as needed)*
¾   cup crustless Italian bread, soaked in water, squeezed to remove moisture, and torn
½   cup extra virgin olive oil
2   tablespoons raspberry vinegar
3   cups cold water
1   cup seedless green grapes, coarsely chopped
1   cup jicama, peeled and diced into ¼" pieces
1   cup cucumber, peeled, seeded, and chopped
2   serrano chile peppers, finely diced
1   red onion, quartered and thinly sliced
½   cup fresh cilantro, chopped

In a blender place the almonds, garlic, salt, and the ¾ cup of water. Purée the ingredients so that they are smooth.

Add the bread and blend it in *(add more water if necessary)*.

With the blender constantly running, slowly dribble in the olive oil.

Add the raspberry vinegar and blend it in. Pour the mixture into a large bowl.

Add the 3 cups of cold water and stir it in.

Add the remainder of the ingredients and stir them in. Serve the soup well chilled.

serves 6

"This is a variation of an old, Mediterranean recipe. It is a very unusual and flavorful soup that tastes rich and creamy, even though there is no dairy in it. A classic white gazpacho has only almonds, garlic, bread, olive oil, and grapes, and everything is puréed. I added the other ingredients to give it more flavor and texture. Lisa Genotti, Adobo's sous chef, suggested using the jicama, which I think really tops the soup off."

"When I cook for myself I love to use a lot of salt, butter, and cream, because that is the way I was brought up. I remember my mother sending me to the creamery to get butter almost every other day. It seems that when I am preparing a dish for myself there is this little tape that goes off in my head and tells me to throw a lump of butter in the pan. But, even though I love rich food, I do appreciate food that is light, healthy, and well prepared. This is the kind of dish that I eat at other restaurants in town."

Jonathan Horst
Adobo Catering

Spicy Squash and Avocado Soup

"This is a wonderful soup because it is very rich and velvety, without having any cream in it. It doesn't taste real squashy.....the avocado flavor is stronger. Also, the spaghetti squash gives it a nice, crunchy texture, and it's neat to bite into it. I serve this dish to my in-laws, who are your basic meat and potato eaters. They don't particularly like vegetables, but they love this soup. It makes a nice, light meal for the summer, and you can serve it heated for the winter. Also, the recipe is foolproof.....it comes out perfect every time."

"When I cook I don't like to use a recipe and then go shopping for the ingredients. Rather, I like to use leftovers, and come up with something original. Of course, I also love fresh ingredients, and will use them as much as possible."

Ernie Bolleter
Inn at Loretto

2	tablespoons olive oil
½	small onion, diced into ¼" pieces
4	cloves garlic, coarsely chopped
1	small zucchini, diced medium
2	small yellow squash, diced medium
3	jalapeño chile peppers, seeded and finely diced
4	cups chicken stock *(recipe on page 295)*
1	small spaghetti squash, cut lengthwise and seeded, steamed until tender, and meat scraped out
2	poblano chile peppers, roasted, peeled, and seeded *(see chef's comments on page 159)*
1	medium ripe avocado, peeled, pitted, and coarsely chopped
4	tablespoons plain yogurt
1	tablespoon lime juice, freshly squeezed
	salt *(to taste)*
½	bunch fresh cilantro, chopped
6	black olives, seeded and chopped

In a large stockpot place the olive oil and heat it on medium until it is hot. Add the onions and garlic, and sauté them for 8 to 10 minutes, or until they turn golden brown.

Add the zucchini, yellow squash, half of the jalapeño chile peppers, and the chicken stock. Simmer the ingredients for 20 minutes, and then let them cool.

In a food processor place the stock with the cooled vegetables, ¾ of the spaghetti squash, the poblano chile peppers, avocado, yogurt, and lime juice. Purée the ingredients so that they are smooth. Chill the soup.

In each of 4 chilled, individual soup bowls place the cold soup. Garnish the soup with the rest of the spaghetti squash, the other half of the jalapeño peppers, the cilantro, and the olives.

serves 4

New Mexican Minestrone

½	pound chorizo, sautéed and drained of all fat
⅔	cup cooked kidney beans
⅔	cup cooked chick peas
1½	pounds tomatoes, diced
½	pound mushrooms, sliced
1	yellow squash, sliced
½	green bell pepper, seeded and diced
¼	stalk celery, diced
¼	large onion, diced
1	tablespoon fresh garlic, minced
1	quart beef stock *(or as needed)*
1	tablespoon ground cumin
1½	teaspoons salt
1	teaspoon black pepper
8	ounces bow tie pasta

In a large stockpot place all of the ingredients *(except for the pasta)*. Simmer them for 45 minutes.

Add the bow tie pasta. Simmer the soup for 8 minutes, or until the pasta is cooked.

serves 6

"I've always loved minestrone, and once I decided to make some that had a Southwestern twist. Instead of Italian herbs, such as basil and oregano, I used cumin. I also used chorizo, which is a hot, spicy Mexican sausage. The chorizo is what gives this soup some kick, so you can use more or less than the recipe calls for, depending on your taste."

Dan Kelley
Peppers Restaurant

"Dan had me taste this soup when he first made it, and I told him that it was the best soup I had ever eaten. The flavor is wonderful.....I think that the chorizo is the key ingredient."

Patricia Helmick
Peppers Restaurant

"Peppers is a fun, lively restaurant, with an upbeat atmosphere. We try to combine the flavors of northern New Mexico with the colors and festivities of Old Mexico. Although our ambiance is lighthearted, we are very serious about serving the best food possible."

Rick Helmick
Peppers Restaurant

Borscht with Beer

2	**slices bacon**
½	**pound stewing lamb, fat removed, and diced**
1	**medium onion, diced**
1	**carrot, diced**
1	**cup celery, diced**
2	**medium beets, peeled and diced**
2	**medium tomatoes, peeled, seeded, and chopped**
1	**tablespoon fresh parsley, minced**
1½	**tablespoons flour**
7	**cups beef broth**
1	**teaspoon nutmeg**
1	**teaspoon salt**
1	**cup red cabbage, thinly shredded**
1	**egg yolk, beaten**
8	**ounces light beer**
4	**dollops sour cream** *(optional)*
4	**slices rye bread**

In a medium large stockpot place the bacon and fry it. Remove the bacon, drain it, mince it, and set it aside.

Remove all but 1 teaspoon of the bacon grease from the stockpot and raise the heat to high. Add the lamb cubes and sear them for 3 to 5 minutes, or until they are lightly browned.

Add the onions, carrots, and celery. Sauté the ingredients for 2 minutes. Add the beets and tomatoes, and sauté them for 15 minutes.

In a small bowl place the reserved bacon, parsley, and flour. Mix the ingredients together, add them to the stockpot, and stir them in. Add the beef broth, nutmeg, and salt. Bring the ingredients to a boil over high heat. Cover the pot, reduce the heat to low, and simmer the soup for 2 hours.

Add the red cabbage and simmer it for 10 to 15 minutes, or until it is tender. Remove the pot from the heat.

In a medium small bowl place the egg yolk. While whisking constantly, slowly add 4 tablespoons of the soup. Continue to whisk and add the beer. Add the mixture to the soup and stir it in.

Serve the soup with a dollop of sour cream and the rye bread.

serves 6

"Although borscht is a classical Russian dish, this is a recipe that I got from a French friend of mine in Europe. The beets are not so dominating in flavor, because the other meat and vegetable tastes come through as well. It's an excellent soup that is both tasty and well balanced in nutrition. It is too rich and hearty for an appetizer, but it is perfect for a light supper."

"In Switzerland there is a very specific way that people are served in a restaurant and all waitpeople go through an apprenticeship to learn it. When I first came to the United States I learned that there is no special serving system here. I nearly had a nervous breakdown trying to train my employees in the European manner. I have made some progress over the years, but I now realize that America and Europe are very different in this way, and there's not much I can do about it."

Marie Jeanne Chaney
Swiss Bakery

Roasted Corn Broth with Pork Potstickers

Roasted Corn Broth

2   **tablespoons olive oil**
1   **yellow onion, diced**
4   **poblano chile peppers, diced**
1   **celery stalk, diced**
5   **cloves garlic**
10   **ears yellow corn, roasted and shucked** *(see chef's comments on this page)*
4   **quarts chicken stock** *(recipe on page 295)*
2   **bunches fresh cilantro, chopped**
      salt *(to taste)*
      black pepper *(to taste)*
      Pork Potstickers *(recipe on next page)*

In a large stockpot place the olive oil and heat it on medium high until it is hot. Add the onions, poblano chile peppers, celery, and garlic. Sauté the ingredients for 5 minutes.

Add the roasted corn ears and chicken stock. Boil the ingredients for 20 minutes. Remove the corn. Add the cilantro, salt, black pepper, and Pork Potstickers.

serves 6 to 8

"This soup has a wonderful, deep, natural corn flavor that is very clean. You can roast the corn in the oven, or preferably, over an outside grill. Either way it will take about 15 to 20 minutes. The husk will start to smoke and turn very dark, and the kernels will start popping, like popcorn. Don't let this frighten you! By leaving the husk and silk on, their flavors will penetrate into the corn. The aromas in your kitchen while the corn is roasting will be pretty exceptional!"

"My father, Robert, was the founder and CEO of the Rosewood Hotels. He taught me that if I wanted something, I had to work hard for it, just like anyone else. To him, there were no free rides in life. So, when I was young he made me get a job, and I started out as a dish-washer in a restaurant. Eventually I graduated up to other positions, and I developed a lot of advanced cooking techniques at a young age. I've always loved cooking because the gratification is so immediate."

Pete Zimmer
Inn of the Anasazi

Pork Potstickers

½	**pound ground pork**
1	**tablespoon fresh ginger root, peeled and minced**
1	**tablespoon fresh garlic, minced**
1	**bunch scallions, thinly sliced**
1	**bunch fresh parsley, chopped**
1	**bunch fresh cilantro, chopped**
1	**tablespoon chile pequin** *(hot red chile flakes)*
2	**tablespoons soy sauce**
1	**tablespoon sesame oil**
3	**eggs, lightly beaten**
½	**teaspoon salt** *(or to taste)*
¼	**teaspoon black pepper** *(or to taste)*
1	**package won ton skins**

In a medium bowl place all of the ingredients *(except for the won ton skins)* and mix them together well.

In the center of each won ton skin place a small amount of the pork mixture. Fold the 4 corners to the center and squeeze them together so that the mixture is completely sealed in.

Steam the won tons in a steamer for 5 to 7 minutes, or until they are firm to the touch.

serves 6 to 8

"Potstickers are little dumplings that are similar to Asian steamed won tons. I like the way the name sounds.....it has a real cowboy feeling to it. They get their name from the fact that the little devils stick to the sides of the pot when you are cooking them."

"In most of my recipes I say 'season to taste'. It is important that you are careful when you season food and that you keep tasting it along the way. Too much or too little can mean the difference between something tasting exceptional or just okay. If the food is raw, as with this pork mix, you should cook a small amount of it in a pan and then taste it for the flavor. What you want to avoid is having someone at your dinner party asking for the salt and pepper to be passed."

Pete Zimmer
Inn of the Anasazi

Santa Fe Stew

1	**16-ounce package frozen posole**
4	**quarts water** *(or as needed)*
2	**tablespoons olive oil**
1	**yellow onion, diced medium**
2	**cloves garlic, minced**
1	**tablespoon paprika**
1	**teaspoon ground cumin**
1	**tablespoon fresh oregano, chopped**
4	**cups tomatoes, diced**
1	**pound frozen green chile peppers** *(mild),* **defrosted and chopped**
12	**cups beef stock** *(or chicken stock)*
2	**tablespoons olive oil**
1	**pound lean pork, fat trimmed off, and cut into ¼" cubes**
¼	**cup fresh cilantro, minced**
	salt *(to taste)*

In a large stockpot place the posole and the water. Cover the pot and bring the water to a boil over high heat. Reduce the heat to low and simmer the posole for 2½ to 3 hours, or until it is tender. Strain the posole and set it aside.

In a medium large sauté pan place the first 2 tablespoons of olive oil and heat it on medium high until it is hot. Add the onions, garlic, paprika, cumin, and oregano. Sauté the ingredients for 4 to 6 minutes, or until the onions are tender.

Add the tomatoes, green chile peppers, beef stock, and cooked posole. Simmer the stew for 30 minutes.

In another medium large sauté pan place the other 2 tablespoons of olive oil. Heat the oil on high until it is hot. Add the pork cubes and sauté them for 4 to 6 minutes, or until they are done.

To the stew add the cooked pork, cilantro, and salt.

serves 8 to 10

"This is basically a posole recipe that has a lot more flavors and spices than normal. It was created as a party dish more than 20 years ago, and now it's a regular item on our menu. There's a definite kick to it, so it's not for the faint of heart. Posole is very popular in Santa Fe, and it's perfect to serve to a large group of people along with chips and salsa."

"You can eliminate the pork, although I've never done so with this recipe. If you want to make it a vegetarian dish, then add some julienned carrots for flavor and color. You can tell when the posole is done because the skins come off and the kernels puff up like popcorn."

Herb Cohen
Steaksmith

Carrot and Sweet Potato Soup

¼	cup peanut oil
½	cup onions, coarsely chopped
2	tablespoons fresh garlic, minced
1½	cups carrots, peeled and coarsely chopped
1	cup dry white wine
3	medium sweet potatoes, peeled and coarsely chopped
2	dried ancho chile peppers, stems and seeds removed
1	tablespoon ground cumin
1	quart chicken stock *(recipe on page 295)*
1	cup milk
	salt *(to taste)*
	black pepper *(to taste)*

In a large saucepan place the peanut oil and heat it on medium until it is hot. Add the onions and sauté them for 6 to 8 minutes, or until they are translucent.

Add the garlic and stir it in.

Add the carrots and white wine. Simmer the ingredients for 5 minutes.

Add the sweet potatoes, ancho chile peppers, cumin, and chicken stock. Simmer the soup for 30 to 40 minutes, or until the carrots and sweet potatoes are tender.

Strain off the liquid and reserve it.

Place the cooked ingredients in a food processor. While adding the reserved liquid in small amounts at a time, purée the ingredients together so that the consistency of a heavy cream is achieved.

Pour the soup back into the saucepan. Add the milk, salt, and black pepper, and stir them in *(if necessary, adjust the consistency with more stock or water)*.

serves 8

Two-Color Beet and Cauliflower Soup

2   tablespoons olive oil
2   large heads cauliflower, cut into florets
1   onion, chopped medium
1   quart chicken stock *(recipe on page 295)*
¼   teaspoon nutmeg
     salt *(to taste)*
2   tablespoons olive oil
2   pounds beets, peeled and diced medium
1   onion, chopped medium
1   quart chicken stock *(recipe on page 295)*
2   tablespoons balsamic vinegar
1   tablespoon sugar
     salt *(to taste)*
     black pepper *(to taste)*

Note: Make both soups at the same time.

In a medium large saucepan place the first 2 tablespoons of olive oil. Heat it on medium until it is hot. Add the cauliflower and the first onion, and sauté them for 8 to 10 minutes, or until they are tender *(don't let them get brown)*.

Add the first quart of chicken stock and the nutmeg. Bring the liquid to a boil and then reduce the heat to low. Simmer the ingredients for 1 hour. Pour the soup into a food processor and purée it so that it is smooth. Season it with the salt.

In another medium large saucepan place the second 2 tablespoons of olive oil. Heat it on medium until it is hot. Add the beets and the second onion, and sauté them for 5 minutes. Add the second quart of chicken stock, balsamic vinegar, and sugar. Bring the liquid to a boil and then reduce the heat to low. Simmer the ingredients for 30 to 45 minutes, or until the beets are tender.

Pour the soup into a food processor and purée it so that it is smooth. Season it with the salt and black pepper.

In each of 8 individual soup bowls pour both soups at the same time *(pour one soup from each hand)* so that they are next to each other. Create a design in the soup with the 2 colors by swirling a toothpick around.

serves 8

"In California they do a lot of two-color soups where the colors are swirled together to make interesting designs. I came up with this recipe when we had a lot of extra cauliflower and beets. Luckily, the two items turned out to be a perfect match. The two soups are very easy to make.....all you need is a food processor. The only trick is to make sure that the consistency is correct.....it should be like heavy cream, but not runny. Also, the consistency should be identical for each soup. It's fun to make this soup for Christmas. You can purée a little green chile pepper and put it on top so that you have the colors red, green, and white."

"I think that it takes a special knack to make a good soup. Some people can make soups all the time, and they never taste exactly right or have the correct consistency. If you want to make a good vegetarian soup, such as this one, you have to sauté the vegetables first so that the flavors marry. Another key is to use enough salt so that the flavors are brought out."

Paul Hunsicker
Paul's Restaurant of Santa Fe

Zuppa di Minestrone

⅓	**cup olive oil**
1	**small zucchini, diced small**
1	**small yellow squash, diced small**
1	**small carrot, diced small**
1	**fennel bulb, diced small**
1	**small red onion, diced small**
½	**red bell pepper, seeded and diced small**
½	**green bell pepper, seeded and diced small**
1	**rib celery, diced small**
1	**tablespoon fresh garlic, chopped**
¼	**cup fresh basil, chopped**
¼	**cup fresh parsley, chopped**
2	**quarts chicken stock** *(recipe on page 295)*
2	**tablespoons lemon juice, freshly squeezed**
	salt *(to taste)*
	black pepper *(to taste),* **freshly ground**

In a large stockpot place the olive oil and heat it on medium high until it is hot. Add the zucchini, yellow squash, carrots, fennel, red onions, red and green bell peppers, celery, and garlic. Sauté the vegetables for 6 to 8 minutes, or until they are tender.

Add ½ of both the basil and parsley, and stir them in.

Add the chicken stock and bring it to a boil. Reduce the heat to low and simmer the soup for 30 minutes.

Add the lemon juice, salt, black pepper, and the rest of the basil and parsley.

serves 8

"Minestrone is an Italian vegetable soup, and this is our version that we serve at the restaurant. You can put any type of good vegetable in it that you want, along with beans or pasta. Get all of the ingredients prepared before you put the soup together. You get a better flavor from the vegetables by first cooking them in hot oil over high heat for several minutes."

"I've always loved Italian cooking because it's very straightforward, with no fluff. It's one of the oldest cuisines in the world, and even though it is simple, it is one of the most flavorful."

Steven Lemon
Pranzo Italian Grill

Green Chile Andalouse

2	poblano chile peppers, halved and cored
½	cup green chile peppers, chopped
3	bell peppers, cored, seeded, and halved
2	onions, peeled and halved
10	tomatoes, cored and halved
3	carrots, coarsely chopped
2	potatoes, peeled and coarsely chopped
½	bunch fresh basil
5	cloves garlic
2	cups tomato juice
	salt *(to taste)*
	black pepper *(to taste)*

In a large saucepan place all of the ingredients *(except the salt and black pepper)*. Add enough water so that they are just covered. Cover the pot with a lid and bring the ingredients to a boil over high heat. Reduce the heat to low and simmer the vegetables for 30 minutes, or until they are tender.

Place the ingredients in a food processor and purée them.

Push the puréed mixture through a fine sieve *(to remove the skins and seeds)*, and then return it to the pan.

Add the salt and black pepper, and stir them in. Heat the soup so that it is hot *(do not let it boil)*.

serves 6

"Andalouse is a well known French soup, and it calls for heavy cream. To make the recipe healthier I eliminated the cream and added an extra potato and carrot, in order to thicken it up. Also, I added the chile peppers, which give it a nice Southwestern zing. The poblano chiles are especially nice because they have a hearty, fresh green taste. The beauty of this recipe is that it is so simple to make, and yet it is so good."

"In my early years I was kind of at odds with myself in terms of what I wanted to do with my life. I toyed with the idea of being a professional writer, or maybe even an artist, but I couldn't seem to commit to either one. Finally I reached a point where I decided it was time to definitely pick a career. So I read the book 'What Color Is Your Parachute', and did all of the little exercises in it. Cooking kept coming up as something I really enjoyed doing and was good at, so it seemed pretty obvious that this was the field I should pursue. From there I got several wonderful apprenticeships, and that is when I really became focused on food."

Isaac Modivah
Ore House

Squash Blossom Soup

"Squash blossoms are exactly what they sound like.....blossoms from the squash plant. Each plant has both female and male flowers on it. The female flowers produce the squash, and the male flowers are just big and showy (typical!). The best time to pick the blossoms is very early in the morning, when the sun is coming up. They don't taste like squash. Rather, they are slightly sweet and a little peppery. The flavor is very refreshing. I came up with this recipe because one day I ordered 100 pounds of squash, and each one had a flower on it. Squash blossoms are gaining in popularity in this country, and they are becoming easier to find in your local market."

"I enjoy finding unusual items that aren't used all of the time and that most people are unfamiliar with. There are over 2500 varieties of vegetables in the world, but we use only something like 100 varieties here. So whenever possible I will promote an unusual item, with the hope of expanding the culinary horizons of our customers."

Karen Woods
Rancho Encantado

6	Roma tomatoes, coarsely chopped
1	English cucumber, peeled, seeded, and coarsely chopped
2	medium yellow squash, coarsely chopped
4	romaine lettuce leaves *(hearts only)*
½	red onion, coarsely chopped
1	yellow bell pepper, seeded and coarsely chopped
1	red bell pepper, seeded and coarsely chopped
1	poblano chile pepper, seeds removed
2	cloves garlic
½	cup fresh cilantro
½	cup fresh basil
½	cup red wine vinegar
2	limes, juiced
	salt *(to taste)*
	black pepper *(to taste)*
3	dozen large squash blossoms, cut into rounds ¼" thick
6	tablespoons olive oil

In a medium large bowl place the Roma tomatoes, English cucumbers, squash, romaine lettuce, red onions, yellow and red bell peppers, poblano chile peppers, garlic, cilantro, basil, red wine vinegar, and lime juice. Combine the ingredients, place them in a food processor, and roughly purée them.

Add the salt and black pepper, and stir them in.

Add the squash blossoms and gently stir them in.

Chill the soup in the refrigerator for 30 minutes.

In each of 6 individual soup bowls place the soup. Dribble on the olive oil.

serves 6

Broiled Tomato Soup

8	large ripe tomatoes, cored
¼	cup olive oil
2	large carrots, cut into 1" long pieces
5	stalks celery, cut into 1" long pieces
1	large yellow onion, cut into 1" pieces
1	tablespoon fresh garlic, finely chopped
4	cups water
3	tablespoons tomato paste
	salt *(to taste)*
	black pepper *(to taste)*
2	tablespoons fresh chives, finely chopped

In a baking pan place the tomatoes and broil them for 2 to 3 minutes on each side, or until the skin turns black *(this also may be done on an outdoor grill)*. Let the tomatoes cool and then remove most of the burnt skin. Place the peeled tomatoes in a bowl and set them aside.

In a large saucepan place the olive oil and heat it on medium high until it is hot. Add the carrots, celery, onions, and garlic. Sauté the ingredients for 4 to 6 minutes, or until the onions are translucent.

Add the water and then turn the heat to high. Let the mixture boil for 10 minutes, or until the liquid is reduced by ⅓.

Add the tomato paste and stir it in.

Reduce the heat to medium. Add the broiled tomatoes *(with their juice)* and stir them in. Cook the ingredients for 5 minutes.

Pour the mixture into a food processor and purée it.

Pour the soup back into the saucepan to heat it, and then season it with the salt and black pepper.

Garnish the soup with the chopped chives.

serves 8

"One day I wanted to make a tomato soup, but I wanted to do something different. I knew that by roasting peppers you get a really wonderful smoky flavor, so I decided to try it with the tomatoes. Now, it's one of my favorite recipes!"

"When you broil the tomatoes they will turn to mush and the skin will get dark and hard. Take off as much of the skin as you can. It's okay if some of it stays on. And, do this over a bowl, so you can save the juice and use it in the soup."

"I use water in this recipe instead of chicken stock, so it is really vegetarian. If you want to use chicken stock it will give the soup a richer flavor."

"This is not a fattening soup, but it is very rich in its flavor and it is very hearty. To really make it good, you can add a little bit of cream. Also, if it is too thick for you, just thin it out with more liquid. I make it so that it is the consistency of a tomato sauce. You can use it instead of a traditional marinara sauce for pasta, chicken, or Eggplant Parmesan."

Adrienne Sussman
Chez What

Southwest Salmon Corn Chowder

¼	cup olive oil
1	cup fresh corn kernels
¼	cup celery, diced medium
¼	cup carrots, diced medium
⅛	cup yellow onions, diced medium
¼	cup yellow bell peppers, seeded and diced medium
¼	cup green bell peppers, seeded and diced medium
½	cup poblano chile peppers, diced medium
2	tablespoons fresh garlic, minced
½	cup white wine
¼	cup red chile powder
1	tablespoon ground cumin
1	tablespoon fresh basil, chopped
1	teaspoon fresh oregano, chopped
1	bay leaf
8	ounces salmon, cubed
2	quarts vegetable stock *(see chef's comments on page 130)*
2	tablespoons salt *(or to taste)*
1	tablespoon black pepper, freshly ground
2	tablespoons roux *(see chef's comments on this page)*

"This is a great soup, with lots of wonderful flavors. You can taste every item in it, from the vegetables, to the spices, to the salmon."

"To make the roux you should melt 2 tablespoons of butter and then stir in 2 tablespoons of flour. Stir the roux on low heat for about 10 minutes."

In a large stockpot place the olive oil and heat it on medium high until it is hot. Add the corn, celery, carrots, onions, yellow and green bell peppers, poblano chile peppers, and garlic. Sauté the ingredients for 3 to 5 minutes, or until the onions are translucent.

Add the white wine, red chile powder, cumin, basil, oregano, and bay leaf. Sauté the ingredients for 3 minutes.

Add the salmon, vegetable stock, salt, and black pepper. Simmer the ingredients for 1 hour.

Add the roux and stir it in so that it is dissolved. Simmer the chowder for ½ hour more.

serves 4 to 6

"The presentation of food is very important to me. My theory is, the food must look good so that people are willing to taste it. I like to use a lot of contrasting colors, shapes, and textures on the plate. And, there should always be a garnish."

Anthony Carpenter
Garfield Grill

Chilled Roasted Tomato and Summer Squash Soups in One Bowl

Chilled Roasted Tomato Soup

1½	tablespoons olive oil
1½	yellow onions, chopped
¼	cup fresh garlic, chopped
3	pounds Roma tomatoes, roasted
1	bunch fresh cilantro
1	tablespoon red chile powder
¼	teaspoon ground cumin
¼	teaspoon allspice
1	bay leaf, ground
1	teaspoon dried Mexican oregano, ground
½	tablespoon salt
1	quart water
	Chilled Summer Squash Soup *(recipe on next page)*

In a medium large saucepan place the olive oil and heat it on medium high until it is hot. Add the onions and garlic, and sauté them for 6 to 8 minutes, or until the onions are translucent. Add the remainder of the ingredients *(except for the Chilled Summer Squash Soup)* and simmer them for 20 minutes.

Place the mixture in a food processor and purée it. Strain the mixture through a fine sieve, and then chill it.

In each of 8 individual soup bowls pour the Roasted Tomato and Summer Squash soups side by side, so that they are next to each other *(use 2 hands and pour both soups at the same time)*.

serves 8

"This is a beautiful, healthy, low calorie soup. When you pour the two soups in the bowl together, you get a nicely defined line, with the yellow separated from the red. You can take a skewer and twirl the 2 soups together to make a design. Or, you can mix some sour cream with milk, and squeeze it out of a bag on top of the soup. Make a tic-tac-toe, write 'Happy Birthday, Joe!', or whatever you want. The recipe calls for the soup to be served cold, but it also is good hot."

"Even though I've always enjoyed cooking, I never dreamed that I would be a chef. All my life I wanted to be a commercial air line pilot, but I had some problems with my eyes, so that didn't work out. After dabbling in a lot of different lines of work I finally settled into cooking, and I'm very happy with what I do. My mother always told me that I should be trained as a chef, because she never saw anyone who loved to eat as much as I do!"

Laszlo Gyermek
Santacafe

Chilled Summer Squash Soup

3	pounds yellow squash, coarsely chopped
2	medium yellow onions
¼	teaspoon ground mustard *(dry)*
⅛	teaspoon nutmeg
¼	teaspoon turmeric
¼	teaspoon ground coriander
½	teaspoon salt
1	cup white wine
1	quart water

In a medium large saucepan place all of the ingredients and simmer them for 10 minutes, or until the squash is tender.

Place the mixture in a food processor and purée it. Strain the purée through a fine sieve and then chill it.

serves 8

> *"I was trained in the classical French way, which I consider to be just a springboard for other types of cooking. When you create and experiment in cooking there are certain parameters that you must remain within.....you must make certain that things work. For instance, you couldn't serve hot curry with vanilla ice cream..... well, maybe you could, but I wouldn't know how!"*
>
> Laszlo Gyermek
> Santacafe

Spanish Gazpacho

4	ripe tomatoes, coarsely chopped
3	cucumbers, peeled and seeds removed
½	bunch scallions
2	ounces Ortega green chile peppers
4	ounces pimientos
1	cup V-8 juice
⅓	cup red wine vinegar
⅓	cup olive oil
2	sprigs fresh tarragon
	salt *(to taste)*

In a food processor place the tomatoes, cucumbers, scallions, green chile peppers, and pimientos, and coarsely purée them.

Place the mixture in a medium bowl. Add the remainder of the ingredients and mix them in.

Chill the soup before serving it.

serves 4 to 6

> *"I love gazpacho.....it is my all time favorite soup. To me, it is like eating salad in a spoon. You have your salad vegetables, which are the tomatoes, cucumbers, scallions, and peppers. Then, when you add the vinegar, oil, and tarragon, it is like the salad dressing."*

> *"Purée this to the consistency that you prefer.....from chunky to smooth."*
>
> Ned Laventall
> El Farol

Chicken and Corn Soup with Saffron, Cilantro, and Poblano Chile

1	3½-pound chicken
3	quarts water
2	medium onions, diced
2	pinches saffron
3	medium carrots, sliced into rounds
2	teaspoons salt
¾	cup celery, diced
2½	cups fresh corn kernels
2	poblano chile peppers, seeds and ribs removed, and cut into thin strips
	salt *(to taste)*
	black pepper *(to taste)*
½	cup fresh cilantro, chopped

In a large stockpot place the chicken, water, onions, saffron, carrots, and the 2 teaspoons of salt. Simmer the ingredients for 1½ hours, or until the carrots are tender and the chicken is cooked.

Remove the chicken from the pot. Remove the skin and take the meat off the bones. Cut the meat into bite size pieces and set it aside.

To the broth add the celery, corn, and poblano chile strips. Simmer the ingredients for 20 minutes.

Add the diced chicken to the broth. Season it with the salt and black pepper. Garnish the soup with the chopped cilantro.

serves 6

"I grew up in the Pennsylvania Dutch part of the country where the Amish and Mennonites live. Their cuisine comes from a melting pot of different European countries, like Germany, Czechoslovakia, and Russia. Usually the food is very heavy, with a lot of dough, noodles, breads, and potatoes. Chicken and corn soup is very popular there, and every household has its own recipe.....kind of like posole or green chile stew in New Mexico. I added chile peppers and cilantro to my family's recipe, to give it a Southwestern twist. And, even though I know that my mother would yell at me if she knew this, I put in carrots because I like the sweetness that they add."

"Saffron is an herb that comes from the stigma of the crocus flower, and it is one of the main ingredients in Pennsylvania Dutch cooking. Every Dutch garden has crocus flowers growing in it, so the supply is abundant. Its unique flavor is embedded in my memory from childhood, and to this day it is my favorite seasoning."

Jonathan Horst
Adobo Catering

Chilled Cucumber Soup

4	cups cucumbers, peeled, seeded, and diced
2	cups plain yogurt
1	clove garlic, chopped
6	fresh mint leaves, chopped
¼	teaspoon dried dill weed
1	tablespoon raw honey
1	teaspoon salt *(or to taste)*
2	cups water
½	cup fresh chives, chopped

In a food processor place all of the ingredients *(except for the chives)* and purée them until they are smooth.

Chill the soup overnight in the refrigerator.

Garnish the soup with the chopped chives.

serves 8

"This is an excellent soup, and all you need to make it is a blender. If you want some additional texture, you can add some diced cucumbers before you serve it."

Walt McDowell
423

Spicy Southwestern Gazpacho

½	cup fresh cilantro, chopped
3	Roma tomatoes, diced
1	cucumber, peeled, seeded, and diced
1	red bell pepper, seeded and diced
1	medium onion, diced
3	jalapeño chile peppers, seeded and minced
3	cups V-8 juice
1	tablespoon tabasco
1	tablespoon balsamic vinegar
3	tablespoons extra virgin olive oil
4	Anaheim chile peppers, roasted, peeled, seeded, and cut into thin strips *(see chef's comments on page 159)*

In a medium large bowl place all of the ingredients *(except for the strips of roasted Anaheim chile peppers)* and mix them together.

Chill the soup for 2 hours in the refrigerator before serving it.

Garnish each bowl of soup with several strips of the roasted chile peppers.

serves 4

"Gazpacho is always a popular soup, and there are a million different ways to make it. I like to use V-8 juice in mine because it provides a very flavorful base. If you look at the label you will see that it is primarily veggies and spices. I put in some olive oil because it adds a really nice, creamy texture, but you can eliminate it if you wish. When you are dicing the vegetables be sure that they are all the same size, except for the jalapeños, which should be minced. The roasted chile strips on top of the soup add a nice, refreshing touch. Serve this with a salad and bread for lunch or a light dinner."

Robert Goodfriend
ek mas

"I looked at a lot of corn chowder recipes, and combined their best elements into this one. I tasted the soup a lot as I was putting it together, and it came out delicious. I think that one mistake many home cooks make is that they don't taste food enough as they are cooking it. They tend to rely too much on the recipe rather than on their own taste. Each person's taste is as valid as another's."

"This soup might curdle if you get it too hot or if you reheat it. If this happens you can reconstitute it in the blender, but then you will lose the texture of the corn kernels and chile peppers."

"I believe that a lot of chefs tend to mystify everything about cooking, and this scares many people away. They try to elevate cooking to an art form comparable to painting or music. I agree that cooking is an art form in its own way, but people can enjoy it and be creative from the very beginning, whereas to be a fine musician or painter takes many years of study. I want the mystery to be taken out of cooking so that everyone feels comfortable creating dishes and trusting their own taste, no matter what their experience or training."

Tom Wright
Galisteo Inn

Roasted Chile Corn Chowder

3	**tablespoons olive oil**
4	**cups red onions, diced**
½	**pound chorizo, casing removed, sautéed, drained of red grease, and crumbled**
1	**pound red potatoes** (skins on), **washed and diced small**
2	**quarts milk**
2	**quarts chicken stock** (recipe on page 295), **reduced to ½ cup** (or use 2 tablespoons chicken base)
3	**cups corn kernels**
6	**green chile peppers, roasted, peeled, seeded, and chopped** (see chef's comments on page 159)
1	**teaspoon ground cumin** (or to taste)
	salt (to taste)
	white pepper (to taste)

In a large stockpot place the olive oil and heat it on medium until it is hot. Add the onions and gently sauté them for 5 minutes, or until they are translucent.

Add the cooked chorizo and sauté it for 1 minute.

Add the red potatoes, milk, and chicken stock. Cook the ingredients for 30 minutes, or until the potatoes are tender.

Add the corn, green chile peppers, cumin, salt, and white pepper. Simmer the soup for 10 minutes, or until everything is heated.

serves 10 to 12

Black Bean Chile

¼	cup olive oil
1	large onion, diced medium
2	tablespoons fresh garlic, minced
1	tablespoon red chile powder
2	teaspoons ground coriander
2½	teaspoons cayenne pepper
2½	teaspoons paprika
1	tablespoon dried oregano
2½	teaspoons ground cumin
1½	pounds frozen green chile peppers, defrosted and chopped
4	cups tomatoes, chopped
4½	cups tomato juice
¼	cup molasses
1½	pounds black beans, washed, cooked *(recipe on page 285),* and drained *(reserve the cooking liquid)*
⅛	cup fresh cilantro, minced
1	tablespoon salt *(or to taste)*
1	cup Monterey Jack cheese, grated *(optional)*
½	cup sour cream *(optional)*

In a large stockpot place the olive oil and heat it on medium high until it is hot. Add the onions and sauté them for 6 to 8 minutes, or until they are translucent.

Add the garlic, red chile powder, coriander, cayenne pepper, paprika, dried oregano, and cumin. Stir the ingredients together.

Add the green chile peppers, tomatoes, tomato juice, and molasses. Stir the ingredients together. Cover the pot and bring the liquid to a simmer.

In a food processor place ⅓ of the cooked black beans and a small amount of the reserved cooking liquid. Purée the ingredients so that a smooth thick liquid is formed *(add the cooking liquid as needed)*.

To the stockpot add the puréed beans, the rest of the cooked beans, the cilantro, and the salt. Stir the ingredients together. Simmer the soup for 10 minutes, or until everything is hot.

In the bottom of each of 8 individual soup bowls place the Monterey Jack cheese. Pour the soup on top. Garnish the dish with a dollop of sour cream.

serves 8

"This is a great party dish that everyone will love. It leaves a nice taste in the roof of your mouth, but it doesn't burn your throat. The recipe is fairly detailed in that there are a lot of steps to it, but there is nothing that is too difficult in making it."

"I have found that many chefs are very sensitive, temperamental people..... much like artists or actors. If you criticize them once, then they will stop cooking for you. That's why many restaurant owners who have chefs don't get too involved in the kitchen."

Herb Cohen
Steaksmith

"You want to know what my philosophy of cooking is? That's easy.....I figure that if I make my boss happy, then I'm doing all right, and that makes me happy!"

Chris Arrison
Steaksmith

Autumn Squash Soup

2	**butternut squash, halved and seeded**
4	**acorn squash, halved and seeded**
1	**tablespoon butter**
2	**large yellow onions, coarsely chopped**
2	**large apples** (Granny Smith), **peeled and coarsely chopped**
1	**tablespoon curry powder**
2	**quarts rich chicken broth** (or as needed), (recipe on page 295)
	salt (to taste)
	black pepper (to taste)

Preheat the oven to 350°.

Place the squash halves, flat side down, on a flat, oiled baking sheet. Bake the squash for 30 minutes, or until they are soft. Let the squash cool. Scrape out the flesh.

In a large sauté pan place the butter and heat it on medium high until it is melted. Add the onions and apples, and sauté them for 6 to 8 minutes, or until the onions are translucent.

In a food processor place the cooked squash flesh, the sautéed onions and apples, curry powder, and chicken broth. Purée the ingredients so that a smooth consistency is achieved (add more broth if necessary).

Season the soup with the salt and black pepper. Gently heat the soup before serving it.

serves 10 to 12

"I love the fall, and I especially love to cook squash during this season. This soup recipe is so good that someone wrote into 'Gourmet' magazine and asked them to get the recipe from me. To let you know how disorganized I am, I recently found the request from 'Gourmet' magazine, dated over a year ago.....I had lost it and forgotten to send in the recipe."

"I think that the cocktail party should be abolished! You should only be allowed to have dinner parties, with lots of courses. The food doesn't have to be elaborately cooked.....it can be simple, peasant food. Take a long time in between courses, enjoy each other's company, and make the evening a memorable experience. If I had my way, everyday eating would be a banquet."

"It's exciting to own my own restaurant and catering business, but it's also incredibly hard work. I get up at dawn, and I'm usually in bed with Dan Rather every evening."

Sylvia Johnson
Celebrations

Chilled Strawberry Soup
with Cumin

2	pints strawberries, hulled
1½	cups pear nectar
1	sprig fresh mint, chopped
½	teaspoon ground cumin
¼	teaspoon salt
1	tablespoon lime juice, freshly squeezed
1	tablespoon corn starch
4	sprigs fresh mint

In a medium large saucepan place the strawberries, pear nectar, chopped mint, cumin, and salt. Cook the ingredients over medium heat for 15 minutes.

In a small bowl place the lime juice and corn starch, and mix them together well so that there are no lumps.

While stirring constantly, slowly add the cornstarch mixture to the cooked strawberries. Cook the mixture for 2 minutes.

Place the mixture in a blender and purée it.

Chill the soup in the refrigerator overnight.

Serve the soup with a mint sprig as a garnish.

serves 4

"This is my recipe that I used in Oklahoma City when we were doing a banquet for a health conscious group. It's one of those wonderful, quick soups that is both elegant and light. Ideally you should make it when fresh strawberries are at their peak, although you could use frozen. There's no trick to making it.....just be sure that you blend it well."

John Davis
Old House

Corn Chowder

"One morning I woke up with the idea to make a corn chowder because people in this part of the country love corn and green chile. Lots of times I wake up with an idea for a new recipe, and then I write it down in my little notebook. It's a good system, and I've come up with a lot of good recipes this way."

"The chowder tastes wonderful, and there is nothing difficult at all in making it. Just don't let the milk boil over. If you like, you can add a bit of cheese."

"My husband is a pastry chef and I am a cook, and together we have the perfect business marriage. He hates to cook and I hate to bake. Together we run the two parts of our restaurant-bakery business, and neither of us trespasses on the other's terrain."

"I hope that when people come to my restaurant they will have a feeling of being in Switzerland. I want them to experience the same atmosphere and to eat the same food that they would have over there."

Marie Jeanne Chaney
Swiss Bakery

1	teaspoon olive oil
½	yellow onion, diced
2	cloves garlic, chopped
8	ounces frozen corn kernels
1	potato, peeled and cubed
½	cup frozen green chile peppers *(hot)*, defrosted and diced
2	cubes beef bouillon
1	quart milk
⅓	cup water
1	egg yolk
¼	cup cream
1	teaspoon fresh cilantro, finely chopped

In a medium large stockpot place the olive oil and heat it on medium high until it is hot. Add the onions and garlic, and sauté them for 5 minutes, or until the onions are translucent.

Add the corn, potatoes, green chile peppers, and beef bouillon cubes. Sauté the ingredients for 10 to 15 minutes, or until the corn is softened.

Add the milk and water, and simmer the ingredients for 45 minutes, or until the potatoes are very soft.

Remove the pot from the heat. Place the soup in a blender and purée it. Return the soup to the pot.

In a small bowl place the egg yolk and cream, and whisk them together. Add the mixture to the soup and stir it in.

Garnish the soup with the cilantro.

serves 4 to 6

Salads & Salad Dressings

Caesar Salad
with Red Chile Dressing

Caesar Salad

1	head romaine lettuce, washed, dried, and cut into 2" long pieces
	Red Chile Dressing (recipe follows)
½	**cup croutons** (see chef's comments on this page)
½	**cup Parmesan cheese, freshly grated**

In a large bowl place the lettuce. Toss it with the Red Chile Dressing.

On each of 4 chilled, individual serving plates place the dressed lettuce. Add the croutons and sprinkle on the Parmesan cheese.

serves 4

Red Chile Dressing

4	anchovies
2	cloves garlic
2	tablespoons Dijon mustard
2	tablespoons Worcestershire sauce
1	tablespoon red chile powder *(mild)*
1	teaspoon paprika
2	tablespoons cider vinegar
2	tablespoons lemon juice, freshly squeezed
1	cup olive oil

In a food processor place all of the ingredients *(except for the olive oil)*, and blend them. With the processor still running, slowly dribble in the oil.

makes 2 cups

"You can make croutons with either stale or fresh bread. Remove the crust, cut the bread into cubes, and put them in a bowl with some olive oil, dried oregano, tarragon, pepper, and garlic salt. Toss them so that they are well coated with the oil and spices. Then, either sauté them until they are crispy brown, or roast them in the oven at 350° for about 10 minutes. Either way, keep a sharp eye on them."

"Anchovies scare a lot of people because they have such a strong, salty, oily taste and a weird texture. Served by themselves they often are overpowering. But, if you chop them up or purée them, they can be an incredible flavor enhancer. Anchovies are in this salad dressing and they really make the tastes come alive. I have never had one complaint about the anchovies.....I've had only many, many compliments on the delicious flavor."

Mark Hawrylak
The Evergreen

"I just love jicama. The first time I ever tried it I thought it was pronounced 'Jim-Ka'. It's such an ugly thing, but when you peel and slice it nicely it is a wonderful vegetable. The texture is crunchy and the flavor is a cross between a coconut and a carrot."

"I like to keep food simple, so that it tastes and looks like what it is. Cooking is like painting, in that if you mix up too many colors you will end up with gray.....and I'm not into gray food."

"This salad dressing is really neat because it's so simple to make. The sweetness of the honey balances out the hotness of the mustard, and when you eat it with the salad you have a lot going on in your mouth. The mustard hits your olfactory nerves so that your sense of smell is stimulated. Most of the nuances of different flavors come from the sense of smell, not from taste. For example, pretend that your nose was stopped up and you were blindfolded. If you ate a piece of chocolate you would not be able to taste what it was. You 'chocoholics' should keep this in mind when you have a cold.....don't waste the calories!"

Walt McDowell
423

423 House Salad

1   head green leaf lettuce, washed, dried, and torn
1   head red leaf lettuce, washed, dried, and torn
     Honey Mustard Dressing *(recipe follows)*
1   cup carrots, grated
1   cup red radishes, grated
1   cup jicama, peeled and julienned
1   cup pine nuts, toasted
1   cup pepitas *(roasted pumpkin seeds)*

In a large bowl place the torn green leaf and red leaf lettuces. Toss them with the Honey Mustard Dressing.

On each of 4 individual salad plates place the dressed lettuce. Artfully arrange the remaining ingredients on top.

serves 4

Honey Mustard Dressing

1   cup raw honey
1   cup Dijon mustard
1   cup white wine vinegar
½   cup dry white wine
½   cup olive oil

In a food processor place all of the ingredients and blend them for 1 minute.

Place the dressing in a covered jar and chill it in the refrigerator. Shake the dressing before using it.

makes 1 quart

Warm Salad of Grilled Wild Mushrooms and Lively Greens

4	cloves garlic, minced
2	tablespoons fresh thyme leaves, stems removed
3	lemons, juiced
½	cup balsamic vinegar
¾	cup olive oil
4	large portabello mushrooms, washed and stems removed
8	shiitake mushrooms, washed and stems removed
2	heads Belgian endive, leaves washed and dried
1	head radicchio, leaves washed and dried
2	large bunches arugula, washed, dried, and ends of stems removed
	black pepper *(to taste)*, freshly ground

In a medium bowl place the garlic, thyme, lemon juice, balsamic vinegar, and olive oil. Mix the ingredients together.

Add the portabello and shiitake mushrooms, and let them marinate for 2 hours at room temperature. Remove the mushrooms. Heat the marinade over low heat.

Grill the mushrooms over medium hot coals for 3 minutes on each side, or until they are heated through.

In a large bowl place the heated marinade, grilled mushrooms, and prepared greens. Toss the ingredients together so that they are well coated with the marinade. Season the salad with the black pepper.

serves 4

"Grilling the mushrooms really brings out their flavor. In order to keep them from falling through the grate, you can take an extra grate and set it on top in a crisscross pattern. You may substitute other herbs, but it is essential that they are fresh, not dried."

"I like to go to the West Coast and eat at different restaurants to see what's new and different. It's really a shot in the arm for me.....they have so many wonderful ethnic cuisines that we don't have here, and my horizons are always expanded. When possible, I take my chef with me."

"When I cook I always look for that partnership of flavors, where things naturally go together well. This requires a lot of dreaming, experience, and trial and error. Our food is emphatic in taste, without being over-powering, and we use organic products whenever possible."

"I remember myself at the age of 4 standing on a chair in the kitchen, stirring pots. Now, as an adult, I am only 5 feet tall and I still find myself standing on a chair in the kitchen so that I can reach things."

Katharine Kagel
Cafe Pasqual's

Steaksmith Spinach Salad
with Hot Citrus Dressing

Steaksmith Spinach Salad

4	cups spinach, stems removed, washed, dried, and torn
1	red onion, sliced into thin rings
12	sections mandarin oranges
4	tablespoons walnuts, chopped
2	tablespoons bacon, cooked and crumbled
½	cup croutons
½	cup Swiss cheese, thinly sliced and cut into 1" squares
	Hot Citrus Dressing (recipe follows)

On each of 4 individual serving plates place the spinach. In this order, artfully add and arrange the red onion rings, mandarin orange sections, walnut pieces, crumbled bacon, croutons, and Swiss cheese.

Serve the salad with the Hot Citrus Dressing on the side.

serves 4

Hot Citrus Dressing

⅓	cup orange juice concentrate
⅔	cup white distilled vinegar
¼	cup honey
1	cup water
1	teaspoon fresh ginger root, peeled and grated
1	dash white pepper
⅔	cup garlic oil (*see chef's comments on this page for instructions*)

In a medium saucepan place the orange juice concentrate, white vinegar, honey, water, ginger, and white pepper. Bring the ingredients to a simmer, and mix them together.

While whisking constantly, slowly dribble in the garlic oil.

makes 3 cups

Tomato and Cucumber Salad

2	tablespoons fresh ginger root, peeled and chopped
2	tablespoons fresh garlic, peeled and chopped
⅓	cup balsamic vinegar
1	cup olive oil
½	head romaine lettuce, washed, dried, and cut
2	cucumbers, peeled, seeded, and thinly sliced
12	yellow teardrop tomatoes, halved
3	Roma tomatoes, quartered
3	scallions, thinly sliced
3	fresh basil leaves, thinly sliced

In a food processor place the ginger and garlic, and purée them together. With the processor running, slowly add the balsamic vinegar and olive oil. Set the vinaigrette aside.

In a medium large bowl place the romaine lettuce, cucumbers, yellow teardrop tomatoes, Roma tomatoes, scallions, and basil leaves. Mix the ingredients together.

Add the vinaigrette and toss it in. Serve the salad immediately.

serves 4 to 6

"This is a light and refreshing salad that you can whip up in a few minutes. The yellow teardrop tomatoes are a variety of the small cherry tomatoes, only they are golden in color and not quite a round shape. They add a nice color to the dish and they are sweet tasting, with almost no acidity. They are a seasonal vegetable, so if you can't find them, then use the regular cherry tomatoes."

Ned Laventall
El Farol

Marinated Vegetable Salad

1	shallot bulb, peeled
1	bunch fresh cilantro, leaves only
¼	cup fresh mint, chopped
2	poblano chile peppers, diced
3	jalapeño chile peppers, diced
½	cup lime juice, freshly squeezed
1	teaspoon salt *(or to taste)*
½	teaspoon white pepper *(or to taste)*
2	cups walnut oil
3	large jicamas, peeled and julienned
1	red bell pepper, seeded and julienned
1	green bell pepper, seeded and julienned
1	yellow bell pepper, seeded and julienned
2	poblano chile peppers, seeded and julienned
2	yellow chile peppers, seeded and julienned
⅛	pound yellow wax beans, strings removed
⅛	pound purple wax beans, strings removed
¼	pound snow peas, strings removed
¼	pound baby corn, husks and silk removed
¼	pound baby carrots
¼	pound cherry tomatoes, stems removed
¼	pound baby cucumbers *(pickling)*
¼	pound baby zucchini

In a food processor place the shallot, cilantro, mint, the first 2 poblano chile peppers, the jalapeño chile peppers, lime juice, salt, and white pepper. Blend the ingredients together. With the food processor running on high, slowly dribble in the walnut oil.

In a large bowl place the vinaigrette and the remainder of the ingredients. Mix everything together well. Let the salad marinate for 24 hours in the refrigerator.

serves 8

New Mexican Pasta Salad with Red Chile Pesto

New Mexican Pasta Salad

1	pound fusilli pasta, cooked al dente, rinsed in cold water, and drained
	Red Chile Pesto *(recipe follows)*
4	large leaves red leaf lettuce, washed and dried
16	calamata olives
1	yellow bell pepper, seeded and julienned

In a medium bowl place the cold pasta and Red Chile Pesto *(to taste)*, and mix them together well.

On each of 4 individual serving plates place a lettuce leaf. Place the pasta on top. Garnish each serving with the calamata olives and yellow bell peppers.

serves 4

Red Chile Pesto

3	cloves garlic
⅛	cup pine nuts
⅛	cup Parmesan cheese, freshly grated
¼	bunch fresh cilantro
¼	bunch fresh basil
⅛	cup red chile powder
⅛	cup chile caribe *(crushed red chile peppers)*
1	teaspoon ground cumin
	salt *(to taste)*
1	cup olive oil

In a food processor place all of the ingredients *(except for the olive oil)* and purée them together. With the processor still running, slowly add the olive oil.

makes approximately 2 cups

"Here is something quick and easy to make that has a wonderful, slightly spicy flavor. Even though the pasta is cold, the pesto will distribute throughout the noodles quite easily."

"I like to think of cooking as being a creative endeavor. You don't necessarily have to follow every single recipe to a 'T' each time you cook. If you can't find one ingredient, then try substituting another that makes sense to you."

"Although my background is in classical French cooking, I like to make cold sauces that use olive oil, such as this recipe, and stay away from creams and butter. This is a Southwestern version of a classical pesto with a little kick to it. It's simple to make, and the flavor is very clean. You can make this several days ahead of time, or you can freeze it."

David Jones
Casa Sena

Garfield Pasta Salad

4	cups cooked tri-colored rotilli pasta, drained and chilled
½	cup red bell peppers, diced
½	cup black olives, thinly sliced
½	cup scallions, thinly sliced
½	cup sun-dried tomatoes, finely chopped
¼	cup piñon nuts *(pine nuts)*, **roasted** *(see chef's comments on page 259)*
1	cup feta cheese, crumbled
1	tablespoon fresh garlic, minced
¼	cup red wine vinegar
¼	cup lemon juice, freshly squeezed
½	cup olive oil
1	tablespoon salt *(or to taste)*
1	teaspoon black pepper, freshly ground

In a medium large bowl place the cooked pasta, red bell peppers, black olives, scallions, sun-dried tomatoes, roasted piñon nuts, and feta cheese. Toss the ingredients together.

In a small bowl place the garlic, red wine vinegar, and lemon juice. While whisking constantly, slowly dribble in the olive oil.

Pour the vinaigrette over the pasta salad *(to taste)* and toss it in well.

Season the salad with the salt and black pepper.

serves 4

"This is really a good recipe for pasta salad. I've been working on it for a long time, trying to perfect it. It's very colorful and festive looking, and it tastes wonderful!"

Anthony Carpenter
Garfield Grill

"Sometimes when people eat at our restaurant they are too tired (or have had a little too much wine!) to walk back to their hotel. Instead of calling a cab, either my wife or I will give them a lift back to their room.....guaranteed! It's nice for them and we enjoy doing it."

Phillip Howell
Garfield Grill

Santa Fe Chicken Pasta Salad

3	pounds boneless chicken breasts, skin removed
	salt *(to taste)*
	black pepper *(to taste)*
1	teaspoon fresh garlic, minced
1	pound fettucini, cooked al dente, rinsed, and cooled
1	pound zucchini, cut into match sticks and blanched
1	can garbanzo beans
2	bunches scallions, thinly sliced
2	bunches fresh cilantro, chopped
3	jalapeño chile peppers, seeded and minced
2	cups crushed tomatoes
1½	teaspoons ground cumin
½	teaspoon salt *(or to taste)*
¼	teaspoon black pepper, freshly ground

Preheat the oven to 350°.

On a lightly oiled baking tray place the chicken breasts. Sprinkle them with the salt, black pepper, and garlic. Bake the chicken for 20 minutes, or until it is done.

Cut the chicken into bite size cubes.

In a medium large bowl place the cooled, cooked fettucini. Add the remainder of the ingredients and toss them together well.

Place the dish in the refrigerator for ½ hour before serving it.

serves 4

"This dish is spicy and it may be too hot for some people. The jalapeño peppers are what give it the heat, so use them to your taste."

"Many times I will visually see a dish in my head before I make it. I feel like an artist painting my foods. I see colors and textures, and then I weave the flavors in."

"I love to use strong, powerful flavors in my cooking. And, I also am a great risk taker in that I use combinations of foods and flavors that I have never seen before. I never follow a recipe verbatim. Instead, I alter it and change things in ways that I think will make it better."

Lisa Sivé
Wild Oats Market

Blackened Chicken Salad with Tamari Sesame Dressing

Blackened Chicken Salad

6	8-ounce chicken breasts, skin and bones removed
	Blackening Spices *(recipe on page 296)*
1	head red leaf lettuce, washed, dried, and torn
1	head green leaf lettuce, washed, dried, and torn
1	bunch arugula, washed, dried, and torn
1	cup mandarin orange sections *(canned or fresh)*
1	cup red flame seedless grapes
	Tamari Sesame Dressing *(recipe follows)*

Dredge the chicken breasts in the Blackening Spices. Place a heavy, seasoned, cast iron skillet on high heat for 10 minutes, or until it is very hot. Add the chicken breasts and cook them for 3 to 5 minutes on each side, or until they are just done. Cut the chicken into thin strips.

In a large bowl place the red and green leaf lettuces, arugula, mandarin orange sections, and grapes. Toss the ingredients with the Tamari Sesame Dressing.

On each of 6 individual serving plates place the dressed salad. Artfully arrange the chicken strips on top.

serves 6

Tamari Sesame Dressing

1	cup balsamic vinegar
⅓	cup red wine vinegar
¼	cup soy sauce
¼	cup sesame seeds, toasted
¾	cup honey
1	teaspoon Dijon mustard
½	cup sesame oil
½	cup salad oil

In a food processor place all of the ingredients *(except for the sesame and salad oils)*. With the food processor constantly running, slowly dribble in the two oils.

makes approximately 4 cups

"The combination of the blackened spice on the chicken with the fruit and the tamari dressing is outstanding. When you cook the chicken in your kitchen, be sure that you have a good exhaust system, because there will be a lot of smoke. If you don't, then I recommend that you blacken the chicken outside."

"I am a writer and an artist, as well as a chef. To me, all of these are art forms that are expressions of who I am as a human being. I like for my life to feel smooth and balanced on the inside, because then the outside things don't seem to matter so much. That's why the images in my paintings flow together, and the flavors in my cooking blend together, with no sharp contrasts."

Isaac Modivah
Ore House

"John Beaupre is the owner of the Ore House, and he loves anything that is blackened. He wanted a blackened chicken salad, but he wanted a special dressing to go with it. So all of us experimented in the kitchen, and finally we came up with this recipe. Now it is the most popular salad dressing that we have."

Daniela Croce
Ore House

Tangy Marinated Chicken Salad with Honeydew Salsa and Herb Balsamic Vinaigrette

Tangy Marinated Chicken Salad

½   medium onion, chopped medium
1   clove garlic, finely chopped
1   teaspoon fresh cilantro, finely chopped
1   lime, juiced
1   cup olive oil
1   dash cayenne pepper
1   teaspoon paprika
2   teaspoons ground cumin
1   teaspoon turmeric
½   teaspoon salt
¼   teaspoon black pepper, freshly ground
2   whole chicken breasts, skin and bones removed, and
        cut in half
½   **pound wild greens** (baby lettuces, arugula, mustard)
       Honeydew Salsa (recipe on next page)
       Herb Balsamic Vinaigrette (recipe on next page)

In a large bowl place all of the ingredients (except for the chicken, wild greens, salsa, and vinaigrette) and mix them together. Add the chicken and let it marinate in the refrigerator for at least 24 hours.

Grill the chicken breasts for 2 to 3 minutes on each side, or until they are just done. Let them cool, and then slice them diagonally.

On each of 4 individual serving plates place the wild greens. Place the grilled chicken slices on top. Circle the Honeydew Salsa around the wild greens. Serve the Herb Balsamic Vinaigrette on the side.

serves 4

"When you let the chicken marinate for 24 hours it gets a real punch to it. The flavors seep inside the meat and they just explode with tanginess when you take a bite. This is a wonderful recipe for grilled chicken breast, even without making it into a salad."

"I've been cooking in restaurants since I was 16. But, I didn't really like cooking until one time when I was given free rein to experiment and use my imagination. From then on, I was hooked!"

Paul Hunsicker
Paul's Restaurant of Santa Fe

Honeydew Salsa

1	honeydew melon, peeled, seeded, and finely chopped
1	medium red onion, finely chopped
1	tomato, chopped medium
1	jalapeño chile pepper, finely chopped
1	tablespoon fresh cilantro, finely chopped
1	lemon, juiced
1/8	teaspoon tabasco
1/8	teaspoon salt

In a medium bowl place all of the ingredients and mix them together. Chill the salsa in the refrigerator for 30 minutes before serving it.

makes 3 to 4 cups

Herb Balsamic Vinaigrette

1	tablespoon fresh basil, minced
2	tablespoons red bell pepper, minced
1	clove garlic, minced
1/4	teaspoon dry mustard
1/3	cup balsamic vinegar
	salt *(to taste)*
	cracked black pepper *(to taste)*
1	cup olive oil

In a small bowl place all of the ingredients *(except for the olive oil)*. While whisking constantly, slowly dribble in the olive oil.

makes 1½ cups

"Although this salsa will not quite knock your socks off, it still is quite spicy. The combination of hot and sweet is very popular these days. You can make this recipe with any kind of fruit that is fresh and good. It should keep in the refrigerator for up to 3 days."

"At the restaurant we use an herb mayonnaise for the salad, but I decided to substitute a vinaigrette, in order to maintain the lighter, healthier theme of this book. If you want to make 1 cup of an herbed mayonnaise, just add 1 tablespoon each of puréed fresh basil, oregano, and tarragon, and mix them in."

Paul Hunsicker
Paul's Restaurant of Santa Fe

Spicy Warm Duck Confit and Wild Mushroom Salad

20	bay leaves, crumbled into small pieces
¾	cup chile caribe *(crushed red chile peppers)*
6	tablespoons dried thyme
2	tablespoons garlic powder
½	cup kosher salt
4	tablespoons black pepper, freshly ground
4	duck breasts
4	cups corn oil *(or as needed)*
2	tablespoons olive oil
2	cups wild mushrooms, cleaned and thinly sliced
3	tablespoons shallots, diced
2	tablespoons fresh herbs *(basil, thyme, marjoram)*, **chopped**
½	cup balsamic vinegar
6	cups mixed salad greens
1	cup garlic croutons *(see chef's comments on this page)*
½	cup pine nuts, toasted

In a small bowl place the crumbled bay leaves, chile caribe, thyme, garlic powder, kosher salt, and black pepper. Mix the ingredients together so they are well combined.

Rub the duck pieces with the spice mixture. Store them in a tight container in the refrigerator for 2 days so that the salt and spices are absorbed into the duck and cure it.

Preheat the oven to 275°.

In a roasting pan place the cured duck pieces and cover them with the corn oil. Cover the pan with a lid. Roast the duck for 5 to 6 hours, or until it is very soft but not crispy. Remove the duck from the pan. Gently remove the skin and pick the meat off the bones. Set the duck meat aside.

In a large sauté pan place the olive oil and heat it on medium until it is hot. Add the duck, wild mushrooms, shallots, and herbs. Sauté the ingredients for 8 to 10 minutes, or until they are heated through. Remove the pan from the heat. Add the balsamic vinegar and toss it with the ingredients.

In a medium large bowl place the duck mixture, salad greens, and garlic croutons, and mix them together well. Garnish the salad with the toasted pine nuts.

serves 4

"Confit is a very old type of food storage that is especially popular in the south of France. It means to cook and store poultry or meat in its own fat and juices. The meat is rubbed with spices and cooked in fat for a very long time at a low temperature. Then it is stored in a cool and dark cellar in its own fat, where it will keep for months and months."

"The dish takes some time to make, but after the duck confit is made and stored, then the rest is easy. When you buy the mixed greens, try to get sturdier kinds that won't wilt when the warm duck is added. This is a wonderful dish and it's perfect for a special dinner salad or an elegant luncheon."

"We use 2-day-old bread when we make the garlic croutons. Cut off the crust and then cut the white part into cubes. Toss them in garlic oil (raw garlic puréed and added to olive oil) and toast them in the oven until they are crispy."

Karen Woods
Rancho Encantado

Mexican Chicken Salad

6	8-ounce chicken breasts, skin removed
6	large tomatoes, diced medium
1	green bell pepper, seeded and diced medium
1	jalapeño chile pepper, seeded and finely chopped
1	medium yellow onion, diced medium
½	cup fresh cilantro, chopped
2	tablespoons fresh garlic, finely chopped
½	cup tomato juice
½	teaspoon ground cumin
½	teaspoon salt
1	teaspoon black pepper, freshly ground
1	large head iceberg lettuce, shredded
1	large avocado, peeled, pitted, and quartered
1	large tomato, cored and cut into 8 wedges
4	tablespoons sour cream *(optional)*

In a large saucepan place the chicken breasts, diced tomatoes, green bell peppers, jalapeño chile peppers, onions, cilantro, garlic, tomato juice, cumin, salt, and black pepper. Cover the pan and cook the ingredients on medium high heat for 10 minutes, or until the chicken is done.

Remove the chicken breas and set them aside to cool.

Continue to cook the ingredients uncovered for 10 minutes more. Pour the mixture into a food processor and purée it. Let the sauce cool.

Remove the cooled chicken from the bones and shred it with your hands.

In a large bowl place the sauce *(reserve 1 cup)* and the lettuce, and toss them together.

On each of 4 individual serving plates place the lettuce. Place the shredded chicken on top. Place the avocado and tomato wedges on top of the chicken. Spoon on the reserved sauce and add a dollop of sour cream.

serves 4 to 6

"I really love Mexican food, and once when I was on a diet I came up with this recipe. Originally I made it as a hot burrito. I used most of the same ingredients, but I didn't purée them. Instead, I rolled them up in a flour tortilla. They were only about 300 calories each and I would eat 3 of them a day. I loved them! One day there were a lot of leftover ingredients, so I decided to make them into a sauce and purée them. It was so good, I can't even tell you!"

"This is a little bit spicy, so if your stomach can't handle the heat, then leave out the jalapeño pepper. And, if you want it hotter, add another pepper. But if you do so, please be careful because jalapeños vary greatly in their heat. Some are quite mild, and some are dynamite. It's best to cut off a small piece of the pepper and touch it to your tongue. If you immediately feel a burning sensation, then you know you have a hot pepper."

Adrienne Sussman
Chez What

Oriental Chicken Salad

½	cup fresh ginger root, peeled and finely diced
5	cloves garlic, chopped
½	medium onion, chopped
1	small celery rib, chopped
½	cup chicken stock *(recipe on page 295)*
1	cup pineapple juice
½	cup soy sauce
⅓	cup brown sugar
2	teaspoons chile caribe *(crushed red chile peppers)*
1	tablespoon cornstarch dissolved in 1 tablespoon water
1	tablespoon balsamic vinegar
¼	cup toasted sesame oil
6	5-ounce chicken breasts, skinned and boned, grilled and cut into long, thin strips
1	small yellow squash, julienned
1	small zucchini, julienned
1	red bell pepper, seeded, julienned, and blanched *(see chef's comments on this page)*
1	yellow bell pepper, seeded, julienned, and blanched
1	green bell pepper, seeded, julienned, and blanched
1	large carrot, peeled, julienned, and blanched
6	celery ribs, julienned and blanched
36	snow peas, strings removed, and blanched
3	ounces water chestnuts *(canned)*, sliced
6	large green leaf lettuce leaves, washed and dried
1	Belgian endive, washed, dried, and leaves separated
1	small can pineapple chunks
¼	cup bean sprouts
¼	cup sesame seeds, toasted
2	tablespoons pickled ginger

In a medium large saucepan place the ginger root, garlic, onions, chopped celery, chicken stock, pineapple juice, soy sauce, brown sugar, and chile caribe. Simmer the ingredients on low heat for 30 minutes.

Add the cornstarch and water mixture, and stir it in. Strain the sauce and then let it cool.

Add the balsamic vinegar and toasted sesame oil, and stir them in.

(continued on next page)

"One day we had a lot of extra chickens in the restaurant, as well as some leftover ginger sauce from a big banquet. I added some ingredients to the sauce and came up with this Oriental Chicken Salad. It proved to be so popular with the customers that we put it on the menu as a permanent item. When a new recipe is met with such success, I find it very satisfying."

"To blanch the vegetables you should use a large amount of water and bring it to a boil. Add a little salt and the vegetables, and cook them for 2 minutes. Pour the vegetables in a strainer and place them in ice water. As soon as they are cool, drain them."

"Pickled ginger can be found in specialty Oriental stores or perhaps in natural food stores. I just love it and I eat it plain or with raw tuna. The kind that I buy is very hot, but other types are sweet because they are packed in syrup. Taste it and then let your imagination come up with possible uses."

Ernie Bolleter
Inn at Loretto

In a medium large bowl place the chicken, yellow squash, zucchini, the red, yellow, and green bell peppers, carrots, celery, snow peas, and water chestnuts. Pour on the desired amount of the sauce and toss the ingredients together.

In each of 6 individual salad bowls place a leaf of the green leaf lettuce. Spoon on the chicken and vegetable mixture. Garnish the dish with the Belgian endive, pineapple chunks, bean sprouts, toasted sesame seeds, and pickled ginger.

serves 6

> *"If you don't put the sauce on the salad, then it will keep for 2 or 3 days. But, once you add the sauce you should serve it right away."*
>
> Ernie Bolleter
> Inn at Loretto

Herring Salad

4	**herring fillets** *("Matjes Herring" if possible),* **chopped**
1	**Granny Smith apple, peeled, cored, and grated**
⅓	**cup dill pickle, chopped**
⅓	**cup beets, cooked, peeled, and grated**
2	**tablespoons mayonnaise**
2	**tablespoons sour cream**
½	**teaspoon Worcestershire sauce** *(or to taste)*
	white pepper *(to taste)*
4	**leaves red lettuce, washed and dried**
1	**Belgian endive, leaves separated**
1	**lemon, cut into 4 wedges**

> *"Matjes Herring is a Scandinavian fish that has a wonderful, unique flavor. It comes in cans and is stored in the refrigerator. This recipe is as simple to make as it sounds. The saltiness of the herring is counterbalanced by the apples and beets. The salad looks very pretty.....it has a nice pink color."*

In a medium bowl place all of the ingredients *(except for the red lettuce, endive, and lemon wedges)* and mix them together.

On each of 4 individual salad plates place a leaf of the red lettuce. Spoon the herring salad on top. Place the endive leaves around the salad. Garnish the dish with a lemon wedge.

serves 4

> *"I love cooking because of the applause I receive at the end. The complete experience is composed of the menu planning, shopping for the various ingredients, preparing the food, putting everything together, and sending the dishes out to the people. Then I wait for the reviews to come in. Nothing makes me happier than to have someone eat my food and then watch their eyes light up."*
>
> Mark Hawrylak
> The Evergreen

Smoked Salmon and Belgian Endive Salad with Ruby Grapefruit and Dill Vinaigrette

Smoked Salmon and Belgian Endive Salad with Ruby Grapefruit

6	ounces smoked salmon *(good quality)*, **cut into 1" squares**
½	**medium red onion, thinly sliced and julienned, soaked in ice water** *(2 minutes)*, **and drained**
4	**Belgian endives, cut into 1" pieces**
2	**ruby grapefruits, peeled, sectioned, and membranes removed**
¼	**cup Dill Vinaigrette** *(recipe on next page)*
4	**sprigs fresh dill**

In a medium bowl place the smoked salmon *(reserve 4 of the pieces for the garnish)*, red onions, Belgian endive pieces, grapefruit sections *(reserve 12 sections)*, and Dill Vinaigrette. Gently toss the ingredients together so that they are well combined.

On each of 4 chilled, individual salad plates place the tossed salad. Place 3 of the reserved grapefruit segments around the edge. Garnish the dish with a reserved piece of the smoked salmon and a sprig of fresh dill.

serves 4

"This is a salad that was on the menu at the Beverly Wilshire Hotel, where I previously worked. It was a very elegant and expensive place.....suites were $3000 a night. I worked 80 to 90 hours a week and there were 120 chefs working under me. You ask if I was stressed? That's putting it mildly! I was happy to get out of Los Angeles and move to Santa Fe, where things are a lot more peaceful."

"When I was a young boy growing up in England I used to love our family holiday traditions. For Christmas dinner we always had what was known as 'Christmas Pudding', and each member of the family had to stir it. A silver coin was put in the pudding, and the person who got it at the dinner table was to have good luck for all of the coming year. My involvement in these traditions helped to develop my love of cooking at a young age. Also, because England has terrible winters I couldn't play outside, so I would amuse myself by fooling around in the kitchen."

Jim Makinson
Bishop's Lodge

Dill Vinaigrette

2	egg yolks
2	tablespoons Dijon mustard
2	tablespoons rice wine vinegar
4	tablespoons aged sherry wine vinegar
2	cups safflower oil
1	red bell pepper, seeded and finely diced
1	teaspoon Pernod
	salt *(to taste)*
	black pepper *(to taste)*

In a medium bowl place the egg yolks and Dijon mustard. Whisk them together so that they are well combined.

Add the two vinegars and whisk them in.

While whisking constantly, slowly add the safflower oil.

Add the red bell peppers, Pernod, salt, and black pepper, and whisk them in.

makes approximately 3 cups

"This vinaigrette can be used on any kind of mixed greens. The flavors marry together very well, and the Pernod gives it a subtle background flavor of licorice."

Jim Makinson
Bishop's Lodge

"Bishop's Lodge has been in my husband's family since 1917. Some of the families that come here are in their sixth generation, which I feel is really a compliment. Over the years we have made many wonderful friends."

Lore Thorpe
Bishop's Lodge

Spicy Shrimp and Black Bean Salad with Citrus Vinaigrette

Spicy Shrimp and Black Bean Salad

¼	cup olive oil
2	pounds medium shrimp, peeled and deveined
2	teaspoons fresh garlic, minced
2	teaspoons red chile powder *(hot)*
1	cup cooked black beans *(recipe on page 285),* **rinsed and drained**
½	red bell pepper, seeded and finely diced
½	green bell pepper, seeded and finely diced
4	scallions, thinly sliced
2	oranges, peeled, sectioned, and membranes removed
2	tablespoons fresh ginger root, peeled and finely chopped
2	tablespoons garlic, finely chopped
	Citrus Vinaigrette *(recipe on next page)*
8	leaves radicchio

In a large skillet place the olive oil and heat it on medium high until it is hot. Add the shrimp, the 2 teaspoons of minced garlic, and the red chile powder. Sauté the ingredients for 2 to 3 minutes, or until the shrimp are opaque.

Remove the skillet from the heat and let the shrimp cool for 15 minutes. Set the skillet in the refrigerator for ½ hour.

In a medium large bowl place the black beans, red and green bell peppers, scallions, orange sections, ginger, and the 2 tablespoons of garlic. Toss the ingredients together.

Add the shrimp and toss them in with the mixture.

Add the Citrus Vinaigrette and toss it in well.

On each of 4 individual salad plates place 2 leaves of the radicchio. Spoon the salad on top.

serves 4

"Black beans are usually served warm, but they also are excellent cold. Pinto beans or white beans may be used as well."

"This is a wonderful salad with many interesting flavors and textures. If you want the dish to be spicier, then substitute a poblano pepper for the green bell pepper."

"Years ago my dad traded chile peppers with the Indians, in exchange for their rugs and pots. He had an old Chevy that he would load with 200 pounds of chiles for trading, and then he would drive way out to the Hopi reservation. When he got hungry, he would open the hood of his Chevy, put a few chile peppers on the engine, along with a can of sausages or something, and then he would drive about 10 miles so that the engine got good and hot. Then he would open up the hood, turn the peppers over, and drive another 10 miles. By this time the chiles were nicely roasted and ready to peel, and the sausages were well heated. It worked great, and it was a lot easier than building a fire!"

Rocky Packard
Francisco's

Citrus Vinaigrette

¼ **cup orange juice, freshly squeezed**
2 **tablespoons lime juice, freshly squeezed**
1 **tablespoon soy sauce**
2 **oranges, zested** *(outer orange part grated off)*
1 **lime, zested** *(outer green part grated off)*
2 **tablespoons balsamic vinegar**
½ **cup salad oil**

In a medium bowl place the orange juice, lime juice, soy sauce, orange zest, lime zest, and balsamic vinegar. Stir the ingredients together.

While whisking constantly, slowly dribble in the salad oil.

makes 1 cup

"This dressing is very light and slightly sweet. It's wonderful with a tossed green salad, and it also works well as a marinade for chicken or fish. Try to use fresh orange and lime juice, instead of frozen, because this will make all the difference in the way it tastes."

Rocky Packard
Francisco's

Sesame Seared Tuna Salad with Asian Vinaigrette

Sesame Seared Tuna Salad

2	tablespoons white sesame seeds
2	tablespoons black sesame seeds
½	teaspoon Szechwan peppercorns, ground
1	teaspoon black peppercorns, ground
½	teaspoon ground cumin
½	teaspoon kosher salt
1	pound tuna *(a whole piece)*, cut into 4 chunks
2	tablespoons sesame oil
4	cups salad greens
	Asian Vinaigrette *(recipe on next page)*

In a small bowl place the white and black sesame seeds, ground Szechwan peppercorns, ground black peppercorns, cumin, and kosher salt. Mix the ingredients together.

Roll each chunk of tuna in the spice mixture so that it is thoroughly coated.

In a large sauté pan place the sesame oil and heat it on high until it is hot. Add the coated tuna chunks and cook them for 1 to 1½ minutes on each side, or until they are seared. Slice each piece of tuna diagonally across the grain into 4 pieces.

On each of 4 individual salad plates place the salad greens. Sprinkle on some of the Asian Vinaigrette. Place the tuna slices on top. Serve the salad with the rest of the Asian Vinaigrette in a ramekin on the side.

serves 4

"This is good to serve as a salad, but it also is great as an appetizer. You can use a tray and lay out all of the tuna slices on top of some greens. Serve it with some tiny forks or toothpicks and a ramekin of the Asian Vinaigrette for dipping. When you sear the tuna it should be cooked from the outside ¼" to ½" to the inside, and it should be blood rare in the center. That way when you slice the pieces diagonally you will have a contrast in color and texture."

Laszlo Gyermek
Santacafe

"Laszlo and Kelly are really hands-on chefs. Instead of running around with a clipboard and pointing at things, they are right in there preparing the food along with everyone else."

Judy Ebbinghaus
Santacafe

Asian Vinaigrette

2	limes, juiced
2	tablespoons teriyaki sauce
1	tablespoon soy sauce
2	tablespoons honey
⅛	cup olive oil
¼	cup light sesame oil

In a medium small bowl place the lime juice, teriyaki sauce, soy sauce, and honey. Whisk the ingredients together.

While whisking constantly, slowly add the olive and sesame oils.

makes 1½ cups

"This dressing would be delicious on cole slaw, a cold pasta salad, or tossed greens. If you don't care for the taste of sesame oil, then you can substitute another kind, such as olive or vegetable oil."

Laszlo Gyermek
Santacafe

Lobster and Chicken Breast Salad with Honey Dressing

Lobster and Chicken Breast Salad

1	tablespoon peanut oil
2	chicken breasts, skin and bones removed
½	pound mixed baby greens
2	1¼-pound Maine lobster tails, steamed, meat removed from shells, cooled, and cut into ¼" slices
½	pound green beans, snipped, blanched, and julienned
¼	pound leeks (white part only), washed, julienned, and blanched
4	Roma tomatoes, skins removed, seeded and diced
	Honey Dressing (recipe follows)

In a large sauté pan place the peanut oil and heat it on medium high until it is hot. Add the chicken breasts and sauté them for 2 to 3 minutes on each side, or until they are barely done. Set them aside to cool, and then cut them into thin slices.

On each of 4 individual salad plates place the mixed baby greens. Place the chicken and lobster on top. Artfully arrange the green beans, leeks, and Roma tomatoes on top. Drizzle on the Honey Dressing.

serves 4

Honey Dressing

3	shallots, minced and blanched
2	tablespoons honey
2	tablespoons lemon juice, freshly squeezed
1	tablespoon lime juice, freshly squeezed
	salt and white pepper (to taste)
2	tablespoons walnut oil
2	tablespoons peanut oil

In a small bowl place the shallots, honey, lemon juice, lime juice, salt, and white pepper. Mix the ingredients together. While whisking constantly, slowly dribble in the walnut and peanut oils, so that they are emulsified.

makes approximately ⅔ cup

Salads & Salad Dressings

"This recipe came into being one day when I needed to use up some chicken and lobster tails. Since then it has become one of our most popular summer dishes."

"I am from Austria, and the cooking profession is very different in Europe than it is here. In Europe, everyone goes through 3 to 4 years of apprenticeships, and there is a lot of self discipline involved. The cooks take great pride in what they do, and they are very much appreciated and valued by the general public. There is a prestige to being a chef in Europe that is lacking in America. However, I think that things are gradually changing here, and Americans seem to be growing more sophisticated in their taste for good food. Along with this is a growing appreciation for the creative talent behind fine restaurants."

"Very little oil is used in this dressing so it is low calorie. The flavor is tangy and pungent, and it's wonderful with all salads. Tasting it, you would never believe how healthy it is."

Martin Lackner
The Palace Restaurant

Salmon Salad with Lemon Yogurt Dill Dressing

"I recently served this dish at a catered party and my client just loved it. We used the whole salmon that she had caught in Alaska. I filleted, deboned, and steamed it, and it was outstanding. It had this wild flavor that you don't get from salmon that is purchased in the store, because they have been commercially farmed and fed."

"I am a big fan of the bamboo steamer because of the way it cooks food. The tastes are concentrated and the cooking is faster. I think that it's way better than using a metal steamer. The steamer sits on top of your pot, and it has its own lid. If you have a gas burner, don't let the flame flicker up the sides, because it will burn the bamboo. When you steam the salmon, be sure that you put the skin side down, so the other side will be pretty and pink."

"This dressing is quite tart, and although it is excellent with the salmon salad, it won't go too well with many other things. If you can, serve this dish with either dill or cottage cheese bread."

Sylvia Johnson
Celebrations

Salmon Salad

4   pounds salmon fillets, deboned
1   large head cauliflower, cut into florets
2   pounds small green beans, strings removed
1   head butter lettuce, washed and dried
1   head red leaf lettuce, washed and dried
1   head green leaf lettuce, washed and dried
1   head radicchio, washed and dried
8   Roma tomatoes, cut into wedges
2   lemons, sliced
    Lemon Yogurt Dill Dressing *(recipe follows)*

Steam the salmon in an oiled bamboo steamer *(see chef's comments on this page)* for 5 minutes, or until it is just done. Let the salmon cool to room temperature. Steam the cauliflower and green beans in a bamboo steamer for 5 to 8 minutes, or until they are just done. Place them in a bowl and let them cool to room temperature.

On each of 8 individual salad plates place the different lettuce leaves. Place the salmon and vegetables on top. Artfully place the Roma tomatoes on the plate. Garnish the dish with the lemon slices. Serve the Lemon Yogurt Dill Dressing on the side.

serves 8

Lemon Yogurt Dill Dressing

1   cup plain yogurt
2   tablespoons lemon juice, freshly squeezed
2   tablespoons olive oil
2   cloves garlic, finely minced
3   tablespoons fresh dill, minced
¾   teaspoon sugar

In a small bowl place all of the ingredients and mix them together well.

makes approximately 1⅓ cups

Smoked Mussel and White Bean Salad with Anchovy Vinaigrette

Smoked Mussel and White Bean Salad

4	slices French bread
2	teaspoons olive oil
1	clove garlic, peeled
	Anchovy Vinaigrette (recipe follows)
2	dozen smoked mussels
3	cups cooked white beans, drained
4	cups bitter greens (arugula, Belgian endive, etc.)
4	thin slices red onion, separated into rings

Brush one side of the French bread pieces with the olive oil. Rub them with the clove of garlic. Toast the bread in the oven so that it is barely golden around the edges and soft in the middle. Cut the bread into bite size cubes.

In a medium bowl place the Anchovy Vinaigrette. Add the toasted bread cubes, smoked mussels, and white beans. Gently fold the ingredients together so that they are well coated with the dressing.

On each of 4 individual salad plates place the bitter greens. Place the smoked mussel mixture on top. Garnish each dish with the red onion rings.

serves 4

Anchovy Vinaigrette

½	tablespoon anchovy paste
3	tablespoons red wine vinegar
2	drops Worcestershire sauce
	salt and black pepper (to taste)
½	cup olive oil

In a small bowl place the anchovy paste, red wine vinegar, Worcestershire sauce, salt, and black pepper. Whisk the ingredients together well. While whisking constantly, slowly dribble in the olive oil.

makes approximately ⅔ cup

"This recipe is similar to a dish that comes from the Tuscan part of Italy. The nickname of the people who live there is 'bean eaters'. You can use either canned or dry beans."

"You can get smoked mussels at a good seafood market, in the section where they sell smoked salmon. I really like them because they have a smoky flavor which permeates the whole dish. Because the flavor is so strong, they are very satisfying, so you only need to eat a few. As you would imagine, the texture is kind of chewy."

"When you toast the bread for the salad, you are not making croutons, which are usually very dry. The pieces should be barely brown around the edges and soft in the center. You also can toast the bread in your toaster. After it pops up, then brush on the olive oil, rub it with the garlic, cut it into cubes, and toss it in the salad."

Wayne Gustafson
Julian's

Grilled Orange Basil Sea Scallop Salad with Spicy Cilantro Lime Vinaigrette

"The presentation of this dish is really nice because the scallops look so nice on the greens, which are slightly wilted from the warmed plate. This makes a rich tasting, full meal, and yet it is not over-whelming. If you reduced the portions it would make an outstanding appetizer. A full order will serve 4 people."

Eric Sanders
Ogelvies

"I enjoy cooking for myself at home. I have 3 sons, and I am teaching them all how to cook. The eldest one works here at the restaurant, and the younger ones help me out when they have time. I will buy them a new pair of shoes or shirt as payment. If they follow in my footsteps I would be very proud. I think that being a chef is a wonderful profession because not only can it give you a good, steady income, but it also is very rewarding."

Frank Peña
Ogelvies

Grilled Orange Basil Sea Scallop Salad

1   cup orange juice, freshly squeezed
4   tablespoons fresh basil, chopped
1¼ pounds jumbo sea scallops, cleaned
1   pound mixed greens
    Spicy Cilantro Lime Vinaigrette *(recipe follows)*
2   Roma tomatoes, sliced into 8 pieces
16 slices English cucumber

In a medium bowl place the orange juice and basil. Add the sea scallops and marinate them for 1 hour at room temperature. Grill the scallops for 1 to 2 minutes on each side, or until they are just done.

In a medium large bowl place the mixed greens and toss them with the Spicy Cilantro Lime Vinaigrette.

On each of 4 hot individual salad plates place the dressed mixed greens. Artfully arrange the grilled scallops, Roma tomato slices, and cucumber slices on top.

serves 4

Spicy Cilantro Lime Vinaigrette

½   tablespoon fresh cilantro, minced
1   serrano chile pepper, seeded and minced
1   clove garlic, minced
1   shallot, minced
1   tablespoon Chinese chile paste
¼   cup sugar
2   tablespoons lime juice, freshly squeezed
2   tablespoons rice wine vinegar
½   cup vegetable oil

In a small bowl place all of the ingredients and whisk them together.

makes approximately 1½ cups

Grilled Tomato Vinaigrette

12	ripe Roma tomatoes, sliced in half lengthwise
2	ounces sun-dried tomatoes
2	tablespoons olive oil
¼	teaspoon salt
¼	teaspoon black pepper, freshly ground
¼	cup fresh basil, chopped
½	cup balsamic vinegar
½	cup red wine vinegar
2	tablespoons brown sugar
3	cups extra virgin olive oil
	salt *(to taste)*
	black pepper *(to taste)*, freshly ground

In a medium bowl place the Roma tomatoes, sun-dried tomatoes, the 2 tablespoons of olive oil, the ¼ teaspoon of salt, and the ¼ teaspoon of black pepper. Toss the ingredients together so that the tomatoes are well coated with the oil. Place the tomatoes on a preheated gas grill and cook them for 3 to 5 minutes, or until they turn dark *(don't move the tomatoes on the grill, or else they will fall apart)*.

Place the grilled tomatoes back in the bowl. Add the basil and stir it in. Set the dish aside.

In another medium bowl place the balsamic vinegar, red wine vinegar, and brown sugar. While whisking constantly, slowly dribble in the 3 cups of olive oil. Add the salt and black pepper, and whisk them in.

In a food processor place a small amount of the grilled tomatoes and vinaigrette, and purée them so that they are smooth. Repeat the process until everything is used up.

makes approximately 1 quart

"This is a wonderful tomato vinaigrette that can be used in many ways. It's good on fresh greens, it can be used as a marinade, and it's good for a raw vegetable dip. You also can add it to your fresh salsa to give it an interesting flavor. I've eaten it as a dressing for cold pasta salad and as a sandwich spread for bread and cheese. The possibilities are endless!"

"My first restaurant job was at the age of 13. I was a dishwasher, and I used to get into trouble because I was never at the dish station.....I was always up on the line, watching the cooks. By the time I was 18 I was in charge of my own kitchen. I've been very fortunate in my cooking career, because people have taken me under their wing and taught me everything they knew. Now I try to do the same for my staff, by passing on all of my knowledge."

Steven Lemon
Pranzo Italian Grill

Roasted Poblano Chile Balsamic Vinaigrette

½ **pound fresh poblano chile peppers, roasted, peeled, seeded, and diced small** *(see chef's comments on page 159)*
½ **cup balsamic vinegar**
¾ **teaspoon ground cumin**
¾ **teaspoon ground coriander**
1 **teaspoon kosher salt**
¾ **cup vegetable oil**
¼ **cup olive oil**

In a small bowl place all of the ingredients *(except for the two oils)* and whisk them together. Let the mixture sit for ½ hour at room temperature.

While whisking constantly, slowly dribble in the vegetable and olive oils.

Store the dressing in a tightly covered jar in the refrigerator. Let the dressing come to room temperature before serving it.

makes 2 cups

"Balsamic vinegar is made in only one place in the world – Modena, Italy. It is aged in wood for many years, and it has a wonderful, sweet flavor. The prices can vary from $3 to over $20 for a bottle, depending upon the aging time. It has a mystique to it, like the art of wine making. For this recipe you can use one of the less expensive brands. The chiles lend a tart flavor to the dressing that is a nice contrast to the sweetness of the balsamic vinegar. This dressing is wonderful on green salads, and it's especially good with spinach. Also, you can use it as a marinade for poultry."

Katharine Kagel
Cafe Pasqual's

Green Onion Vinaigrette

1 **egg**
2 **teaspoons sugar**
8 **scallions, coarsely chopped**
⅛ **cup fresh mint leaves, packed**
½ **teaspoon tabasco**
½ **cup rice vinegar**
½ **teaspoon salt**
¼ **teaspoon white pepper**
1¼ **cups vegetable oil**

In a food processor place all of the ingredients *(except for the oil)*.

With the food processor constantly running, slowly dribble in the oil.

makes 2 cups

"If this dressing comes out too thick for your taste, then you can thin it down by adding some water. It's not as spicy as it sounds, and it's excellent on any kind of green salad. I've also used it as a marinade for both fish and chicken."

Paul Constantine
Chez What

Sauces, Dips, & Condiments

Avocado Tomatillo Salsa

8	tomatillos, husks removed, and coarsely chopped
4	cloves garlic, coarsely chopped
2	jalapeño chile peppers, coarsely chopped
1	medium yellow onion, diced
	salt *(to taste)*
	black pepper *(to taste)*
2	medium avocados, peeled, pitted, and diced into ¼" pieces
½	bunch fresh cilantro, leaves only, finely chopped

In a food processor place the tomatillos, garlic, jalapeño chile peppers, onions, salt, and black pepper. Purée the ingredients so that they are roughly smooth. Add the avocados and cilantro, and stir them in. Let the salsa sit for 2 hours before serving it.

makes approximately 2 cups

> "We used to serve this with chips, and then I discovered that it was delicious with fish.....especially fish that is breaded or mesquite grilled. It's very tasty, and the sourness of the tomatillos really contrasts well with the bland, smooth richness of the avocados."
>
> *Marc Greene*
> *Old Mexico Grill*

Salsa de Arbol

½	cup butter, clarified
½	ounce arbol chile peppers, stems removed
9	medium, ripe tomatoes, broiled till brown
2	whole cloves
½	medium yellow onion, coarsely chopped
2	cloves garlic, coarsely chopped
1	tomato, diced
¼	cup tomato juice
1	tablespoon salad oil

In a medium saucepan place the clarified butter and heat it on medium until it is hot. Add the arbol chile peppers and sauté them for 5 minutes, or until they are lightly brown *(don't breathe the fumes)*.

In a food processor place the sautéed arbol chile peppers and the remaining ingredients. Purée the ingredients together.

makes approximately 3 cups

> "The other day I served this salsa with grouper, which was breaded in a mixture of dark red chile powder and bread crumbs, quickly seared, and then finished off in the oven. It was outstanding! The arbol chiles are extremely hot, and they will have very different flavors, depending on how you cook them. If you fry them they will taste completely different from those that are roasted over a grill. Serve this with chips, or any fish or meat entrée."
>
> *Marc Greene*
> *Old Mexico Grill*

Zesty Melon Salsa

cups ripe melon *(cantaloupe or honeydew)*, **peeled, seeded, and diced medium**
1   jalapeño chile pepper, seeded and minced
2   tablespoons fresh cilantro, minced
¼   teaspoon chile pequin *(hot red chile flakes)*
½   teaspoon lime zest *(outer green part grated off)*
2   tablespoons lime juice, freshly squeezed
2   tablespoons lemon juice, freshly squeezed
¼   teaspoon salt

In a medium bowl place all of the ingredients and mix them together. Cover the bowl and refrigerate the salsa for 1 hour before serving it.

makes approximately 1½ cups

"I suggest using only one kind of melon because you will get a cleaner, more direct flavor that way. Be sure that the melon is ripe. The end should be soft enough so that you can press it in slightly and it should have a flowery, melon smell. Also, be sure to cut your ingredients evenly, so that the salsa looks beautiful."

Lynn Walters
The Natural Cafe

Salsa de Ancho

6   dried ancho chile peppers, washed and toasted in the oven until very brittle
1   medium yellow onion, finely chopped
½   cup olive oil
½   cup red wine vinegar
1   teaspoon salt

Remove and discard the seeds from 3 of the toasted ancho chile peppers.

Crush all of the chile peppers into tiny pieces with your hands and place them in a medium bowl.

Add the remaining ingredients and mix them together. Chill the salsa in the refrigerator for 1 hour.

makes approximately 1½ cups

"I really love this salsa. It's very different tasting in that it has more of a vinaigrette flavor. It is wonderful as an alternative to a basic tomato salsa with chips. The ancho chiles are poblano peppers that have been dried. Be sure that you wash all dried chile peppers before you use them."

Marc Greene
Old Mexico Grill

Sauces, Dips, & Condiments

Light Jicama-Melon Salsa

½   cup honeydew melon, diced small
½   cup cantaloupe, diced small
½   cup Crenshaw melon, diced small
½   cup fresh pineapple, diced small
½   cup jicama, peeled and diced small
2   red jalapeño chile peppers, finely chopped
1   tablespoon light brown sugar
½   cup lime juice, freshly squeezed
1   lime, zested *(outer green part grated off)*

In a medium bowl place all of the ingredients and gently toss them together. Refrigerate the salsa for 30 minutes before serving it.

makes 3 cups

Pineapple Nopales Cactus Salsa

8   fresh cactus leaves, thorns carefully cut out
1   large fresh pineapple, peeled, cored, and diced medium
1   large red onion, finely diced
1   red bell pepper, seeded and finely diced
1   bunch scallions, finely chopped
8   jalapeño chile peppers, seeded and finely diced
1   large shallot, finely diced
1   bunch fresh cilantro, stems removed, and chopped
3   tablespoons sherry vinegar
½   cup extra virgin olive oil
     salt *(to taste)*

Grill the cactus leaves for 5 minutes on each side, or until they are tender. Cut them into thin strips.

In a medium bowl place the cactus strips and the remainder of the ingredients, and mix them together. Let the salsa sit for 30 minutes before serving it.

makes 3 to 4 cups

"Most people think of salsa as being something you serve with chips. But nowadays with the nouvelle cuisine dishes, it's a term that is used for all kinds of fruit medleys, sauces, relishes, and whatever. I would not recommend serving this salsa with chips. However, it is excellent with all kinds of fish, meats, and poultry. If you can't find red jalapeño chile peppers, that's okay. Just substitute green or yellow ones."

Ernie Bolleter
Inn at Loretto

"This is a healthy, fresh, flavorful salsa that uses cactus leaves and pineapple with chile peppers.....and the combination is outstanding. You can find fresh cactus leaves in some produce or specialty markets. Or, you can buy them in jars. Cactus leaves taste almost like cucumbers, but they also take on a lot of the flavor of the grill."

"Being a professional chef is a high stress job. I have seen chefs scream, yell, and throw pots and pans across the room. Although I realize that people handle stress in different ways, it is best if you are the kind of person who thrives on the tension that is inherent in this profession."

David Jones
Casa Sena

Cactus Pear Salsa

*"I used to see cactus pears
when I was growing up in
Arizona, but I never
thought about eating them
until several years ago.
Now they are one of those
new Southwestern fads.
Each pear has hundreds of
tiny, hard seeds in it. I like
to eat the seeds because I
enjoy the texture, but some
people don't. That's why I
say to crush them with a
mortar and pestle. Or, you
can push the meat through
a fine sieve. Be sure to
wear gloves when you are
peeling the pears, because
they have vicious, tiny
thorns."*

Jonathan Coady
Piñon Grill

4	"crimson" cactus pears, peeled and mashed with a mortar and pestle so that the seeds are ground
1	papaya, peeled, pitted, and finely diced
1	tablespoon dried chives, finely minced
2	teaspoons white sugar
1½	tablespoons champagne vinegar
2	tablespoons Herradura Silver Tequila

In a medium bowl place all of the ingredients and gently mix them together. Refrigerate the salsa for ½ hour before serving it.

makes 2½ to 3 cups

Mint Chutney

*"This is a very delicious,
spicy chutney, and it goes
with any kind of food you
can think of.....except
maybe for desserts. We
even eat it with our
Kentucky Fried Chicken!"*

Baldev Singh
India Palace

1	bunch scallions, coarsely chopped
1	bunch fresh mint
1	teaspoon fresh ginger root, peeled and chopped
2	bunches fresh cilantro
1	green bell pepper, seeded and coarsely chopped
5	jalapeño chile peppers
1	tablespoon lemon juice, freshly squeezed
1	teaspoon ground cumin
1	teaspoon ground coriander
½	teaspoon garam masala *(see chef's comments on page 230)*
2	teaspoons salt
½	cup yogurt

In a food processor place all of the ingredients *(except for the yogurt)* and purée them. Add the yogurt and mix it in.

makes approximately 2 cups

Papaya, Mango, and Chile Guajillo Marmalade

2	**dried chile guajillos**
¼	**cup orange juice, freshly squeezed**
¼	**cup sweet port wine**
¼	**leek** (*white part only*), **washed and cut into very thin strips**
1	**large papaya, peeled, seeds removed, and diced**
1	**mango, peeled and finely diced**
½	**lime, squeezed**
⅛	**teaspoon red chile powder** (*medium hot*)

In a small bowl place the chile guajillos, orange juice, and sweet port wine. Let the chiles soak overnight. Place the ingredients in a food processor and purée them.

In a medium bowl place the chile purée and the remainder of the ingredients, and gently mix them together with your hands. Refrigerate the marmalade for at least 2 days before serving it.

makes approximately 3 cups

Black Bean Dip

2	**cups cooked black beans** (*recipe on page 285*)
1	**jalapeño chile pepper, minced**
1	**small onion, chopped**
1	**tablespoon fresh garlic, chopped**
1	**cup sour cream**
1	**teaspoon ground cumin**
	salt (*to taste*)
	black pepper (*to taste*)

In a food processor place the black beans and purée them.

Add the remainder of the ingredients and purée them so that the dip is smooth.

Chill the bean dip in the refrigerator.

makes 3 cups

"When this dish marinates, all of the flavors blend together and the mixture becomes almost jellied. It goes well with both smoked and raw fish, such as oysters on the half shell. The flavor is spicy, sweet, and sour, all at the same time. It really wakes up your mouth!"

"I was trained in the classical way, and it was a thrill for me to learn how to make all of the traditional sauces and dishes. But now I really enjoy veering off in my own direction, and trying flavor combinations that I have never seen used before."

Jonathan Coady
Piñon Grill

"One day a customer who had previously ordered a black bean dip at the restaurant wanted to have it again. It wasn't on the new menu, so I threw some items together and came up with this recipe.....and she loved it! You can substitute yogurt for the sour cream. It won't be as rich or creamy tasting, but it still will be good."

Paul Hunsicker
Paul's Restaurant of Santa Fe

"Paul is a genius. He can make anything and it's always wonderful!"

Carol Moberg
Paul's Restaurant of Santa Fe

Corn Relish

2	tablespoons olive oil
4	ears corn, kernels scraped off
6	Roma tomatoes, finely chopped
1	large onion, finely chopped
1	tablespoon fresh cilantro, minced
	salt *(to taste)*
	black pepper *(to taste)*

In a medium large sauté pan place the olive oil and heat it on medium until it is hot. Add the remainder of the ingredients and sauté them for 10 minutes, or until the corn is done.

makes approximately 4 cups

"Try to use fresh corn if you can. When you remove the kernels scrape off the milky substance as well. This adds flavor and helps to steam the relish. Serve this as an accompaniment to everything from steaks and chops to hamburgers."

Sylvia Johnson
Celebrations

Tomatillo Ketchup

¼	cup olive oil
1	yellow onion, diced medium
2	pounds tomatillos, hulled
⅜	cup champagne vinegar
2	tablespoons sugar
	salt *(to taste)*
	black pepper *(to taste)*

In a large sauté pan place the olive oil and heat it on medium high until it is hot. Add the onions and sauté them for 6 to 8 minutes, or until they are clear.

Reduce the heat to low. Add the tomatillos, champagne vinegar, and sugar. Simmer the ingredients for 15 to 20 minutes, or until the liquid is reduced by ½.

Push the mixture through a fine sieve into a bowl. Season the ketchup with the salt and black pepper.

makes approximately 1 quart

"I developed this recipe because I wanted a ketchup that was unique. It has a different flavor from regular ketchup in that it is not as sweet, because the tomatillos are more tart than tomatoes. We serve this on a grilled fillet of beef, and it is excellent."

"My ideas for recipes come to me out of the blue, at any time of day or night, and I have to write them down or else I forget them. Also, I have over 400 cookbooks and I subscribe to every cooking magazine there is."

Laszlo Gyermek
Santacafe

Really Good Tartar Sauce

2   egg yolks
2   teaspoons Dijon mustard
¾   cup olive oil
1   tablespoon balsamic vinegar
3   tablespoons shallots, minced
1½   tablespoons capers, minced
3   tablespoons sour pickles, minced
2   anchovy fillets, rinsed and finely diced
1   serrano chile pepper, minced
1½   tablespoons fresh cilantro, minced
       salt and black pepper *(to taste)*

In a medium bowl place the egg yolks and Dijon mustard, and whisk them together.

While whisking constantly, slowly dribble in ½ of the olive oil, or enough so that the sauce begins to thicken. Whisk in ½ of the balsamic vinegar. While continuing to whisk constantly, dribble in the remainder of the olive oil and the vinegar *(the sauce should be the consistency of mayonnaise)*.

Add the remainder of the ingredients and stir them in so that they are well combined. Store the sauce in the refrigerator.

makes approximately 2 cups

"I promise you, this is really, really good tartar sauce! Be sure that you use the anchovies. You can't exactly taste them, but they are essential to the good flavor of the end product."

"We developed this recipe for the occasional customers who can't eat their fish without tartar sauce. We said, 'Okay, if we have to make a tartar sauce, then we're going to make it really gourmet!'"

"To be successful as a professional chef you must be slightly twisted. The hours are crazy and there are continuous catastrophes. But, it's also a wonderfully creative and satisfying work."

Don Fortel
Francisco's

Green Chile Sauce

¼   cup vegetable oil
½   cup onions, finely diced
2   cloves garlic, minced
2   tablespoons flour
1   cup chicken stock *(recipe on page 295)*, **heated**
1½   cups green chile peppers, roasted, peeled, seeded, and diced *(see chef's comments on page 159)*
1   tomato, diced
1   teaspoon ground coriander
1   tablespoon fresh cilantro, chopped
       salt *(to taste)*

(continued on next page)

"Northern New Mexico has a unique cuisine that is very regional, and it is different from the rest of the country, including the southern part of the state. The Santa Fe School of Cooking offers people a chance to learn about the history of the cuisine, and how to prepare it. People

(continued on next page)

In a medium saucepan place the vegetable oil and heat it on medium high until it is hot. Add the onions and garlic, and sauté them for 5 minutes, or until the onions are tender.

Add the flour and whisk it in for 3 minutes.

While whisking constantly, slowly add the heated chicken stock. Continue to whisk the sauce for 5 minutes, or until it thickens.

Add the green chile peppers, tomatoes, coriander, and cilantro. Cook the sauce for 20 minutes more. Add the salt to taste.

makes approximately 1 quart

have a lot of interest and they love to be able to return to their homes, wherever in the world that may be, and recreate some of the dishes they enjoyed while visiting Santa Fe."

Susan Curtis
Santa Fe School of Cooking

"This sauce can be used over burritos, enchiladas, eggs, potatoes, or anything else you can think of. People here eat green or red chile with breakfast, lunch, dinner, and even dessert! We make a green chile key lime pie that is really excellent."

"Here in New Mexico we make our enchiladas flat instead of rolling them. Place a layer of the green chile sauce in the bottom of a baking dish, and then layer on corn tortillas. Cover these with more sauce, add the filling (cooked chicken or beef), and spread on grated cheese. Add another layer of tortillas, lots more sauce, and then put cheese on top. Bake the enchiladas at 350° for 30 to 45 minutes, or until they are hot."

Peter Raub
Santa Fe School of Cooking

Red Chile Sauce

¼	cup vegetable oil
⅓	cup onions, finely diced
2	cloves garlic, minced
2	tablespoons flour
½	cup red chile powder
½	teaspoon ground cumin
½	teaspoon ground coriander
2	cups chicken stock *(recipe on page 295)*, **heated**
	salt *(to taste)*

In a medium saucepan place the vegetable oil and heat it on medium high until it is hot. Add the onions and garlic, and sauté them for 5 minutes, or until the onions are tender.

Add the flour and whisk it briskly for 3 minutes. Add the red chile powder, cumin, and coriander, and whisk them for 2 minutes.

While whisking constantly, slowly add the heated chicken stock. Continue to whisk the sauce for 5 minutes, or until it thickens. Add the salt and whisk it in.

makes 2½ to 3 cups

Fresh Tomato Sauce

24	large, ripe Roma tomatoes
¼	cup olive oil
1	tablespoon butter
1	small yellow onion, diced small
2	cloves garlic, minced

With a paring knife score an "X" in the bottom of each tomato.

In a pot of boiling water place the scored tomatoes for 30 seconds, or until the skin loosens. Remove the tomatoes with a slotted spoon. Peel off the skins. Cut the tomatoes in half horizontally.

Place a fine sieve over a medium bowl. Squeeze out the seeds into the sieve and discard them *(save the juice in the bowl)*.

Dice the tomatoes into ¼" pieces and place them in the sieve over the bowl. Let them sit for 5 minutes.

In a medium stockpot place the olive oil and butter, and heat them on medium until the oil is hot and the butter is melted. Add the onions and garlic, and sauté them for 6 to 8 minutes, or until the onions are translucent.

Add the tomato juice in the bowl and simmer the ingredients on low heat for 10 minutes. Add the diced tomatoes and simmer them for 1 hour *(stir them occasionally)*.

makes approximately 2 quarts

"This is a basic tomato sauce, to which you can add any kind of fresh herbs that you want. It is rather chunky, so if you use it for a pizza sauce I would recommend puréeing it so that it is smooth. Otherwise, it's an easy sauce to make for a light pasta dinner."

"Ever since I can remember I have loved to cook. My mom used to bake bread when I was small, and she would give me small scraps of dough to roll out. I would drop them on the floor, but we always baked them anyway. Usually they came out black."

Steven Lemon
Pranzo Italian Grill

Traditional Basil Pesto

1	teaspoon fresh garlic, chopped
¼	pound fresh basil
¼	cup pine nuts
¼	cup Parmesan cheese, freshly grated
1½	cups olive oil

In a blender place all of the ingredients and purée them. Keep the pesto refrigerated *(it will keep for up to 2½ weeks)*.

makes 2 cups

"Pesto can be used with so many different things. I love to eat it with bread..... it's a meal in itself!"

Jane Stacey
Pranzo Italian Grill

Marinara Sauce

2	tablespoons olive oil
2	yellow onions, chopped medium
¼	cup fresh basil, chopped
¼	cup fresh oregano, chopped
1	bay leaf
⅛	cup white wine
1	6-ounce can tomato paste
3	cups water
	salt *(to taste)*
	black pepper *(to taste)*, **freshly ground**

In a medium large saucepan place the olive oil and heat it on medium high until it is hot. Add the yellow onions and sauté them for 4 to 6 minutes, or until they are transparent.

Add the basil, oregano, bay leaf, white wine, and tomato paste. Stir the ingredients together.

Add the water, salt, and black pepper, and stir them in.

Simmer the sauce for 30 minutes, or until it is the consistency of a heavy cream.

makes approximately 1 quart

"This is a typical marinara sauce that can be used with any kind of pasta. You can add sautéed mushrooms, other fresh herbs, or even baked eggplant that is cut up."

"In our kitchen we have a lot of fun. We joke around, and we even talk to our food. For instance, if the vegetables are especially nice we will compliment them and thank them for being so beautiful. Sometimes when we make a dish we will be out of an ingredient, so we will have to improvise and change it. Often the result will be even better than the original recipe, so we say things like, 'Oh the food gods are smiling on us today!' We tend to have a very personal relationship with the food."

Lisa Sivé
Wild Oats Market

Guadalupe Red Chile Sauce

5   **cups water** *(or as needed)*
½   **cup red chile powder** *(hot)*
½   **cup red chile powder** *(mild)*
3   **cloves garlic, finely minced**
1½   **pounds chuck roast, cooked, fat trimmed off, and diced into ¼" pieces**
      salt *(to taste)*

In a food processor place the water, the hot and mild red chile powders, and garlic. Blend the ingredients together well. *(Add more water if the sauce is too thick.)*

Pour the puréed mixture into a medium large saucepan. Add the chuck roast and salt, and simmer the ingredients for 10 minutes.

makes approximately 4 quarts

"This chile sauce recipe is very healthy because it has no fat. It is thickened with its own chile powder instead of with flour. I think that the flavor of chile is so marvelous that I don't alter it by adding other herbs, spices, or chicken stock. Most people love it, so I figure I must be on the right track!"

Isabelle Koomoa
Guadalupe Cafe

Oriental Sauce

2	**teaspoons butter**
2	**teaspoons flour**
¼	**cup sugar**
¼	**cup soy sauce**
¼	**cup dry sherry**
½	**cup hoisin sauce** *(see chef's comments on this page)*
¼	**cup sesame oil**

In a small saucepan place the butter and melt it on medium heat. Add the flour *(to make a roux)* and stir it in for 5 minutes.

In another small saucepan place the remainder of the ingredients and heat them until they are hot. While stirring constantly, slowly add the hot liquid to the roux. Stir and cook the sauce for 5 minutes, or until it is thickened.

makes 1½ cups

"Hoisin sauce is very popular in Chinese cooking. It is made from soybeans, flour, sugar, water, spices, garlic, and chile. You will find it in the Oriental section of your grocery store."

"This sauce is delicious with the pork brochettes and pasta pillows. It will store in the refrigerator for a long time, and it can be used with chicken, beef, or as a flavor enhancer in any stir-fry dish."

Frank Peña
Ogelvies

Eggs, Cheese, & Vegetarian

Vegetarian Quesadilla

¼	**cup olive oil**
1	**red onion, thinly sliced**
1	**red bell pepper, seeded and julienned**
1	**green bell pepper, seeded and julienned**
5	**carrots, julienned**
1	**bunch broccoli, cut into small florets**
¾	**pound mushrooms, thinly sliced**
¼	**cup fresh cilantro, minced**
5	**cloves garlic, minced**
6	**flour tortillas** (thick)
1½	**cups Monterey Jack cheese, grated**
1½	**cups cheddar cheese, grated**
2	**tomatoes, thinly sliced**
	Green Chile Sauce (recipe on page 114)

In an extra large skillet place the olive oil and heat it on medium high until it is hot. Add the red onions, red and green bell peppers, carrots, broccoli, mushrooms, cilantro, and garlic. Sauté the vegetables for 4 to 6 minutes, or until they are tender.

On top of each tortilla sprinkle ⅛ cup of both the Monterey Jack and cheddar cheeses. Spoon on the sautéed vegetables. Place the tomato slices on top. Sprinkle on another ⅛ cup of both the two cheeses.

Heat a medium size skillet on medium. Rub the bottom of the pan with a paper towel dipped in oil (do this for each quesadilla). One at a time, place a quesadilla inside and cover the pan with a lid. Cook the quesadilla for 6 to 7 minutes, or until the tortilla is crisp and the cheese is melted. (Keep the finished quesadillas in a warm oven until they all are made.) Cut each quesadilla into 8 wedges.

Serve the quesadilla with the Green Chile Sauce on the side.

Note: This also may be served as an appetizer.

serves 6

"One day my chef, Chris Arrison, and I went to another restaurant in town for lunch where we both had their vegetarian quesadilla. It was just excellent, and that's where we got the idea for this recipe. We made it different from the common quesadilla in that it is open faced and served like a pizza. Also, instead of being baked in the oven the tortilla is lightly fried so that it is crispy. These are so easy to make that even little kids can do it.....they think it's great fun!"

"People come to the Steaksmith because the food is good and consistent. But they also come so that they can relax, have a good time, and enjoy a smooth running and hassle free service. Our customers are primarily locals, with maybe 30 percent being from out of town."

Herb Cohen
Steaksmith

Baked Polenta and Cheese

4	**cups water** *(or as needed)*
1	**red bell pepper, seeded and diced small**
1	**yellow bell pepper, seeded and diced small**
1	**poblano chile pepper, seeded and diced small**
¾	**cup fresh cilantro, chopped**
1	**teaspoon salt** *(or to taste)*
½	**teaspoon black pepper** *(or to taste)*
2	**cups rough cornmeal**
6	**ounces Bel Paese cheese** *(see chef's comments on this page),* **cut into 6 squares**
2	**tablespoons olive oil** *(or as needed)*

In a medium large saucepan place the water, red and yellow bell peppers, poblano chile peppers, cilantro, salt, and black pepper. Bring the water to a boil. While stirring constantly, slowly add the cornmeal.

Reduce the heat to low. While stirring frequently, cook the polenta for 15 minutes *(add more water if it gets too thick)*, or until it is very thick but not lumpy *(be careful not to scorch it, which is easy to do)*.

In each of 6 oiled, individual ramekins place the polenta. Place a piece of cheese in the center. Let the polenta cool and then unmold it.

Preheat the oven to 350°.

Place the polenta *(cheese side up)* on a flat sheet and bake it for 10 minutes, or until the cheese melts.

serves 4 to 6

Gnocchi alla Piemontese

1¾   **pounds potatoes, baked and then cooled overnight**
1   **egg**
¾   **cup flour** *(or as needed)*
¼   **cup olive oil**
2   **cloves garlic, crushed**
¼   **medium onion, diced**
1½   **medium carrots, diced**
1   **stalk celery, diced**
¾   **pound tomatoes, peeled, seeded, and diced**
1   **tablespoon fresh basil, chopped**
       salt and black pepper *(to taste)*
1   **teaspoon salt**

Scoop out the pulp from the baked potatoes. Push it through a fine sieve *(or pass it through a meat grinder)*. Push it again through an even finer wire mesh sieve.

On a lightly floured surface place the potatoes. Make a well in the center. Add the egg and ½ of the flour, and knead them in. Continue to add more flour *(as needed)* and knead it in so that the dough forms a semi-firm ball. Cut the ball into quarters. Roll out each quarter into a sausage shape so that it is ½" in diameter. Cut the gnocchi into ¾" pieces. Sprinkle them with some flour.

In a large sauté pan place ½ of the olive oil and heat it on medium high until it is hot. Add the garlic, onions, carrots, and celery. Sauté them for 6 to 8 minutes, or until they are lightly browned.

Add the tomatoes and sauté them for 20 minutes *(add some water if necessary)*.

Place the sauce in a food processor and purée it. Place the sauce back into the pan. Add the basil, salt, black pepper, and the rest of the olive oil. Keep the sauce warm.

Fill a large stockpot ⅔ full of water. Add the 1 teaspoon of salt and bring the water to a boil. Very carefully add the gnocchi and cook them for 2 minutes, or until they have risen to the top and are done *(see chef's comments on this page)*. Remove them with a slotted spoon and add them to the sauce.

serves 4

"Gnocchi is an old Italian potato dish that is a nice alternative to pasta. When I make it I never measure anything. I add the flour until I see that the dough has the right consisency. It must get to the point where you can roll it out, but it should not be overworked because then the gluten comes out and the dough gets sticky. You may need some experience in working with the dough, but it's really not that hard. When you cook the gnocchi they will sink to the bottom of the pot and then rise back to the top. Let them cook a little longer than this, but not to the point where they fall apart. You want the flour to get cooked."

"The sauce in this recipe is typically Italian. It is fairly mild, but you could add more garlic, some olives, and maybe even some anchovies."

"I always enjoy getting positive feedback from our customers, but when I get a compliment from someone with a truly sophisticated palate..... then I really am happy."

Martin Lackner
The Palace Restaurant

Sweet Potato and Pear Tamale

⅓	cup butter, softened
1	pound prepared masa *(follow the directions on the box)*
½	teaspoon salt
½	teaspoon baking powder
¼	cup hot water
1	teaspoon achiote *(see chef's comments on this page)*
½	sweet potato, diced medium and cooked
2	pears, cored and diced medium
¼	cup golden raisins
¼	teaspoon cinnamon
¼	teaspoon ground cumin
¼	teaspoon salt
8	corn husks, soaked in warm water until pliable

In a medium bowl place the butter and then cream it.

Add the prepared masa, salt, and baking powder, and mix them in. Add the hot water *(as needed)* and mix it in so that the masa is pliable. Add the achiote and stir it in.

In another medium bowl place the sweet potatoes, pears, golden raisins, cinnamon, cumin, and salt. Mix the ingredients together well.

For each tamale lay a soaked corn husk on a flat surface, lengthwise. Spread the masa down the center so that it is ¼" thick. Spread the fruit filling on top. Fold the bottom of the husk over the filling, and then fold over the top. Fold the ends over, toward the center. Tie the tamale around the center with a thin strip of the husk so that it does not open.

Place the tamales in a steamer. Place a damp cloth on top of the pan and put a tight lid on top. Steam the tamales for 30 to 45 minutes, or until they are very hot and the masa is cooked.

serves 4

"We developed this recipe as a vegetarian dish, so we left the meat out and substituted fruit for the filling. It's almost dessert-like, although it's best served as an entrée, appetizer, or side dish."

"Achiote can be found in the dried spice section, or in the Mexican section. It is ground annatto seeds, and it tastes like the earth."

"At the Santacafe we felt that it was important to get in touch with our local growers, so I have taken it upon myself to make a weekly morning trip to our outdoor farmers' market. All of the growers are there with their produce and other goods, and I have become friends with my favorite ones. They are wonderful people.....calm, gentle, straightforward, and into the earth. They don't give me a discount, but if I buy a lot they throw some extra stuff in my basket!"

Kelly Rogers
Santacafe

Autumn Harvest Feast with Grilled Tomato Salsa and Bean Ragoût

Autumn Harvest Feast

⅓   cup balsamic vinegar
⅔   cup olive oil
       salt *(to taste)*
       black pepper *(to taste),* freshly ground
4   ears corn, husked and blanched
2   tomatoes, thickly sliced
1   large red onion, peeled and quartered
1   red bell pepper, seeded and quartered
1   yellow bell pepper, seeded and quartered
4   New Mexican green chile peppers
1   acorn squash, peeled, quartered, and blanched
1   large Idaho potato, cut into 4 pieces and boiled al dente
1   apple, quartered
2   cups salad greens
4   flour tortillas, lightly grilled
       Grilled Tomato Salsa *(recipe on next page)*
       Bean Ragoût *(recipe on next page)*

In a large bowl place the balsamic vinegar, olive oil, salt, and black pepper.

Whisk the ingredients together so that they are well blended. Add the corn, tomatoes, red onions, red and yellow bell peppers, green chile peppers, acorn squash, potatoes, and apples. Mix the ingredients so that they are well coated with the vinaigrette. Let them sit for 60 minutes.

Remove the vegetables from the marinade *(reserve it)* and then grill them for 30 to 60 seconds on each side, or until they are somewhat charred and heated through.

Toss the salad greens with some of the reserved marinade.

On ½ of each flour tortilla place the dressed salad greens with the grilled vegetables on top. Place the Grilled Tomato Salsa on part of the uncovered tortilla. Place the Bean Ragoût on the remaining uncovered part of the tortilla.

serves 4

"This is a wonderful dish that really fills the vegetarian gap. I think that a lot of times vegetarians get left holding the short end of the stick, because many restaurants will add a meatless dish only as an afterthought. I am not a vegetarian, but I don't eat meat for lunch. If I have something as heavy as that, then I want to go home and sleep instead of going back to work! My solution is to eat New Mexican vegetarian green chile with a tortilla. It tastes delicious and it's extremely good for you."

Judy Ebbinghaus
Santacafe

"We have built this dish around fresh autumn fruits and vegetables from northern New Mexico. You can substitute things that grow in whatever part of the country you live in, but it's important to the concept that they be both fresh and local. Cut the vegetables large enough so that you can handle them like a piece of meat and turn them with your grilling tongs. When you grill the vegetables the oil burns into the fire and flames shoot up and char them, which gives them a really good flavor."

Kelly Rogers
Santacafe

Grilled Tomato Salsa

2	tablespoons balsamic vinegar
2	tablespoons olive oil
4	tomatoes, cored and sliced into ½" thick pieces
¼	red onion
1	green chile pepper
	salt and black pepper *(to taste)*

In a medium bowl place the balsamic vinegar and olive oil, and whisk them together.

Add the tomatoes, red onions, and green chile peppers. Toss the vegetables so that they are well coated, and then let them sit for 30 minutes.

Remove the vegetables and then grill them for 30 to 60 seconds on each side, or until they are somewhat charred and heated through.

Dice the grilled vegetables and place them back in the bowl with the vinegar and oil. Add the salt and black pepper.

makes approximately 1½ cups

Bean Ragoût

1	cup cooked black beans *(recipe on page 285)*
1	cup cooked white beans
½	tablespoon fresh basil, chopped
½	tablespoon fresh parsley, chopped
½	tablespoon fresh oregano, chopped
½	tablespoon fresh chives, chopped
¼	cup water
2	tablespoons butter
	salt and black pepper *(to taste)*

In a medium saucepan place the black and white beans, basil, parsley, oregano, chives, and water. Simmer the ingredients for 5 minutes, or until they are heated. Add the butter and stir it in. Season the ragoût with the salt and black pepper.

serves 4

Quesadillas with Goat Cheese, Red Chile, and Pine Nuts

½   cup white, semi-soft goat cheese
½   cup ricotta cheese
4   flour tortillas
3   red chile peppers *(Anaheim, Chimayo, or Hatch)*, **roasted, peeled, seeded, and julienned small** *(see chef's comments on page 159)*
2   medium zucchinis, sliced lengthwise into ¼" thick strips, lightly grilled, and then cut into ½" long pieces
¼   cup pine nuts, toasted

Preheat the oven to 350°.

In a small bowl place the goat cheese and ricotta cheese, and mix them together.

On each of the 4 flour tortillas spread on the mixed cheeses to within ¼" of the edge. Artfully arrange the red chile pepper strips, grilled zucchini pieces, and toasted pine nuts on top.

Place the quesadillas on a flat sheet and bake them for 6 to 8 minutes, or until the cheese is melted and the tortillas start to brown slightly. Fold the quesadillas in half and cut each one into 3 pieces.

serves 4

"This is Edgar Catanach's recipe. There are 14 kids in his family and each male is named a variation of Ed.....Edward, Edwin, Edloy, Edrick. They all live in Santa Fe and have umpteen grandchildren, but I think they broke away from the 'Ed' tradition in naming them."

"These are great appetizers because they are so easy to make. Also, they are a fun and colorful variation of the basic quesadilla. If you can, use New Mexican Coon Ridge goat cheese. It's very soft and smooth, and it's easier to spread than cream cheese. Ricotta cheese is very stiff, so when you mix it with the goat cheese you will have to use some muscle."

Michael Nelsen
Zia Diner

"A lot of young, talented chefs have cooking come very easily to them, as was the case with myself. In order to rise to another level of ability they need to mature and achieve a degree of discipline. There is no limit to which the integrity of cooking can be carried. The more that I am in this business the more obsessed with attention to detail I become. It is tempting to cheat and make things easier on yourself, but the integrity will be sacrificed."

Sarah Alvord
Zia Diner

Marinated Vegetable Brochette with Whole Roasted Garlic

"This recipe is for an entrée, but you can make smaller portions and serve it as an appetizer. Cut the vegetables so that they are all the same size. This way they will look good and cook in the same time, more or less. Feel free to use other vegetables. As you can see, other than the butter on the roasted garlic, this is a very healthy recipe."

"I used to work in Berkeley, California at Chez Panisse. Every year we celebrated Bastille Day, and part of the celebration included the garlic festival. I learned to use garlic in every imaginable way, from appetizers, to entrées, to desserts. If you are a garlic lover, you will just die when you taste this dish. The roasted garlic gets very, very sweet, and you can squeeze the cloves out, just like butter. The flavor is so delicious I can't explain it. Serve it with some crusty bread so that you can soak up the juice."

Karen Woods
Rancho Encantado

Marinated Vegetable Brochette

1	yellow squash, cut into thick rounds
1	zucchini, cut into thick rounds
1	large red onion, diced large
1	red bell pepper, seeded and diced large
1	yellow bell pepper, seeded and diced large
1	Anaheim chile pepper, seeded and diced large
1	cup olive oil
½	cup red wine vinegar
1	tablespoon black pepper
	Whole Roasted Garlic *(recipe follows)*

On each of 16 small bamboo skewers place, in an alternating pattern, the yellow squash, zucchini, red onions, red and yellow bell peppers, and Anaheim chile peppers.

In a medium large bowl place the olive oil, red wine vinegar, and black pepper. Add the vegetable brochettes and marinate them for 2 to 6 hours. Grill the vegetable brochettes for 5 minutes on each side, or until grill marks appear and they are cooked al dente. In each of 4 small bowls place 4 of the grilled vegetable brochettes and a roasted garlic bulb. Pour in some of the roasting juices.

serves 4

Whole Roasted Garlic

4	bulbs garlic, outer skin rubbed off with bulb still intact
1	cup sweet butter, softened
10	sprigs fresh thyme
2	cups chicken stock *(recipe on page 295)*

Preheat the oven to 250°. Rub the butter all over the garlic bulbs so that they are well coated and you can't see the tips. Place the bulbs in a roasting pan with the root side down. Sprinkle the fresh thyme on top. Pour in the chicken stock. Cover the pan with foil and bake the garlic for 5 hours, or until it is very soft.

serves 4

Vegetarian Green Chile Stew

2	tablespoons olive oil
2	large onions, coarsely chopped
4	cloves garlic, minced
3	stalks celery, chopped
½	teaspoon turmeric
1	teaspoon red chile powder (mild)
¼	teaspoon cinnamon
1	tablespoon dried oregano
1	teaspoon ground cumin
½	teaspoon salt
¼	teaspoon black pepper
6	cups vegetable stock (see chef's comments on this page)
2	medium white potatoes, peeled and coarsely chopped
2	large sweet potatoes, cut into ½" cubes
⅔	cup frozen corn
⅔	cup frozen peas
1½	cups mild green chile peppers, roasted, peeled, and chopped (see chef's comments on page 159)
1	tablespoon molasses

In a large stockpot place the olive oil and heat it on medium high until it is hot. Add the onions, garlic, and celery. Sauté the ingredients for 5 minutes, or until the onions are translucent.

Add the turmeric, red chile powder, cinnamon, oregano, cumin, salt, and black pepper. Sauté the ingredients for 2 minutes. Remove the pot from the heat and set it aside.

In a medium large saucepan place the vegetable stock and white potatoes. Bring the liquid to a boil over high heat. Reduce the heat to low and simmer the potatoes for 15 to 20 minutes, or until they are tender.

In a food processor place the cooked potatoes and 1 cup of the stock (reserve the rest of the stock). Purée the mixture so that it is smooth.

Place the stockpot with the sautéed vegetables back on medium low heat. Add the potato purée and stir it in. Add the rest of the stock and stir it in. Add the remainder of the ingredients. Simmer the stew for 30 minutes, or until the sweet potatoes are tender.

serves 4 to 6

"This is a fabulous tasting stew, and it's very healthy because there is no dairy in it. Not to give vegetarian dishes a bad rap, but many people perceive them as being quite bland. They think, 'Well, maybe I can force myself to eat this and it will taste okay, but I'd sure rather have something else.' This isn't one of those dishes. It's spicy and rich tasting, and everyone loves it."

Michael Nelsen
Zia Diner

"To make a vegetable stock you can use most of the vegetables in your refrigerator that are going bad. Potato peelings are excellent, as are onions, garlic, carrots, celery, and parsley. Some vegetables to avoid are bell peppers, cabbage, broccoli, cauliflower, and tomatoes. Another good idea is to freeze vegetable scraps until you are ready to use them. Then, cover the vegetables with water and let them simmer for several hours. After the stock is done, strain the liquid."

"This recipe is from one of our talented and innovative chefs, Kristy Rawson. She makes all of our soups and a lot of our vegetarian specials."

Sarah Alvord
Zia Diner

Greek Hash Brown Bake

1	tablespoon olive oil
1	medium onion, diced medium
½	green bell pepper, seeded and diced medium
½	medium tomato, peeled, seeded, patted dry, and diced medium
2	teaspoons Cavender's Greek Seasoning *(see chef's comments on this page)*
	salt and black pepper *(to taste)*
¼	cup flour
½	teaspoon paprika
2	tablespoons fresh parsley, finely chopped
2	tablespoons cream cheese, softened
2	tablespoons sour cream
2	tablespoons yogurt
1	tablespoon milk
1	egg, beaten
4	medium, red potatoes, boiled, drained, cooled, peeled, and grated
4	eggs
2	tablespoons red bell peppers, finely chopped
1	tablespoon fresh parsley, finely chopped

"This is a really fun, easy dish to make. It's tasty, healthy, and people just love it. For a nice, light meal, serve it with a salad and some fruit. Another option is to eliminate the eggs, and then serve the potatoes as a side dish."

"If you object to the cream cheese, you can substitute ricotta. That would make the dish lighter."

"You should be able to find Cavender's Greek Seasoning in most good supermarkets. If not, use some basil, thyme, and oregano."

Louise Stewart
Grant Corner Inn

In a large skillet place the olive oil and heat it on medium high until it is hot. Add the onions and green bell peppers, and sauté them for 2 minutes. Add the tomatoes and sauté them for 2 minutes. Add the Cavender's Greek Seasoning, salt, and black pepper, and stir them in. Set the mixture aside.

In a medium bowl place the flour, paprika, and the 2 tablespoons of parsley. Stir the ingredients together so that they are well blended.

In this order, gradually blend in the cream cheese, sour cream, yogurt, milk, and beaten egg. Add the sautéed vegetables and gently fold them in. Add the cooked, grated potatoes and gently fold them in.

Preheat the oven to 400°. Place the mixture in a shallow baking pan and pat it down. Make 4 "wells" in the mixture with the back of a spoon. Break one egg into each well. Bake the dish for 12 to 15 minutes, or until the eggs are set. Sprinkle the red bell peppers and the 1 tablespoon of parsley on top.

serves 4

Tortilla Española
with Romesco Sauce

Tortilla Española

10	**medium white potatoes, peeled and thinly sliced** (store them in cold water until ready to use)
½	**cup olive oil**
1	**medium onion, halved and thinly sliced**
6	**large eggs**
¼	**teaspoon salt**
	Romesco Sauce (recipe on next page)

Preheat the oven to 350°.

In a small roasting pan place the potatoes and olive oil, and toss them together. Cover the pan and bake the potatoes for 20 minutes.

Very carefully (because of the steam) uncover the pan. Add the onions and spread them around evenly. Re-cover the pan and cook the potatoes for 10 minutes more, or until they are done. Remove the pan from the oven and let the potatoes cool.

In a medium large bowl place the eggs and salt, and lightly beat them. Fold the potatoes and onions into the eggs.

Add a small amount of olive oil (from the roasting pan) to a large sauté pan (nonstick) and heat it on high until it is hot. Very carefully add the potato and egg mixture. Gently shake the pan for 1 minute so that the eggs set. Reduce the heat to the lowest temperature possible and cook the ingredients for 15 to 20 minutes, or until the eggs are ⅔ done. Place a plate on top of the pan and very carefully turn the tortilla out of the pan and onto the plate.

Reheat the sauté pan on high. Slide the tortilla back into the pan. Reduce the heat to low and cook it for 10 minutes, or until it is firm to the touch.

Cut the tortilla into wedges and serve them with the Romesco Sauce.

serves 6 to 8

"This is a very typical Spanish dish that is wonderful for breakfast or brunch. It is one of the best potato dishes that I know."

"As with most of our dishes at the restaurant this requires some skill to make. However, if you like to cook and you are a real 'foodie', then by all means I encourage you to try it, because this definitely is a do-able recipe. The hardest part is turning the tortilla out onto the plate. This is very stressful. Don't panic if the tortilla breaks, because it still will taste good. You have to kind of shake the pan and twist it at the same time."

Ned Laventall
El Farol

Romesco Sauce

2	chile pequin pods
2	cloves garlic
¼	cup sliced almonds, toasted
¾	cup olive oil *(not extra virgin)*
4	red bell peppers, roasted, peeled, and seeded *(see chef's comments on page 159)*
¼	cup red wine vinegar
½	teaspoon salt

In a small pan place the chile pequin pods. Toss them on high heat for 5 to 6 minutes, or until they are lightly toasted *(do not breathe the fumes)*. Let the chiles cool.

In a food processor place the toasted chile pods, garlic, toasted almonds, and olive oil. Coarsely chop the ingredients. Add the roasted red bell peppers, red wine vinegar, and salt. Purée the ingredients together so that a smooth consistency is achieved.

makes approximately 2 cups

"This sauce goes well with so many things. It is especially good with fried items that are browned and crispy. When you roast the chile pequin pods, stand back from the stove so that you don't breathe the fumes, and don't let small children in the kitchen. It's a good idea to let the chiles cool outside, but first test the wind direction so that the fumes don't blow back in your face. As a man who speaks from experience, I can assure you that this is a most unpleasant occurrence! Another option, of course, is to wear a gas mask."

Ned Laventall
El Farol

Four Cheese Pizza

1	12" pizza round *(recipe on page 299)*
	Traditional Pesto *(recipe on page 116)*
2	Roma tomatoes, thinly sliced
1	ounce Fontina cheese, grated
1	ounce provolone cheese, grated
1	ounce mozzarella cheese, grated
1	ounce Parmesan cheese, freshly grated

Preheat the oven to 350°.

Spread the pizza round with a thin layer of the pesto. Place the Roma tomato slices on top. Sprinkle on the four cheeses.

Bake the pizza for 15 to 18 minutes, or until the cheese is hot and bubbly.

serves 1

"A good trick is to chill the cheese in the freezer so that it will grate easily..... especially the Fontina."

Steven Lemon
Pranzo Italian Grill

Cheese, Spinach, and Green Chile Egg White Omelette

4	teaspoons margarine
8	egg whites, whisked until frothy
1	cup Monterey Jack cheese, diced small
2	cups spinach, cleaned and chopped
1	cup green chile peppers, roasted, peeled, seeded, and diced

(see chef's comments on page 159)

Heat a small nonstick omelette pan on medium high until it is hot. For each omelette place 1 teaspoon of the margarine in the pan and melt it. Add ¼ of the egg whites. Pull the omelette from the sides with a spatula so that the uncooked part gets cooked. Cook the omelette in this manner for 4 minutes.

Place the cheese, spinach, and green chile peppers on top. Reduce the heat to low and cover the pan. Cook the omelette for 2 minutes more, or until the ingredients are hot. Fold the omelette over.

serves 4

"This omelette is made without any egg yolks. I swear that if you were blindfolded and tasted this omelette, you would not be able to tell the difference from one that was made the usual way.....except that this one might be lighter and fluffier. The color of food really influences how it tastes to you. It's exciting to come up with really non-fat, healthy meals that taste great and leave you feeling completely satisfied.....not like you have eaten some spartan health food meal."

Isabelle Koomoa
Guadalupe Cafe

Eggplant Parmesan

3	medium eggplants, cut into ½" thick discs
1	tablespoon canola oil
1	tablespoon olive oil
1	pound mushrooms, sliced
2	carrots, grated
1	teaspoon fresh garlic, minced
	salt *(to taste)*
1	pound spinach, stems removed, washed, dried, and chopped
1	pound Roma tomatoes, cut into thin discs
2	cups Marinara Sauce *(or as needed), (recipe on page 117)*
1	cup mozzarella cheese, grated
1	cup Parmesan cheese, freshly grated

Preheat the oven to 350°.

On a flat, lightly oiled baking sheet place the eggplant slices. Brush them with the canola oil. Bake the eggplant slices for 1 hour, or until the centers are tender. *(Leave the oven on for baking the casserole after it is assembled.)*

In a large sauté pan place the olive oil and heat it on medium high until it is hot. Add the mushrooms, carrots, garlic, and salt. Sauté the ingredients for 5 minutes, or until the mushrooms are tender.

In the bottom of a large, lightly oiled baking dish place ½ of the baked eggplant slices. On top of each slice, in this order, layer on the spinach, Roma tomatoes, and mushroom mixture.

Spoon on ½ of the Marinara Sauce.

Place the other eggplant slice on top of each stacked eggplant. Spread on the remainder of the sauce.

In a medium bowl place the mozzarella and Parmesan cheeses, and toss them together. Sprinkle the cheeses on top of the casserole.

Bake the dish for 25 to 30 minutes, or until the eggplant is hot and the cheese is melted.

serves 6

"This recipe differs from a traditional Eggplant Parmesan in several ways. First, each serving is in an individual medallion form, and you can see each layer of the different foods. Second, it has extra vegetables in it, like the spinach and carrots, so it is especially healthy. Third, the eggplant is baked instead of fried in oil, so it is obviously much better for you."

"For me, the hardest part in making this dish is to use the right amount of the marinara sauce. The other ingredients are so flavorful that you want the sauce to accent, not dominate them. You will have to use your own judgment and learn by experience."

"Years ago I was a single parent and supported myself by waitressing. I worked in the best restaurants with the top chefs, and so I was exposed to a lot of excellent food. This inspired me to learn how to cook, which I did by apprenticing with several great chefs. I worked for them for free, and eventually I learned how to combine and balance flavors. I find cooking to be both exciting and sensual!"

Lisa Sivé
Wild Oats Market

Eggs Norvegiennes with
White Sauce and Red Sauce

Eggs Norvegiennes

4   **English muffins, sliced in half horizontally and toasted**
1   **8-ounce can smoked Norwegian salmon**
8   **eggs, poached**
     White Sauce (recipe follows)
     cayenne pepper (to taste)
     Red Sauce (recipe on next page)

On each of 4 heated, individual serving plates place 2 English muffin halves. Place some smoked salmon on each piece. Place a poached egg on top of each half. Spoon on the White Sauce and then sprinkle on some cayenne pepper. Spoon the Red Sauce next to each English muffin half.

serves 4

White Sauce

4   **tablespoons butter**
4   **tablespoons flour**
2   **cups milk, heated**
2   **teaspoons white wine**
     salt (to taste)
     white pepper (to taste)

In a medium saucepan place the butter and heat it on low until it is melted. Add the flour and stir it in for 5 minutes, or until it is well blended and the flour is cooked.

While stirring constantly, slowly add the milk. Cook and stir the sauce for 5 to 8 minutes, or until it is thickened. Add the wine and stir it in. Season the sauce with the salt and white pepper.

makes 2 cups

"The name of this recipe comes from the Norwegian salmon that is used, instead of it being a dish that is served in Norway. The taste is wonderful with the two sauces, and the colors are very pretty. I would serve it for a Sunday brunch with some potatoes on the side, and some very good champagne.....it would be perfect!"

"An easy way to poach eggs is to carefully place them in a pot of boiling water, to which several drops of vinegar have been added. For some reason the vinegar causes the eggs to shrink and become nicely rounded."

"When I first came to Santa Fe and tasted the green chile, I said 'Ugh! Never let me eat that again!' Now I am addicted, and I have to have it. Even when I travel to my home in Switzerland, I don't go without my cans of green chile."

Marie Jeanne Chaney
Swiss Bakery

Red Sauce

1	teaspoon olive oil
1	clove garlic, minced
1	shallot, minced
½	teaspoon dried basil
2	large tomatoes, chopped
	salt *(to taste)*
	black pepper *(to taste)*

In a small saucepan place the olive oil and heat it on medium high until it is hot. Add the garlic, shallots, and basil. Sauté the ingredients for 2 minutes.

Add the tomatoes and simmer the sauce for 15 minutes, or until the tomatoes are of a puréed consistency.

Season the sauce with the salt and black pepper.

makes approximately 1 cup

"When I was a teen-ager in Switzerland I used to work in a restaurant as a waitress. I was always very interested in cooking, and on my hours off between lunch and dinner I would hang out in the kitchen, watching the cooks work. I asked lots of questions and memorized how they made different dishes. Because I wasn't able to take a chef's apprenticeship, this is one way I learned a lot about cooking."

Marie Jeanne Chaney
Swiss Bakery

Baked Eggs with Shrimp

3	**tablespoons olive oil**
3	**medium onions, finely chopped**
3	**green bell peppers, seeded and finely chopped**
3	**medium tomatoes, peeled, seeded, and finely chopped**
1	**teaspoon red chile powder**
	salt *(to taste)*
	black pepper *(to taste)*
12	**large eggs**
6	**large shrimp, cooked, shelled, and deveined**

Preheat the oven to 350°.

In a large skillet place the olive oil and heat it on medium high until it is hot. Add the onions and green bell peppers, and sauté them for 2 to 3 minutes, or until they are tender.

Add the tomatoes and sauté them for 3 to 5 minutes, or until they are softened.

Add the red chile powder, salt, and black pepper, and stir them in.

In the bottom of 6 individual ramekins spoon a small amount of the sauce. Break 2 eggs into each dish and then place one shrimp on top.

Bake the eggs for 10 minutes, or until they are set.

Spoon the remainder of the sauce on top.

serves 6

"I hate to admit this, but I am one of the few people in the world who doesn't like shrimp. However, I needed some good recipes for the restaurant, so I asked an old family friend to develop one for me, and this is it. I've never tasted it myself, but I get rave reviews from everyone who eats it!"

"When people walk into my restaurant I want them to feel that they are in a place where people really care about them. And when they eat their meal I want them to feel that they are experiencing something very special. After all, there is no reason why breakfast cannot be as exciting a meal as dinner."

Louise Stewart
Grant Corner Inn

Green Chile Macaroni and Cheese

2	**Anaheim chile peppers, seeded and chopped**
1	**bunch fresh cilantro, washed and coarsely chopped**
2	**cups romaine lettuce, washed and chopped**
½	**cup water** *(or as needed)*
4	**cups elbow macaroni, cooked and drained**
1	**cup sharp cheddar cheese, grated**
½	**cup milk**
2	**tablespoons butter**
	salt *(to taste)*
	black pepper *(to taste)*

In a food processor place the Anaheim chile peppers, cilantro, romaine lettuce, and some of the water. Blend the ingredients together so that a smooth purée is achieved *(add the water as needed so that it is the consistency of a heavy cream)*.

In a large saucepan place the purée, cooked macaroni, cheddar cheese, milk, butter, salt, and black pepper. Heat the ingredients on medium *(stir frequently to prevent the cheese from sticking to the bottom of the pan)* for 10 minutes, or until the cheese is melted and everything is hot.

serves 4

"Macaroni and cheese is wonderful stuff.....it reminds me of my childhood. In the restaurant we use 1 cup of heavy cream that has been reduced (instead of the milk), and ½ cup of butter (instead of 2 tablespoons). The texture of the cream and butter is just excellent. So, if you want to make this recipe really special and delicious, this is the way."

"When I work in the kitchen I wear 3 chef's jackets at the same time, and I wrap my hair up turban-style, with several wildly colored scarves. If I come into the dining room I frighten the customers. It has been suggested that I resemble someone from the Grateful Dead."

"Our customers have a wonderful access to the kitchen, and we appreciate their feedback. One evening I was working with my back to the door, and a customer came in to ask what I was making. I didn't see who it was, and I said, 'Bugs. We're having bug pasta tonight.' He freaked out and said, 'What!? You're cooking bugs!?' I guess that some of our food is so far out that he thought I was serious."

Lawrence McGrael
Geronimo Lodge

Black Bean Enchiladas

12	**blue corn tortillas** *(fresh)*
2	**cups cooked black beans** *(recipe on page 285),* **heated**
¾	**cup Monterey Jack cheese**
	Guadalupe Red Chile *(recipe on page 118),* **heated**
½	**cup Monterey Jack cheese, grated**

Preheat the oven to 450°.

Across the center of each tortilla place 3 tablespoons of the black beans and 1 tablespoon of the ¾ cup of cheese. Roll each enchilada up and place them in a lightly oiled baking pan.

Pour the Guadalupe Red Chile Sauce on top. Sprinkle on the ½ cup of cheese.

Bake the enchiladas for 10 minutes, or until the cheese is melted.

serves 4 to 6

"A lot of recipes tell you to quick-fry the tortillas in oil to soften them, but this is not necessary. Just be sure that they are fresh and pliable. My daughter, who is very physically fit and health conscious, taught me this. She has been very influential in helping me to develop recipes that are low in fat and yet taste delicious."

Isabelle Koomoa
Guadalupe Cafe

Spinach and Cheese Burrito

"We have a problem in our restaurant because a lot of people want their chile on the side. We won't serve it this way, because whatever they are ordering will be dry and not good. So I ask them to try just a small amount. Sometimes the people will leave, but usually we can talk them into trying it our way..... and 95% of these people walk out of the restaurant on cloud nine."

"I grew up in an extremely wealthy family with chauffeurs, maids, and limousines. I lived in boarding schools from the time I was six, I was spoiled rotten, bored with everything, and I found food to be very unexciting. At the age of 16, to the horror of my family, I got a job as a waitress. Every day our chauffeur would drive me to work in my little white uniform, and he would pick me up later to drive me home. My grandmother made me use the servant's quarters because I had the uniform on. Now in my later life I am paying my dues, because I spend most of my time cooking in the restaurant.....but, I love it!"

Isabelle Koomoa
Guadalupe Cafe

1	teaspoon margarine
1	cup mushrooms, sliced
4	cups fresh spinach, stems removed, washed and chopped
4	flour tortillas
1	cup Monterey Jack cheese, grated
	Guadalupe Red Chile Sauce *(recipe on page 118)*

Preheat the oven to 450°.

In a large sauté pan place the margarine and heat it on medium high until it is melted and hot. Add the mushrooms and spinach, and sauté them for 3 to 4 minutes, or until the mushrooms are tender and the spinach is wilted. Drain off the liquid.

In the center of each flour tortilla place ¼ of the mushroom-spinach mixture. Add ⅛ cup of the cheese. Roll the burrito up.

Spoon the Guadalupe Red Chile Sauce on top. Sprinkle on another ⅛ cup of the cheese.

Heat the burrito for 5 minutes, or until the cheese is melted.

serves 4

LP CALDWELL

Pasta

Spicy Seafood Fettucini

1	cup poblano chile peppers, diced
1	cup red bell peppers, seeded and diced
1	cup green bell peppers, seeded and diced
1	cup red onions, thinly sliced
4	cups Roma tomatoes, diced
½	cup calamata olives, diced
4	tablespoons fresh mixed herbs (thyme, basil, oregano, etc.), chopped
1	teaspoon fresh garlic, chopped
½	cup white wine
½	cup extra virgin olive oil
8	green lip mussels, washed
20	clams, washed
12	jumbo prawns, shelled and deveined
1	pound fettucini, cooked al dente and drained
4	tablespoons Romano cheese, freshly grated
1	lemon, cut into 8 wedges

"The seafood that we use in this dish will vary, depending upon what pieces we have on hand. It's excellent with any kind of fish or shellfish that is fresh. The peppers and fresh herbs make it both spicy and flavorful."

Eric Sanders
Ogelvies

In a medium large bowl place the poblano chile peppers, red and green bell peppers, red onions, Roma tomatoes, calamata olives, fresh herbs, garlic, white wine, and olive oil. Mix the ingredients together and let them marinate for 24 hours.

In a large saucepan place 1 cup of the marinade mixture and heat it on medium high until it is hot. Add the mussels, clams, and prawns. Cover the pan and cook the ingredients for 3 minutes, or until the shells open.

Add the remaining marinade and heat it until it is hot.

In the center of each of 4 individual plates place the fettucini. Surround the pasta with the shellfish. Spoon the heated vegetable sauce on top. Sprinkle the Romano cheese on top of the sauce. Garnish the plate with 2 lemon wedges.

serves 4

"There is a saying in the restaurant business..... 'You don't feed 'em to fatten 'em. You feed 'em to keep 'em happy and comin' back.'"

Frank Peña
Ogelvies

Jalapeño Pasta with Scallop Sauce

Jalapeño Pasta

2	cups all purpose flour
¾	cup semolina flour
5	fresh eggs
¼	cup milk
2	teaspoons canned jalapeño chile peppers, puréed
1	pinch salt
	Scallop Sauce *(recipe follows)*

In a large mixing bowl place all of the ingredients and knead them with an electric mixer *(use the dough hook)* for 10 minutes, or until a soft dough is formed. On a flat, floured surface roll out the dough so that it is ⅛" thick. Cut the dough lengthwise into ¼" wide strips. Hang the strips over a wooden rod *(like a broom handle)* for 2 hours *(minimum)* so that they dry. Cook the pasta al dente and drain it. Serve it with the Scallop Sauce on top.

serves 6

Scallop Sauce

2	tablespoons olive oil
2	cloves garlic, smashed and minced
2	pounds sea scallops, cleaned
1	tablespoon fresh cilantro, minced
1	teaspoon dried tarragon
1½	cups dry white wine

In a large skillet place the olive oil and heat it on medium high until it is hot. Add the garlic and sauté it for 45 seconds, or until it begins to turn brown. Add the sea scallops and cook them on 1 side for 1 minute. Remove the scallops and place them on a warm plate. To the skillet add the cilantro, tarragon, and white wine. Cook the ingredients for 5 minutes, or until the sauce is reduced by ½. Add the scallops *(place the uncooked sides down on the pan)* and cook them for 4 minutes.

serves 6

Angel Hair Pasta with Shallots and Basil on a Savory Tomato Sauce

Angel Hair Pasta with Shallots and Basil

2   tablespoons extra virgin olive oil
2   tablespoons fresh garlic, finely chopped
2   tablespoons shallots, finely chopped
2   tablespoons fresh basil, julienned
¼   cup tomatoes, skins and seeds removed, and diced
1   pound angel hair pasta, cooked al dente and drained
       cracked black pepper *(to taste)*
½   cup **Savory Tomato Sauce** *(recipe on next page),* **heated**
4   sprigs fresh basil
½   cup Parmesan cheese, freshly grated

In a large skillet place the olive oil and heat it on medium high until it is hot. Add the garlic, shallots, julienned basil, and tomatoes. Sauté the ingredients for 2 to 3 minutes, or until the tomatoes are soft but still hold their shape.

Add the angel hair pasta and cracked black pepper, and toss them in.

In the bottom of each of 4 individual soup bowls place 2 tablespoons of the Savory Tomato Sauce. Place the pasta on top. Garnish the dish with a sprig of basil.

Serve the pasta with the Parmesan cheese and cracked black pepper on the side.

serves 4

"This is a California cuisine type of dish.....no cholesterol, lots of intense flavors, and a very good presentation. Employees at the Bishop's Lodge just love it. They are supposed to have their meal between 4 and 5 o'clock, and we always have something special prepared for them. However, a lot of times they pretend that they are busy during this time, and then they call up at 6 o'clock to ask if we can make this dish. I don't mind making it for 1 or 2 people, but when 15 ask for it, I tend to get a little crazy. However, I am flattered that they like it so much."

"When I was at the Beverly Wilshire I once prepared a dinner for the Music Awards Association where the cost was $100,000 per plate. Madonna, Michael Jackson, President Reagan, and all sorts of celebrities attended. Experiences like that were quite thrilling, and that's one of the things that I do miss about not working in Los Angeles."

Jim Makinson
Bishop's Lodge

Savory Tomato Sauce

2	**tablespoons extra virgin olive oil**
¼	**cup onions, coarsely chopped**
2	**tablespoons fresh garlic, coarsely chopped**
2	**tablespoon shallots, coarsely chopped**
2	**tablespoons fresh basil, coarsely chopped**
2	**teaspoons fresh rosemary**
½	**cup fresh tomatoes** *(in their juice),* **chopped**
2	**tablespoons V-8 juice**
1	**teaspoon sugar**
½	**teaspoon nutmeg**
¼	**cup white wine**
	salt *(to taste)*
	black pepper *(to taste)*

In a medium saucepan place the olive oil and heat it on medium high until it is hot. Add the onions, garlic, and shallots. Sauté the ingredients for 3 to 4 minutes, or until the onions are translucent.

Add the basil and rosemary, and sauté them for 1 minute.

Add the remainder of the ingredients. Cook the sauce slowly on medium low heat for 15 minutes.

Pour the sauce into a food processor and blend it. Strain the sauce through a fine sieve.

makes approximately 2 cups

Fresh Vegetable, Herb, and French Goat Cheese Pasta

¼   **cup olive oil**
1   **red onion, chopped medium**
2   **cloves garlic, finely chopped**
1   **tablespoon fresh basil, chopped**
1   **tablespoon fresh oregano, chopped**
1   **small can of artichoke hearts, drained**
1   **small green bell pepper, seeded and chopped medium**
1   **small red bell pepper, seeded and chopped medium**
1   **small yellow bell pepper, seeded and chopped medium**
3   **medium tomatoes, chopped medium**
1   **cup mushrooms, sliced**
½   **teaspoon salt** *(or to taste)*
¼   **teaspoon black pepper** *(or to taste)*
1½ **pounds farfalle** *(bow tie)* **pasta, cooked al dente and drained**
8   **ounces French goat cheese, cut up**
1   **cup pecans, chopped**

In a large sauté pan place the olive oil and heat it on medium high until it is hot. Add the red onions, garlic, basil, and oregano. Sauté the ingredients for 2 minutes, or until the onions are tender.

Add the artichoke hearts, green, red, and yellow bell peppers, tomatoes, and mushrooms. Sauté the vegetables for 5 minutes, or until they are tender. Add the salt and black pepper, and stir them in.

Add the sautéed vegetables to the cooked pasta and toss them together so that everything is well mixed.

On each of 4 individual serving plates place the pasta. Place the goat cheese on top. Sprinkle on the pecans.

serves 4

"I like bow ties for the pasta, but if you don't care for them you can use fettucini or linguini, or whatever suits your fancy. This is a wonderful dish that's fresh and light tasting, and yet it is filling. The goat cheese melts into the pasta and the bell peppers combine with the other flavors beautifully. It's very important that you use all of the vegetables that are called for in the recipe, because each one is necessary for the total taste of the dish."

Paul Hunsicker
Paul's Restaurant of Santa Fe

"We try to use fresh everything in the restaurant.....what comes in the back door fresh goes out to the customer fresh. And, we always buy the best ingredients that we can find."

Carol Moberg
Paul's Restaurant of Santa Fe

Asian Flavor Linguini with Prawns and Sweet Peppers

½	**teaspoon chile pequin** (hot red chile flakes)
1	**tablespoon sugar**
2	**tablespoons Thai fish sauce** (see chef's comments on this page)
2	**tablespoons toasted sesame oil**
2	**tablespoons lime juice, freshly squeezed**
3	**tablespoons water**
2	**tablespoons peanut oil**
1	**pound prawns, shelled and deveined**
2	**tablespoons fresh garlic, minced**
2	**tablespoons fresh ginger root, peeled and minced**
1	**medium red onion, chopped small**
1	**large red bell pepper, seeded and chopped small**
1	**bunch fresh cilantro, large stems removed, and chopped small**
1	**pound linguini, cooked al dente and drained**

In a small bowl place the chile pequin, sugar, Thai fish sauce, toasted sesame oil, lime juice, and water. Mix the ingredients together and set it aside.

Heat a large sauté pan on medium high until it is hot. Add the peanut oil and coat the pan. Add the prawns, garlic, and ginger. Gently toss the ingredients for 30 seconds.

Add the red onions and red bell peppers. Sauté the ingredients for 2 to 3 minutes, or until the prawns are just done.

Add the cilantro and fish sauce mixture, and mix them in so that they are heated.

Add the linguini and toss it in well.

serves 4

Southwestern Pasta Primavera

3	tablespoons olive oil
1	yellow bell pepper, seeded and diced small
1	red bell pepper, seeded and diced small
1	jalapeño chile pepper, minced
¼	cup green chile peppers, roasted, peeled, seeded, and diced *(see chef's comments on page 159)*
1	medium zucchini, cut lengthwise and then into ⅛" thick pieces
1	tablespoon fresh garlic, minced
6	Roma tomatoes, skinned, quartered, and coarsely chopped *(save the juice)*
¼	cup corn kernels
2	tablespoons fresh cilantro, chopped
1	teaspoon ground cumin
3	tablespoons white wine
	salt *(to taste)*
	black pepper *(to taste)*
1	pound pasta, cooked al dente and drained
4	tablespoons Parmesan cheese, freshly grated

In a large sauté pan place the olive oil and heat it on medium until it is hot. Add the yellow and red bell peppers, jalapeño and green chile peppers, zucchini, and garlic. Sauté the ingredients for 2 to 3 minutes, or until the peppers soften.

Add the tomatoes *(with the juice)*, corn, cilantro, and cumin. Sauté the ingredients for 2 minutes.

Add the white wine and deglaze the pan. Add the salt and black pepper.

Add the sauce to the cooked pasta and toss it in well. Serve the pasta with the Parmesan cheese sprinkled on top.

serves 4

"I am a real pasta lover. It's my specialty and I love to make it. I just can't resist the temptation to cook fresh tomatoes in hot olive oil and then add some white wine.....the whole experience is addictive!"

"When I cook food for other people I am not just making and selling a product. Rather, I am providing something that is necessary for their survival, as well as giving them something that they really do enjoy. The greatest thing in the world is when a waiter comes back into the kitchen and tells me that a customer claimed that my pasta was the best he has ever eaten. That makes my whole day worthwhile."

"As a native of Santa Fe, I am a lover of hot green chile.....so much so that I have to watch myself in the restaurant and keep my food toned down. I think that I went right from my baby bottle to a Hatch green chile!"

"I was in high school when I first started cooking, and I thought that it was really neat. My friends would ask me where I worked, and I would tell them in a restaurant. They would ask if I was a bus boy and I would say, 'No, I'm a cook!' "

Rocky Durham
Zia Diner

Linguini with Shrimp and Saffron

¼	cup olive oil
4	tablespoons celery, chopped
4	tablespoons onions, chopped
4	tablespoons fresh garlic, chopped
1	cup tomatoes, chopped
2	teaspoons fresh oregano, chopped
½	cup fresh Italian parsley, chopped
4	pinches saffron
24	medium shrimp, peeled and deveined
	salt *(to taste)*
	black pepper *(to taste)*
1	pound linguini, cooked al dente and drained

In a large sauté pan place the olive oil and heat it on medium high until it is hot. Add the celery, onions, and garlic. Sauté the ingredients for 5 minutes, or until the onions are translucent.

Add the tomatoes, oregano, parsley, and saffron. Bring the ingredients to a simmer.

Add the shrimp, cover the pan with a lid, and cook the shrimp for 2 minutes, or until they are done. Add the salt and black pepper, and stir them in.

On each of 4 individual serving plates place the linguini. Spoon on the shrimp with the sauce on top.

serves 4

"Traditionally Parmesan or Romano cheese is not served with seafood pasta. Just imagine if I served the shrimp in this dish all by themselves. They would be salty and flavorful enough, with all of the other ingredients, so that no one would think of putting a big sprinkling of cheese on top. But, if a serving of pasta is put underneath the shrimp, then some psychological perversion happens to Americans, and they think that it needs cheese."

"My mother is a marvelous Italian cook.....the kind that you would give anything to be invited to her house for dinner. Her recipes were passed down from generation to generation, and nothing was ever written down. As a little boy I used to love spending time in the kitchen watching her cook, and sometimes helping her. However, I couldn't get away with this too often, because since I was a boy I was supposed to be out in the garden or doing more 'manly' work. I remember that on Sunday mornings, if we were having meatballs for dinner, there would be 2 of them waiting for me to eat before they were put in the sauce.....pink in the middle and with no tomatoes!"

Ken Calascione
La Traviata

Radiator Pasta with Spicy Mushroom Sauce

2	cups Roma tomatoes, peeled, seeded, and chopped
10	sun-dried tomatoes, reconstituted and finely chopped
1	cup white wine
2	teaspoons chile pequin *(hot red chile flakes)*
1	teaspoon sugar
¼	cup olive oil
10	cloves garlic, thinly sliced
½	medium yellow onion, diced small
1	pound mixed mushrooms *(oyster, shiitake, Chanterelle, etc.)*
2	tablespoons fresh oregano, coarsely chopped
2	tablespoons fresh thyme, coarsely chopped
1	cup fresh Italian parsley, coarsely chopped
½	cup white wine
	salt *(to taste)*
	black pepper *(to taste)*
1	pound radiator pasta, cooked al dente and drained
½	cup Romano cheese, freshly grated

In a medium saucepan place the Roma tomatoes, sun-dried tomatoes, the 1 cup of white wine, chile pequin, and sugar. Simmer the ingredients on low heat for 20 minutes, or until the liquid is reduced by ½. Keep the sauce warm.

In a large skillet place the olive oil and heat it on medium high until it is hot. Add the garlic and the onions, and sauté them for 8 to 10 minutes, or until they begin to brown.

Add the mushrooms and sauté them for 5 minutes, or until they begin to brown.

Add the oregano, thyme, Italian parsley, the ½ cup of white wine, salt, black pepper, and warm tomato sauce. Stir the ingredients together and heat them until they are hot.

On a serving platter place the cooked pasta. Pour the sauce on top. Sprinkle on the Romano cheese.

serves 4

"Radiator pasta is made in the shape of little coils and I just love them. It's funny about pasta, because even though all sizes and shapes are made out of the same ingredients, some shapes definitely taste better than others. Make sure that you use a premium quality semolina pasta that is made with eggs. This is the only kind of pasta that will not fall apart right after you cook it. This is a pretty spicy dish, so be careful. I think I've been around my cooks from Chimayo too long.....everything they cook has hot peppers in it!"

"This recipe will work with any kind of mushrooms, but it is best with a mixed variety of the wild ones. Commercially grown mushrooms lack that wonderful woodsy flavor, but they will work in a pinch. If you pick your own mushrooms, be EXTREMELY CAREFUL! I never will forget when I was a little boy and my parents went mushroom hunting. They were experts, but this time they made a mistake and ate a bad one. They were rushed to the hospital, had their stomachs pumped, and were in critical condition for several days. It scared me to death."

Ernie Bolleter
Inn at Loretto

Spaghetti alla Puttanesca

½	cup olive oil
4	whole anchovies
4	cloves garlic, chopped
8	plum tomatoes, peeled, seeded, and coarsely chopped
20	calamata olives
3	tablespoons fresh parsley, chopped
½	teaspoon cayenne pepper *(or to taste)*
	black pepper *(to taste)*
1	pound spaghetti, cooked al dente and drained

In a large sauté pan place the olive oil and heat it on high until it is hot. Add the anchovies and sauté them for 30 seconds, or until they are broken. Add the garlic and sauté it for 10 seconds.

Add the plum tomatoes, calamata olives, ½ of the parsley, cayenne pepper, and black pepper. Sauté them for 1 to 2 minutes, or until they are heated through.

Toss the spaghetti with the sauce, sprinkle on the rest of the parsley, and serve it immediately.

serves 4

Linguini with Clams

4	tablespoons olive oil
1	tablespoon fresh garlic, minced
1	tablespoon shallots, minced
1	teaspoon fresh oregano, chopped
28	baby clams *(see chef's comments on this page)*
½	cup clam juice
1	tablespoon lemon juice, freshly squeezed
	salt *(to taste)*
	black pepper *(to taste)*
1	pound linguini, cooked al dente and drained

In a large sauté pan place the olive oil, garlic, and shallots. Heat the ingredients on medium high until the oil is hot, and then sauté them for 2 minutes. Add the oregano and sauté it for 30 seconds.

Add the clams, clam juice, lemon juice, salt, and black pepper. Cook the ingredients for 2 minutes, or until the clams open.

Add the pasta and toss it well.

serves 4

"If you are using clams in the shell, then take a knife and cut through the muscle that holds the shell closed, so that they will be slightly opened before you cook them."

"I enjoy cooking much more than baking, because I don't like to be restricted to exact measurements. I remember once when I worked at a restaurant in Denver and was baking bread. The hostess went to the chef and told him that the bread was terrible. He tasted it, and then came back to where I was working. The dough was growing on the table really, really fast, and I was having to work double time to knead it. He took one look and said, 'No salt in the bread today, eh, Steven?' I looked at him and answered, 'No sir, I just didn't feel like using it today.' 'What does salt do to baking, Steven?' 'It controls the growth of the yeast in the dough, sir.' 'That's right, Steven, it controls the growth of the yeast in the dough.' I had 25 dozen loaves of bread in pans ready to be baked, and he made me take out all of the dough and rework it with the proper amount of salt. That's the last time I ever neglected to follow a baking recipe correctly!"

Steven Lemon
Pranzo Italian Grill

Linguini alla Amatriciana

"This is a great pasta dish because it tastes wonderful, and it's quick and easy to prepare. To make it really good you should cook the onions for a long time so that they caramelize. In fact, the longer you cook them the better the dish is going to taste, because more of the natural sugar will be released."

"When you add vodka it is important that you first remove the pan from the heat. Then, when you return the pan to the stove be careful and stand back because the flame will flash up, and you don't want to burn off your eyebrows! One time a guy who worked here poured brandy into a pan while it was still on the stove. The flame traveled back into the bottle and it exploded in his hand. If you have an electric stove, then the heat has to be hot enough for the vodka to flambé. Shake the pan around a little bit, and if this doesn't work, you can always light a match to it."

Steven Lemon
Pranzo Italian Grill

6	tablespoons olive oil
1	tablespoon fresh garlic, minced
1	tablespoon shallots, minced
1	medium yellow onion, halved and thinly sliced
½	teaspoon chile caribe *(crushed red chile peppers)*
2½	ounces prosciutto, diced
2	ounces vodka
3	cups Fresh Tomato Sauce *(recipe on page 116)*
¼	cup fresh parsley, chopped
	salt *(to taste)*
	black pepper *(to taste)*
1	pound linguini, cooked al dente and drained

In a large sauté pan place the olive oil, garlic, shallots, and onions. Heat the ingredients on medium heat until the oil is hot, and then sauté them for 10 minutes.

Add the chile caribe and prosciutto, and sauté them for 2 minutes.

Remove the pan from the heat and add the vodka. Return the pan to the heat and carefully flambé it *(see chef's comments of this page)*.

Add the Fresh Tomato Sauce, parsley, salt, and black pepper. Cook the sauce until everything is heated.

Add the pasta and toss it with the sauce.

serves 4

Spago con Melanzane

1	tablespoon olive oil
2	tablespoons lemon juice
1	medium eggplant, sliced into ¼" medallions
6	tablespoons olive oil
1	tablespoon fresh garlic, minced
1	tablespoon shallots
1½	cups tomatoes, peeled, seeded, and diced
4	tablespoons fresh basil, chopped
2½	cups Fresh Tomato Sauce *(recipe on page 116)*
3	ounces dry vermouth
	salt *(to taste)*
	black pepper *(to taste)*
1	pound spaghettini, cooked al dente and drained
1	ounce Gorgonzola cheese, crumbled

In a small bowl place the 1 tablespoon of olive oil and the lemon juice, and mix them together. Brush the eggplant slices with the mixture. Grill them for 2 to 4 minutes on each side, or until they are tender. Dice them and set them aside.

In a large sauté pan place the 6 tablespoons of olive oil, garlic, shallots, and tomatoes. Heat the oil until it is hot and then sauté the ingredients for 2 minutes.

Add the eggplant, basil, Fresh Tomato Sauce, dry vermouth, salt, and black pepper. Cook the ingredients for 4 minutes, or until a sauce-like consistency is achieved.

Add the pasta and toss it with the sauce. Sprinkle the Gorgonzola cheese on top.

serves 4

"This is one of our most popular pasta recipes. What makes it so special is the grilling of the eggplant, which really gives it a good flavor. If you don't have an outdoor grill, or if it's wintertime and too cold to be outside, then you can broil them in the oven. In this case use just a small amount of the olive oil-lemon juice mixture, because you don't want the oil to catch fire in your oven. Another key to the delicious flavor is the Gorgonzola cheese."

"Pranzo is very involved in charitable benefits and causes. One thing we do that I especially enjoy is to have a special Christmas lunch for the Big Brothers and Big Sisters of Santa Fe, along with their little brothers and sisters. Most of these kids have never seen anything fancier than a Burger King for eating out, so this is a real experience for them. Santa Claus comes and passes out candy and T-shirts, and the kids come back in the kitchen to help cook. Everyone has a lot of fun and it's a real heart warming experience."

Steven Lemon
Pranzo Italian Grill

Greek Style Bow Tie Pasta

4	**ounces sun-dried tomatoes** *(dried, not packed in oil)*
4	**tablespoons olive oil**
2	**medium leeks** *(white part only),* **cut into long, thin strips and washed**
2	**tablespoons fresh garlic, minced**
¾	**cup calamata olives, pitted and finely diced**
½	**cup feta cheese, crumbled**
1	**pound farfalle pasta, cooked al dente and drained**
	salt *(to taste)*
	black pepper *(to taste)*

In a small saucepan place the sun-dried tomatoes and cover them with water. Bring them to a boil and then simmer them for 5 minutes, or until they are softened. Strain the tomatoes *(reserve the cooking liquid)* and cut them into thin strips. Set them aside.

Heat a large sauté pan on medium high until it is hot. Add the olive oil and leeks, and sauté them for 2 minutes, or until the leeks begin to soften.

Add the garlic, calamata olives, sun-dried tomatoes, and ¼ cup of the reserved cooking liquid. Cook the ingredients for 1 minute.

Add the feta cheese, pasta, salt, and black pepper. Toss the ingredients together and cook them for 1 minute.

serves 4

"The kind of food that I like to fix has different moods and it affects people in different ways. Sometimes I make 'challenging food', where you have to think about what you are eating to determine the flavors and decide if you like it or not. For instance, one time I made lamb raisin raviolis with turmeric. Another kind of food is what I call 'comfort food', and it reminds you of your childhood and what mom used to make. Examples are macaroni and cheese, meat loaf, and tapioca pudding. And then there is 'playful food', which is clean, light-hearted, tasty, and fun, with no heavy emotional overtones. This recipe is an example of the latter."

"I get my ideas for recipes in a lot of different ways. My peers and I bounce ideas off each other, I read cookbooks and food magazines, and I walk around town and look at the menus of other restaurants. If I eat out I try to notice the different combinations of flavors and take one or two ideas home with me. But, I never take notes.....that's cheating!"

Sarah Alvord
Zia Diner

Peasant Style Pasta

6	tablespoons olive oil
¼	pound panchetta *(Italian bacon),* **thinly sliced and diced**
¼	cup red onions, diced small
2	tablespoons fresh garlic, minced
1	cup mustard greens, washed and coarsely chopped
1	cup escarole, washed and coarsely chopped
1	pound farfalle pasta, cooked al dente and drained
½	cup feta cheese, crumbled
	salt *(to taste)*
	black pepper *(to taste)*

In a large sauté pan place the olive oil and heat it on high until it is hot. Add the panchetta and sauté it for 1 minute. Add the red onions, garlic, mustard greens, and escarole. Toss the ingredients for 2 minutes, or until the greens begin to wilt.

Add the pasta, feta cheese, salt, and black pepper. Toss the ingredients over medium heat for 1 minute, or until everything is well mixed.

serves 4

"I adapted this recipe from a traditional Italian peasant salad. It has greens in it, which were considered to be a lower class vegetable. The flavor of the pasta is nice and light, and the feta cheese really brings out the taste of the greens. When you are cooking them in the hot oil, just be careful that they don't overcook. They should retain their bright color and be just barely wilted. If you are deft, you can toss them in your pan, or else you can use tongs to turn them."

"Panchetta is an Italian bacon that has less fat than American bacon. It comes in rolls at the deli and can be sliced to your specifications."

Rocky Durham
Zia Diner

Angel Hair Pasta with a Sweet Red Pepper and Lime Purée

"This is a nice, light pasta that has a bit of zip to it because of the lime juice and cayenne pepper. The flavor of the roasted red bell peppers comes through and it is well balanced by the lime juice. There is a nice yin-yang quality to the dish."

"When you roast peppers the skin should get black and blistered all over. This can be achieved by broiling the peppers in the oven, placing them over an open flame on your gas stove, or grilling them outside on a barbecue. Another method is to cut the peppers in half, place them on a flat sheet with the skin side up, and bake them in the oven for about 30 minutes at 425°. After the skins are well blistered, put the peppers in a bowl, cover them tightly with plastic wrap, and let them sit for about 15 minutes. Then you can easily peel off the skin."

"The angel hair pasta takes only a few minutes to cook so that it is al dente. As soon as it is done you must drain and serve it immediately."

Sarah Alvord
Zia Diner

6	large red bell peppers, roasted, peeled, and seeded *(see chef's comments on this page)*
1	teaspoon fresh garlic, chopped
¼	cup fresh cilantro, chopped
¼	cup lime juice, freshly squeezed
½	teaspoon cayenne pepper
½	teaspoon salt
2	tablespoons olive oil
1	pound angel hair pasta, cooked al dente and drained
½	cup Parmesan cheese, freshly grated

In a food processor place the roasted red bell peppers, garlic, cilantro, lime juice, cayenne pepper, and salt. Blend the ingredients for 60 seconds, or until they are roughly puréed.

In a medium large sauté pan place the olive oil and heat it on medium high until it is hot. Add the purée mixture and sauté it for 5 minutes, or until it is hot.

Add the angel hair pasta and quickly mix it with the purée.

Add the Parmesan cheese and mix it in.

serves 4

Pasta

Fish & Shellfish

New Mexican Seafood Sauté

2	tablespoons olive oil
⅔	pound medium shrimp, peeled and deveined
⅔	pound scallops
⅔	pound halibut steak, skin and bones removed, and cut into bite size chunks
6	cloves garlic, finely minced
10	Roma tomatoes, diced medium *(with the juice)*
6	scallions, thinly sliced
⅓	cup fresh cilantro, finely minced
4	serrano chile peppers, finely minced
1	cup fume blanc wine
2	limes, quartered
	salt *(to taste)*
	black pepper *(to taste)*

In a large sauté pan place the olive oil and heat it on medium high until it is very hot *(so that a few drops of water flicked into the pan sizzle loudly)*. Add the shrimp, scallops, and halibut chunks. Toss them rapidly with a spatula for 20 to 30 seconds, or until they are seared.

Add the garlic and sauté it with the fish for 30 seconds.

Add the tomatoes, scallions, cilantro, and serrano chile peppers *(stir lightly after each addition)*.

Add the fume blanc and stir it in.

Squeeze the juice of the limes into the pan. Add 4 of the rinds and stir them in.

Simmer the fish for 2 to 3 minutes more, or until it is just cooked through. Season it with the salt and black pepper.

serves 4

"I get a lot of compliments from customers who eat this dish. One man told me that these were the best scallops he had ever put into his mouth. You can make this recipe with only one of the seafood items, but my favorite is to use a combination. If you are watching your cholesterol, it's probably best to use just the fish."

Sarah Alvord
Zia Diner

"I believe that for most people ⅓ of the dining experience is the food. The other ⅔ is the atmosphere, service, conversation, and other intangibles that do not have a price tag on them. People like to eat here because they are not intimidated by our food."

"I am a carpenter as well as a chef. One thing that I like about cooking is that no matter how exact I am with my measurements, each time I make an item it comes out a little bit different. This is because in cooking there are so many uncontrollable variables. I enjoy that element of spontaneity in cooking. Whereas in carpentry, the more precise I am in my measurements, the more predictable the outcome will be."

Michael Nelsen
Zia Diner

Seafood Enchiladas

1	**stick margarine**
½	**cup flour**
1	**cup milk**
1	**quart fish stock, reduced to 1 cup** *(see recipe and chef's comments on page 294)*
1	**bunch fresh cilantro, chopped**
3	**tablespoons lime juice, freshly squeezed**
1	**teaspoon Old Bay Seasoning**
½	**teaspoon white pepper**
1	**tablespoon olive oil**
¾	**pound white fish, cut into bite size pieces**
¾	**pound shrimp, peeled and deveined**
¾	**pound snow crab, cooked**
12	**blue corn tortillas**
1	**cup Monterey Jack cheese, grated**
2	**cups cooked black beans** *(recipe on page 285)*
1	**cup head lettuce, chopped**
1	**cup tomatoes, chopped**

In a medium saucepan place the margarine and heat it on medium until it is melted. Add the flour and stir it in for 5 minutes.

While stirring constantly, slowly add the milk and fish stock. Cook the sauce for 5 minutes or until it thickens.

Add the cilantro, lime juice, Old Bay Seasoning, and white pepper, and stir them in. Keep the sauce warm.

In a large sauté pan place the olive oil and heat it on medium high until it is hot. Add the white fish and shrimp, and sauté them for 2 minutes. Add the crab and sauté it for 1 to 2 minutes, or until it is heated, and the fish and shrimp are done.

Preheat the oven to 375°.

In a large, flat baking dish place 6 of the tortillas. Place the seafood on top of them. Place the other 6 tortillas on top. Spread on the sauce. Sprinkle on the cheese. Bake the enchiladas for 30 to 45 minutes, or until they are hot and bubbly.

Serve the enchiladas with the black beans. Garnish the dish with the lettuce and tomatoes.

serves 4 to 6

"Sometimes people will tire of New Mexican food. They feel they don't want to ever see another red or green chile. This recipe is an excellent alternative, because it is assembled like a traditional enchilada dish, but there is no chile in it at all. You get the distinctive flavor of the blue corn tortillas, and the sauce is very smooth and subtle. Eat this with a glass of white wine.....it's heavenly!"

Patricia Helmick
Peppers Restaurant

"This dish is made by laying out the tortillas flat. If you roll them up, first dip them in hot oil so that they will be pliable and won't break. Also, when you are cooking the sauce don't let it boil or else it might separate."

Dan Kelley
Peppers Restaurant

"Dan is the first chef I have ever worked with who is humble, with very little ego. We are fortunate to have found such an easy-going guy who also is an excellent cook. He is almost too humble for his own good.....I practically have to hit him over the head to make him understand the extent of his talent. It's a refreshing change!"

Rick Helmick
Peppers Restaurant

Shellfish Stew

6	tomatillos, husked
6	Roma tomatoes
1	large red onion, julienned
¾	cup dry white wine
12	manilla clams
12	green lip mussels
6	shrimp, peeled and deveined
6	large scallops
2	red bell peppers, roasted, peeled, seeded, and julienned *(see chef's comments on page 159)*
2	yellow bell peppers, roasted, peeled, seeded, and julienned
2	poblano chile peppers, roasted, peeled, seeded, and julienned
2	tablespoons chipotle chile peppers in adobo sauce, puréed
6	cloves garlic, roasted *(see chef's comments on this page)* **and crushed**
3	tablespoons fresh herbs, chopped
6	ounces crab meat
¼	cup fresh cilantro, chopped
6	wedges lime
6	pieces garlic bread

In two large sauté pans, separately place the tomatillos and Roma tomatoes. Turn the heat on high and cook them for 15 to 20 minutes, or until the skins are burnt *(turn the tomatillos but not the Roma tomatoes)*. Roughly chop them and then set them aside.

In a medium large sauté pan place the onions. Cook them on high heat for 8 to 10 minutes, or until they are slightly scorched *(stir occasionally)*. Set them aside.

In a large stockpot place the white wine, clams, and mussels. Cover the pot with a lid and steam the ingredients for 6 to 7 minutes on high heat, or until the shellfish open.

Add the shrimp and scallops, and cook them for 2 to 3 minutes, or until they are just done.

Add the scorched onions, charred tomatoes and tomatillos, red and yellow bell pepper strips, poblano chile pepper strips, puréed chipotle chile peppers, roasted garlic, and chopped herbs. Quickly bring the ingredients to a high simmer and then remove the pot from the heat. Add the crab and stir it in.

(continued on next page)

"Although this is a rather long and time consuming recipe, there are no special skills required to make it. It's a great thing to serve at a dinner party, along with a crisp, green salad."

"In general, when you blacken the tomatillos and tomatoes your pans will get dark, but they can be easily cleaned. Don't turn the tomatoes because if you do, the skins will break, the juices will be released, and they will steam instead of getting brown."

"Roast the garlic in a pan on top of the stove or in the oven, on a very low heat. Keep turning the cloves so that they get soft and brown."

Karen Woods
Rancho Encantado

"I get feedback all of the time from my waitpeople, but I also like to go out on the floor. I'm the chef that comes to your table and asks you how everything is. People are usually surprised to see that the head chef is a woman, and that I am so young."

Karen Woods
Rancho Encantado

In each of 6 individual serving bowls ladle in the stew. Sprinkle on the cilantro. Serve the stew with a lime wedge and a piece of garlic bread.

serves 6

Crab Meat Louisianne

"The Crab Meat Louisianne is a signature dish of our restaurant. It was developed years ago when my wife and I had a restaurant in Florida. We were a real mom and pop operation back then.....we didn't even have a real kitchen! We cooked everything in woks, back yard grills, and crock pots. I believe that this recipe comes out best if you use a wok, which is the way we used to cook it."

1	**stick butter**
2	**cups jumbo lump crab meat**
1⅔	**cups scallion tops, chopped medium**
1	**cup sliced almonds, toasted**
2	**tablespoons New Orleans Spice Mix** *(recipe on page 296)*
4	**tablespoons fresh parsley, chopped medium**
4	**lemons, juiced**
2	**cups long grain white rice, cooked and mixed with a pinch of saffron** *(or use a packaged saffron rice mix)*

In a large skillet place the butter and heat it on high until it is melted. Add the crab meat, scallion tops, toasted almonds, and New Orleans Spice Mix. Gently stir the ingredients together.

Add the parsley and lemon juice. Gently sauté the ingredients for 2 to 3 minutes, taking care not to break the crab meat.

On each of 4 individual serving plates place the rice. Spoon the crab meat mixture on top.

Note: If possible, make only 2 servings of the crab meat mixture at a time, to keep it from getting too dry.

serves 4

"To get the true flavor of this dish you should use butter, or at least margarine. It is possible to use oil, but if you do then add more of the spice mixture so that the flavor is enhanced."

Skip Kirkland
Pontchartrain

Grilled Shellfish with Pestoso Butter

Grilled Shellfish

24	**jumbo shrimp, shelled and deveined**
36	**jumbo scallops, cleaned**
3	**tablespoons olive oil** *(or as needed)*
½	**cup Pestoso Butter** *(recipe follows)*, **melted**
2	**cups white rice, cooked**

In an alternating manner, place the shrimp and scallops on twelve 8" long bamboo skewers. Brush the seafood with the olive oil. While basting constantly with the Pestoso Butter, grill the seafood for 2 minutes on each side, or until it is just done. Serve the seafood on top of the rice.

serves 6

Pestoso Butter

½	**tablespoon fresh garlic**
¼	**cup pine nuts**
¼	**cup Parmesan cheese, freshly grated**
⅛	**cup Romano cheese, freshly grated**
2	**teaspoons dried basil**
½	**teaspoon dried tarragon**
½	**teaspoon salt**
4	**dried red chile pods, stemmed, seeded, and ground into a coarse powder**
1	**cup olive oil** *(or as needed)*
1	**pound butter, warmed to room temperature, and cut into small pieces**

In a food processor place the garlic and finely chop it. Add the pine nuts and finely grind them. Add the Parmesan and Romano cheeses, basil, tarragon, and salt, and purée them together. Add the ground chile pods and purée them with the other ingredients. Add the olive oil and purée it so that a loose paste consistency is achieved. With the food processor running, add the pieces of butter one at a time.

Note: This butter may be frozen.

makes approximately 1½ pounds

"The idea for this recipe came from John Beaupre, the owner. He is not a professional chef, but he has a wonderful palate. He can taste a dish and tell you exactly what's in it or what it needs to make it better."

Daniela Croce
Ore House

"I really like working at the Ore House. Daniela Croce, our manager, is wonderful because she creates the perfect work atmosphere.....it's honest, dedicated, and enjoyable. Also, I think that our staff is very special because we all work together to improve our own lives, both inside and outside of the kitchen."

"This pestoso butter is somewhat spicy, and it can be used on lots of different things. It is especially good with 'steaky' fish like marlin or swordfish. It's also a nice spread for bread that is toasted and then cut into triangles for hors d'oeuvres. When you baste the shellfish with the butter during the grilling process, they really become infused with the flavor. If you are watching your fat intake, or if you are sensitive to spicy things, then don't baste the fish..... just brush on a little at the end."

Isaac Modivah
Ore House

Marinated Shrimp Casino

1	medium red onion, coarsely chopped
1	red bell pepper, seeded and coarsely chopped
1	yellow bell pepper, seeded and coarsely chopped
1	green bell pepper, seeded and coarsely chopped
4	small tomatoes, coarsely chopped
3	cloves garlic, minced
1	tablespoon fresh basil, chopped
1	tablespoon fresh oregano, chopped
1	cup olive oil
2	cups white wine
½	teaspoon salt
¼	teaspoon black pepper
20	medium shrimp, shelled and deveined
8	strips bacon, slightly undercooked, drained, and chopped
3	cups cooked white rice

In a large bowl place the red onions, red, yellow, and green bell peppers, tomatoes, garlic, basil, oregano, olive oil, white wine, salt, and black pepper. Mix the ingredients together. Add the shrimp and marinate them in the refrigerator for 6 hours.

Preheat the oven to 400°.

In a shallow pan place the marinated shrimp mixture and bake it for 5 minutes.

Sprinkle on the bacon and bake the shrimp for 5 minutes more.

On each of 4 individual serving plates place the white rice. Place the shrimp on top. Spoon on the vegetables with the marinade.

serves 4

"I used to live in Connecticut, and that's where I got this recipe. The marinade is wonderful, and you can use it for other things. For instance, you can heat it up on the stove, add some clams, and toss it all in with pasta. I prefer for the bell peppers to be crunchy, although they can be overcooked with no harm. Just be sure not to overcook the shrimp."

"This is one of those dishes that really has a lot of character.....there is nothing timid about the flavors, which is the way I like my food."

Paul Hunsicker
Paul's Restaurant of Santa Fe

Prawn and Scallop Brochette with Cashew Sauce, Bok Choy Stir-Fry, and Ginger Rice Cakes

Prawn and Scallop Brochette

12   **large shrimp, peeled and deveined**
8   **large scallops, cleaned**
1   **teaspoon olive oil**
      Cashew Sauce *(recipe follows)*
      Bok Choy Stir-Fry *(recipe on next page)*
      Ginger Rice Cakes *(recipe on next page)*

On each of 4 bamboo skewers place 3 shrimp and 2 scallops. Lightly brush the seafood with the olive oil. Grill the brochettes for 2 minutes on each side, or until they are just done.

On each of 4 individual serving plates place the Cashew Sauce so that it covers ⅓ of the surface. Remove the shrimp and scallops from the skewer and place them, in an alternating manner, on top of the sauce. Place the Bok Choy Stir-Fry down the center ⅓ of the plate. Place the Ginger Rice Cakes on the other ⅓ of the plate.

serves 4

Cashew Sauce

1   **cup cashews, roasted**
1   **teaspoon fresh garlic, chopped**
1   **teaspoon walnut oil**
½   **cup coconut milk**
1   **teaspoon cayenne pepper**
¼   **teaspoon salt**
½   **cup water** *(or as needed)*

Place all of the ingredients *(except for the water)* in a food processor and blend them for 1 minute. Let the mixture sit for 5 minutes. With the food processor running, slowly add enough of the water so that a smooth, pourable sauce is achieved.

makes approximately 2 cups

Fish & Shellfish

"I think that food is the ultimate art because you can eat it.....and you can't eat a canvas. To me, the visual presentation should be just as dramatic to your eyes as the flavors are to your palate. Jim Bibo (who is one of the restaurant's owners and its founder) and I have a lot of input as to what the artistic presentation of each plate should be. We are both manic, hyperactive people. You talk about type A and type B personalities.....well, we are definitely double A!"

Judy Ebbinghaus
Santacafe

"I had this recipe in my head for some time, and finally I made it to go with the prawn and scallop brochette.....and, it worked perfectly. We make this with an east Indian red chile pepper mixture, called sambal chile, but cayenne pepper also works well. This sauce is spicy and delicious!"

Kelly Rogers
Santacafe

Bok Choy Stir-Fry

2	tablespoons peanut oil
1	head bok choy, outer leaves removed, bottom chopped off, washed, dried, and cut into ½" wide strips
1	red bell pepper, seeded and thinly julienned
½	large red onion, thinly julienned
1	poblano chile pepper, seeded and thinly julienned
½	teaspoon salt *(or to taste)*

Heat a seasoned wok on high until it is very hot. Add the peanut oil. Add the bok choy, red bell peppers, red onions, and poblano chile peppers. Stir-fry the ingredients for one minute, or until they are heated through but still crispy. Add the salt and toss it in.

serves 4

"This is a simple, straightforward stir-fry dish that takes only minutes to prepare. The same quick method of cooking can be used for any kind of vegetables, as long as they are thinly julienned or sliced."

Ginger Rice Cakes

2	cups botan rice *(or white short grain)*, rinsed
4	cups water
¼	cup plum wine
¼	teaspoon salt
¼	cup rice wine vinegar
½	cup pickled ginger
1	teaspoon black sesame seeds

"If you follow this recipe the rice should come out sticky, which I think is fun, because then you can play with it on your plate. Cut the rice cakes into any shapes that you want. We use the triangles because we like the way they look next to the other items on the plate."

In a medium saucepan place the rice, water, plum wine, and salt. Bring the ingredients to a boil over high heat. Cover the pan, reduce the heat to low, and simmer the rice for 20 minutes, or until all of the liquid is absorbed.

Place the cooked rice in a medium bowl. Add the rice wine vinegar and pickled ginger, and mix them in.

Press the rice mixture into a small baking pan. Chill it in the refrigerator for 30 minutes. Before serving it, bring it back to room temperature.

Cut the rice into triangles. Sprinkle on the black sesame seeds.

serves 4

"When I was 12 years old I took my first cooking class in school with all of the girls. It was an experimental program that allowed boys, and there were a few guys in the class besides myself. I went on to be a chef in Santa Fe, and the other guys are probably all IBM executives earning six figure salaries."

Kelly Rogers
Santacafe

Shrimp Fajitas with Guacamole and Pico de Gallo

Shrimp Fajitas

2   pounds medium shrimp, peeled and deveined
1   bunch fresh cilantro, tough stems removed
3   cloves garlic, chopped
4   jalapeño chile peppers, seeded and chopped
1   cup olive oil
2   red bell peppers, seeded and cut into thin strips
2   green bell peppers, seeded and cut into thin strips
4   medium yellow onions, each one cut into 6 wedges
8   flour tortillas, heated
     Guacamole *(recipe on next page)*
     Pico de Gallo *(recipe on next page)*

In a medium bowl place the shrimp, cilantro, garlic, jalapeño chile peppers, and olive oil. Let the shrimp marinate for 2 to 8 hours.

In a large, heavy skillet place 2 tablespoons of the oil from the marinade, and heat it on high until it is hot. Add the red and green bell peppers and the onions, and sauté them for 3 to 4 minutes. Remove the shrimp from the marinade and add them to the skillet. Sauté them for 2 minutes, or until they are done.

Serve the shrimp and vegetables with the tortillas, Guacamole, and Pico de Gallo.

serves 4

"This recipe was developed by me and some of my cooks from Chihuahua, Mexico. In the beginning they couldn't speak English, but now they speak and understand the language quite well. On the other hand, the only thing that I can say in Spanish is 'por favor'."

"The fajitas are incredibly simple to make, and everyone loves them. After you heat the tortillas either wrap them in foil or place them in a tortilla warmer, because they will dry out immediately. To eat the fajitas you put some shrimp and vegetables on a tortilla along with some guacamole and pico de gallo, roll it up, and eat it by hand or with a fork."

"We get many locals at our restaurant, and some of them have standing reservations. When tourists come they sit like little mice, with their eyes and ears wide open in fascination. They listen to locals talk about paintings and art shows, and watch everyone table hopping. Sometimes a well known artist or other personality will come in and visit with all of their friends in the restaurant, and the tourists are always asking the waitpeople, 'Who's that? Who's that?'"

Sylvia Johnson
Celebrations

Guacamole

2	large ripe avocados, peeled, pitted, and mashed
1	tablespoon fresh cilantro, minced
4	jalapeño chile peppers, seeded and finely minced
1	lime, juiced

In a small bowl place all of the ingredients and mix them together well.

makes approximately 1 to 2 cups

Pico de Gallo

1	tomato, diced medium small
½	red onion, diced medium small
3	serrano chile peppers, minced
1	tablespoon fresh cilantro, minced
2	teaspoons lemon juice, freshly squeezed
2	tablespoons water

In a small bowl place all of the ingredients and mix them together.

makes approximately 2 cups

Cinnamon and Chile Crusted Scallops with Wild Field Greens and Spicy Mango Salsa

Cinnamon and Chile Crusted Scallops with Wild Field Greens

2	tablespoons Spanish paprika
2	tablespoons sugar
2	tablespoons cayenne pepper
3	tablespoons coriander seeds, crushed
2	tablespoons cinnamon
2	tablespoons salt
1	tablespoon olive oil
32	jumbo sea scallops, cleaned
½	pound mesclun (wild, baby greens)
	vinaigrette dressing (your favorite)
	Spicy Mango Salsa (recipe on next page)
4	sprigs fresh cilantro

In a jar with a tight fitting lid place the Spanish paprika, sugar, cayenne pepper, crushed coriander seeds, cinnamon, and salt. Shake the ingredients together so that they are well mixed.

Dust the scallops with the spice mixture so that they are well covered.

In a large sauté pan place the olive oil and heat it on medium high so that it is hot. Add the dusted scallops and sauté them for 2 to 3 minutes on each side, or until they are barely done.

Toss the mesclun with your favorite vinaigrette.

In the center of each of 4 individual serving plates place the dressed greens. Arrange the scallops around the greens in a circle. Place a small dollop of the Spicy Mango Salsa next to each scallop. Garnish the plate with a sprig of the cilantro.

serves 4

"When you sprinkle the spice mixture on the scallops they will turn dark as you grill them. The outsides will sear, the juices will remain inside, and they will have a fantastic flavor. You can prepare this dish in minutes, and it's a feast!"

"To me, cooking is a celebration of life, and it is very dear to me. I realize that my talent is something I have been given, through no effort on my part, and I am just the recipient. For this I am very humble, and very grateful."

"Sometimes my fellow chefs think I am nuts when I talk to them about food. I tell them to pretend that the food is the love of their life, and they must have passion when dealing with it."

Pete Zimmer
Inn of the Anasazi

Spicy Mango Salsa

1   cup mango, diced
2   poblano chile peppers, diced
1   red bell pepper, seeded and diced
1   small red onion, diced
1   bunch fresh cilantro, leaves removed from stems and chopped
1   tablespoon honey
1   tablespoon olive oil
     salt *(to taste)*

In a medium bowl place all of the ingredients and mix them together.

makes 2 to 3 cups

"I never had any formal training in cooking, and many times I bluffed my way through jobs by pretending I knew how to do things, which I really didn't. But, I always found out how, and I never got caught in my little white lies. Eventually I learned how to do everything I had previously bluffed my way through.....and now I do them very well!"

Dolly Nevada Hand
Inn of the Anasazi

Ginger Orange Sea Scallops with Scallion Watercress Pancakes

Ginger Orange Sea Scallops

2	tablespoons fresh garlic, chopped
2	tablespoons fresh ginger root, peeled and grated
2	tablespoons orange zest *(outer orange part grated off)*, **blanched twice for 30 seconds, and dried in the oven**
1	tablespoon peanut oil
20	jumbo sea scallops, cleaned
1	cup Scallop Broth *(recipe on page 294)*
1	tablespoon butter
	salt and black pepper *(to taste)*
1	tablespoon peanut oil
2	bunches spinach, stems removed, washed and coarsely chopped
2	tablespoons fresh ginger root, peeled, thinly julienned, blanched for 30 seconds, and deep fried for 30 seconds
	Scallion Watercress Pancakes *(recipe on next page)*

In a food processor place the garlic, grated ginger, and orange zest. Purée the ingredients together and then set them aside.

In a large sauté pan place the first tablespoon of peanut oil and heat it on high until it is hot. Add the sea scallops and sear them for 30 seconds on each side.

Add the puréed spice mixture and stir it in. Add the Scallop Broth and deglaze the pan. Add the butter and stir it in. Cook the scallops for 1 minute more, or until they are done. Remove the scallops and keep them warm. Cook the sauce for 5 minutes, or until it is reduced and thickened. Season it with the salt and black pepper.

In another large sauté pan place the second tablespoon of peanut oil and heat it on medium high until it is hot. Add the spinach and sauté it for 1 minute, or until it has just wilted.

On each of 4 individual serving plates place the wilted spinach. Place the scallops on top. Spoon on some of the sauce. Sprinkle on the fried ginger. Serve the dish with the Scallion Watercress Pancakes next to the spinach and scallops.

serves 4

"This recipe may look involved, but actually it is quite simple. You need to assemble the ingredients, like the spice mix and scallop broth, but these items can be prepared in advance and then stored. The presentation of this dish is just as beautiful as the food is flavorful."

Frank Peña
Ogelvies

"Frank has a lot of artistic talent, and this is reflected in the presentation of his dishes. He is somewhat shy when speaking with words, but when he is working with food, his hands speak as eloquently as the finest orator."

Eric Sanders
Ogelvies

Scallion Watercress Pancakes

2	eggs
¼	cup sesame oil
½	teaspoon salt
¼	teaspoon black pepper
8	flour tortillas
½	cup scallions, chopped
½	cup watercress, chopped
3	cups vegetable oil *(or as needed)*

In a medium bowl place the eggs, sesame oil, salt, and black pepper, and whisk them together well. Brush the mixture on the top and bottom of the tortillas so that they are very well coated.

Sprinkle the scallions and watercress on top of 4 of the tortillas. Place the other 4 tortillas on top and press them down so that they will stick together.

In a medium large saucepan place the vegetable oil and heat it on medium high until it is hot. Deep fry the "pancakes" for 30 seconds, or until they are golden brown. Drain them on paper towels. Cut each one into 4 wedges.

serves 4

"The flavors of the sesame oil, the flour tortillas, scallions, and watercress really combine well. These pancakes have a delicious flavor, are simple to make, and yet they appear to be exotic.....something you have never eaten before."

Frank Peña
Ogelvies

Marinated Grilled Sea Scallops with Sautéed Capellini

Marinated Grilled Sea Scallops

½	cup fresh ginger root, peeled and coarsely chopped
¼	cup fresh garlic, coarsely chopped
4	shallots, coarsely chopped
1	cup fresh oregano leaves, stems removed
6	limes, juiced
¼	cup rice wine vinegar
1	teaspoon sugar
2	cups olive oil
2	pounds sea scallops, muscles removed
	Sautéed Capellini (recipe on next page)

In a blender place the ginger root, garlic, shallots, oregano leaves, lime juice, rice wine vinegar, and sugar. Blend the ingredients together.

With the blender constantly running at medium speed, slowly dribble in the olive oil.

Skewer the scallops on eight 6" long bamboo sticks.

Pour the marinade in a large, shallow glass dish. Add the skewered scallops and let them marinate for 15 minutes at room temperature.

Grill the scallops for 1 to 2 minutes on each side, or until they are opaque. Brush the scallops with the marinade.

On each of 4 individual serving plates place 2 skewers of the scallops and 1 Sautéed Capellini "pancake".

serves 4

"This recipe is from our chef, Jason Aufrichtig, who is very young, but a rare artist in the kitchen. When he first came to work here, he immediately commanded the respect of the rest of the staff because of the extremely high regard he has for food products. He sees great potential for everything he puts his hands on. His recipes reflect the kind of person he is, which is young, lively, innovative, and daring. If you try this dish you will know what I mean, because the scallops likely will be the best you have ever eaten."

"When I was 2 years old my best friend was a little 3-year-old boy who lived across the street. His mother started a vegetable garden for us, and we tended it for years, all by ourselves. We had tiny little tools and our patch of ground was the size of a small table, but we loved it. We never brought the food inside. Instead, we would pull up a carrot, brush off the dirt, sit down in the dirt, and eat it. These are precious memories, and to this day I feel that planting and harvesting your own food is an ultimate experience."

Katharine Kagel
Cafe Pasqual's

Sautéed Capellini

3   **tablespoons toasted sesame oil** *(or as needed)*
½   **pound capellini, cooked al dente and drained**

In a small, nonstick sauté pan place approximately 2 teaspoons of the toasted sesame oil *(use just enough to barely coat the bottom of the pan)* and heat it on medium high until it is hot. Add ¼ of the cooked pasta and cook it for 5 to 7 minutes on each side, or until the "pancake" is crisp and golden brown.

Repeat the process 3 times more so that 4 pancakes are made.

Note: Keep the finished pancakes in a warm oven until you are ready to use them.

serves 4

"If you are making a stir-fried dish, this makes a delightful alternative to rice. Just be sure that you use a good quality nonstick pan."

"When people come to our restaurant I want all of their senses to be engaged. That's why we have colorful murals on the wall and serve strongly flavored food. We have respect for traditional New Mexican products, but we like to prepare them in innovative ways."

Katharine Kagel
Cafe Pasqual's

Tortilla Crusted Snapper with Cilantro Lime Salsa

Tortilla Crusted Snapper

6   **5-ounce snapper fillets**
1   **cup flour** (or as needed)
4   **eggs, beaten**
10   **corn tortillas** (½ blue and ½ yellow), **cut into ⅛" wide strips**
½   **cup olive oil**
     Cilantro Lime Salsa (recipe follows)

Preheat the oven to 350°.

Dust the snapper fillets with the flour. Dip them in the beaten eggs. Press the fillets firmly into the tortilla strips so that they are completely embedded.

In an extra large sauté pan place the olive oil and heat it on high until it is hot. Sauté the crusted snapper fillets for 30 to 40 seconds on each side, so that they are seared.

Bake the fish for 3 to 5 minutes, or until it is just done. Serve the snapper fillets with the Cilantro Lime Salsa on top.

serves 6

Cilantro Lime Salsa

2   **cups fresh corn kernels**
1   **red bell pepper, seeded and diced**
1   **green bell pepper, seeded and diced**
2   **tomatoes, diced**
½   **teaspoon fresh garlic, minced**
½   **bunch fresh parsley, chopped**
1   **bunch fresh cilantro, chopped**
6   **limes, juiced**
2   **teaspoons Hot Desert Seasonings Mix** (recipe on page 297)
1   **tablespoon olive oil**
½   **tablespoon balsamic vinegar**

In a medium bowl place all of the ingredients and mix them together.

makes approximately 4 cups

"I have always loved textures on fish. This crust will be very crispy, and it makes an excellent contrast to the soft flesh of the fish. I like to use a mix of blue and yellow tortillas because the blue imparts a stronger flavor. Also, the two colors together look very striking, so that nothing much else needs to be done for the presentation of the dish. Cut the tortilla strips as thin as possible, and really pack them into the fillets. The tortilla flavor will get seared into the fillets..... almost like they grew that way!"

"Do you have a friend or relative who always salts their food before tasting it? A good remedy is to serve them something that you have saturated with salt. After they salt it and bite into it, they will gag. Hopefully, this will teach them a lesson!"

"A lot of times when people are cooking from a recipe they are rather nervous about it and keep double-checking the instructions. With this salsa recipe you don't have to worry about anything, not even the proportions. Just cut everything up, throw it in a bowl, season it, and you will have an exceptional salsa."

Pete Zimmer
Inn of the Anasazi

Pescado ala Chorrillana

1	tablespoon olive oil
1	large red onion, cut into 10 wedges
1	teaspoon fresh garlic, minced
¼	teaspoon salt
½	teaspoon black pepper
2	tablespoons olive oil
4	6-ounce red snapper fillets, dusted in flour
1	green chile pepper, seeded and cut into thin strips
2	tablespoons fresh cilantro, chopped
1	lime, juiced
1	tomato, cut into thin wedges
1	tablespoon fresh parsley, chopped

In a large sauté pan place the 1 tablespoon of olive oil and heat it on medium high until it is hot. Add the red onions, garlic, salt, and black pepper. Sauté the ingredients for 2 to 3 minutes, or until the onions are slightly tender. Set the mixture aside.

In another large sauté pan place the 2 tablespoons of olive oil and heat it on medium high until it is hot. Add the flour-dusted fish fillets and sauté them for 2 minutes on each side, or until they are lightly browned.

Place the sautéed fish on top of the onions in the first sauté pan. In this order, place on top of the fish fillets the green chile pepper strips, cilantro, lime juice, tomato wedges, and parsley.

Cover the pan and steam the ingredients on medium low heat for 8 to 10 minutes, or until the fish is done.

serves 4

Baked Salmon with Potato Basil and Chile Tarragon Sauce

Baked Salmon with Potato Basil

½   cup fresh basil
2   tablespoons olive oil
1   cup potatoes, peeled, cooked, and stiffly mashed
4   6-ounce salmon fillets
     Chile Tarragon Sauce *(recipe follows)*

Preheat the oven to 350°.

In a food processor place the basil and olive oil. Purée the ingredients so that a pesto consistency is achieved.

In a medium bowl place the puréed pesto. Add the mashed potatoes and beat them together so that they are well combined.

In a medium baking pan place the salmon fillets. Spread the potato-basil mixture on top of each fillet. Bake them for 20 minutes, or until they are just done *(do not overcook)*.

In the center of each of 4 individual serving plates spread on the Chile Tarragon Sauce. Place a salmon fillet on top.

serves 4

Chile Tarragon Sauce

2   cups demi-glace *(see chef's comments on this page)*
1   tablespoon fresh tarragon, chopped
2   tablespoons red chile powder
¼   cup white wine
     salt *(to taste)*
     black pepper *(to taste)*

In a medium saucepan place all of the ingredients and stir them together. Simmer the sauce for 1 hour, or until it is the consistency of heavy cream.

makes approximately 1½ cups

"This dish is a very interesting combination of different flavors. It's also quite colorful, because the fish is pink, the crust is green, and the sauce is red."

"One thing I love about cooking is that it provides me with instant gratification. I make a dish, it looks and smells beautiful, the customer eats it, and hopefully loves it and goes away happy. I know immediately that what I have just created is good. In many lines of work people have no idea if what they are doing is good or bad."

"We make our own demi-glace in the restaurant by reducing a veal stock. However, that is way too involved for most home cooks, so I advise you to buy it in the grocery store. Demi-glace has a wonderful, rich flavor, and you can use it in many sauces."

Paul Hunsicker
Paul's Restaurant of Santa Fe

Baked Salmon on a Plank with Peanut Chipotle Sauce

"Baking food on a plank of wood is a rustic idea that is popular in New Orleans, and somewhat on the East Coast. The flavor of the wood imparts itself to the salmon, which gives it a really interesting flavor. The more you use your plank the better it gets, because it will start to become charred, and then that flavor also gets into the food. You can cook any kind of meat or fish on the plank. It's a fun and different way to cook food, and people get a kick out of it. Just be sure that you get untreated wood.....don't get it from a lumber yard."

"I have always enjoyed the flavors of peanuts and smoked peppers in Thai food, so I decided to create my own recipe using these ingredients. The sauce is spicy, and it goes well with chicken or tuna, or any other kind of hearty fish."

"To be a good chef means to be a good kitchen manager. You need to stick your neck out for your employees and fight for their rights. You need to instill a pride in their work and teach them culinary skills. Without the family of kitchen employees, from the top to the bottom, there would be no restaurant business."

Karen Woods
Rancho Encantado

Baked Salmon on a Plank

4   8-ounce salmon fillets, skin and bones removed
     salt (to taste)
     black pepper (to taste)
     Peanut Chipotle Sauce (recipe follows)

Soak a slab of apple wood or pecan wood (approximately 2" thick, 12" long, and 5" wide) in water for 2 days.

Preheat the oven to 400°. Sprinkle the salmon fillets with the salt and black pepper. Place the fish fillets on the soaked wood plank and bake them for 15 to 20 minutes, or until they are barely done.

On each of 4 individual serving plates place a salmon fillet. Spoon the Peanut Chipotle Sauce on top.

serves 4

Peanut Chipotle Sauce

3   **tablespoons chipotle chile peppers** (canned in adobo sauce), chopped
3   **tablespoons tomatoes, diced**
3   **tablespoons dry white wine**
1   **tablespoon heavy cream**
1   **tablespoon peanut butter** (smooth)
½   **cup unsalted butter, softened**
     salt (to taste)
     black pepper (to taste)

In a small saucepan place the chipotle chile peppers, tomatoes, white wine, and heavy cream. Whisk the ingredients together and bring them to a boil. Remove the pan from the heat.

Add the peanut butter and whisk it in.

While whisking constantly, add the butter in small pieces.

Season the sauce with the salt and black pepper.

makes 1 cup

Pan Seared Salmon with Charred Tomato Sauce

Pan Seared Salmon

1   tablespoon olive oil
4   6-ounce salmon steaks
     salt and black pepper *(to taste)*
     Charred Tomato Sauce *(recipe follows)*

In a large, seasoned cast iron skillet place the olive oil and heat it on high until it is very hot *(so that it just starts to smoke)*. Add the salmon steaks and cook them for 2 minutes on each side, or until they are barely done.

On each of 4 individual serving plates spread on some of the Charred Tomato Sauce. Place a seared salmon steak on top. Serve the rest of the sauce on the side.

serves 4

Charred Tomato Sauce

1   **large onion**
1   **whole bulb garlic**
3   **pounds Roma tomatoes**
½   **cup fresh basil** *(or cilantro)*, **finely chopped**
     salt and black pepper *(to taste)*

Preheat the oven to 350°. Wrap the onion and garlic head in foil. Bake them for 1 hour, or until they are very soft. Let them cool, and then peel them.

Preheat the oven to broil. Place the Roma tomatoes on a flat baking sheet and broil them for 5 to 10 minutes, or until the skins are black and charred *(rotate the tomatoes so that the skin is charred all over)*.

In a food processor place the charred tomatoes, baked onion, baked garlic, and basil. Purée the ingredients. Add the salt and black pepper, and stir them in.

makes approximately 3 cups

Fish & Shellfish

"I really hate for salmon to be overcooked because it gets a dry, chalky, gummy quality, and I can't stand that. Check the center and if there is a 1" diameter that is red, then take it off the heat."

"One of my most pleasurable experiences is cooking in my kitchen at home, being creative, listening to good music, and maybe sipping (or should I say 'quaffing'?) some nice wine. Cooking should be fun, creative, and invigorating.....it shouldn't be drudgery. Playing around with different flavors is one of the freest forms of expression that there is."

"You want to char the living hell out of these tomatoes. Get them really black on the outside so that the sugar caramelizes on the inside. Lately I've been experimenting with roasting vegetables and then puréeing them, instead of poaching or steaming them to get them soft. The dry heat of the roasting really adds a lot of natural sweetness. Use this sauce with pasta, seafood, or a charred rib steak."

"When I lived in Spain I saw all of the tremendous bounty in their markets. This is when I first got serious about food and saw the endless possibilities."

Robert Goodfriend
ek mas

Ore House Grilled Salmon with Spinach Pecan Pesto

"What I really like about this recipe is the way the pesto seeps into the fish and infuses it with flavor. The pesto tends to dry up a little bit and makes a crust, which gives the fish an interesting texture. I have always loved the flavor of pecans in spinach salads, and so I decided to use the two ingredients to make a pesto. The flavor of the pecans blends really well with the salmon. This pesto also is excellent with trout, as well as pasta. We used to serve it to our employees to put it on their fish, but they started using it with pasta instead."

"As a little boy I grew up with only my father. He wasn't passionate about very many things in life, but cooking was the one exception. When he was in the kitchen preparing food, something extra came out of him. He seemed happy and involved, and he became much more lovable to me. I used to watch him be playful with the food, and these were my happiest times with him. I remember that even if he was fixing something as ordinary as a can of soup, he would always throw extra things in it. This is where I got the idea that experimenting with food was the right thing to do."

Isaac Modivah
Ore House

Ore House Grilled Salmon

6   8-ounce salmon steaks
3   tablespoons olive oil
    salt *(to taste)*
    black pepper *(to taste)*
    Spinach Pecan Pesto *(recipe follows)*

Brush both sides of the salmon steaks with the olive oil. Sprinkle on the salt and black pepper.

Grill the salmon steaks with the flesh side down for 2 minutes. Turn the steaks over and spread on a thick layer of the Spinach Pecan Pesto. Grill the fish for 2 to 4 minutes more, or until it is just done.

serves 6

Spinach Pecan Pesto

2   cloves garlic
½   bunch spinach, cleaned and stemmed
½   bunch fresh basil
½   cup pecans
¼   cup Parmesan cheese, freshly grated
1   tablespoon lemon juice, freshly squeezed
2   tablespoons red wine vinegar
¼   teaspoon salt
¼   teaspoon black pepper
¾   cup olive oil

In a food processor place each ingredient one at a time, and purée it so that finally a loose paste is formed *(if the mixture gets too thick during this process, then add some of the olive oil to loosen it up)*.

makes approximately 2½ cups

Grilled Swordfish and Tomato Coulis with Tomatillo Salsa

Grilled Swordfish and Tomato Coulis

3	large ripe tomatoes, cored and coarsely chopped
2	teaspoons shallots, chopped
3	tablespoons white wine
½	cup water
½	teaspoon salt *(or to taste)*
½	teaspoon black pepper *(or to taste)*
4	8-ounce swordfish steaks
2	tablespoons olive oil
1	teaspoon garlic powder
	salt *(to taste)*
	black pepper *(to taste)*
	Tomatillo Salsa *(recipe on next page)*

In a small saucepan place the tomatoes, shallots, white wine, and water. Heat the ingredients on high heat and boil them for 5 minutes.

Pour the mixture into a blender and purée it. Strain the purée into a small bowl through a fine sieve so that the pulp *(but not the seeds and skins)* comes through. Add the ½ teaspoon of both the salt and black pepper, and stir them in. Set the coulis aside.

Brush the swordfish steaks with the olive oil. Sprinkle both sides with the garlic powder, salt, and black pepper.

Grill the fish for 2 to 3 minutes on each side, or until it is just done.

On each of 4 individual serving plates spread on the tomato coulis. Place the swordfish on top. Spoon the Tomatillo Salsa on top.

serves 4

"Coulis is the French word for a puréed sauce, and it can be either hot or cold. This tomato coulis has a nice, light, fresh taste, and you can use it with any kind of fish."

"The only trick is not to overcook the swordfish. The center should be a little bit translucent. If you cook it all the way through, it will be really dry, just like canned tuna."

"I like to keep my cooking simple and elegant, using the freshest and best ingredients available. If you can't get the best ingredients for a certain recipe, don't use something sub-standard.....make something else. And, don't mix too many flavors together so that you kill the palate."

"I've been cooking since I was 4 years old, when I used to help my mom in the kitchen. I'm very lucky because I love being a chef and I'm good at it. My friends think I'm crazy because what I enjoy doing the most on my days off is.....you guessed it..... cooking!"

Adrienne Sussman
Chez What

Tomatillo Salsa

10	**tomatillos, husked and finely diced**
1	**medium red onion, finely diced**
3	**serrano chile peppers, seeded and finely diced**
¼	**cup fresh cilantro, chopped**
2	**tablespoons lime juice, freshly squeezed**
2	**tablespoons peanut oil** *(or vegetable oil)*
	salt *(to taste)*
	black pepper *(to taste)*

In a medium bowl place all of the ingredients and mix them together well.

Let the salsa sit in the refrigerator for 2 hours before serving it.

makes approximately 1½ cups

"This salsa is delicious with all kinds of fish, grilled chicken, and grilled steaks. It's also great to put on salads. It tastes good with chips, too, only it's hard to scoop it up with a chip. The salsa will keep for up to 3 days."

Adrienne Sussman
Chez What

Grilled Norwegian Salmon with Chinese Mustard Glaze

1	teaspoon light sesame oil
¼	pound spinach, washed and stems removed
2	teaspoons sesame oil
1	small leek, washed and finely julienned *(white part only)*
1	small yellow bell pepper, seeded and finely julienned
1	small red bell pepper, seeded and finely julienned
1	ounce haricots vert *(or green beans)*, strings removed, and blanched
4	8-ounce salmon fillets
	salt and black pepper *(to taste)*
2	tablespoons Chinese mustard *(dry)*
2	tablespoons soy sauce
4	tablespoons honey
¼	pound new potatoes, boiled and peeled
4	sprigs fresh Italian parsley

In a medium skillet place the 1 teaspoon of sesame oil and heat it on medium high until it is hot. Add the spinach and sauté it for 2 minutes, or until it is just wilted. Set the spinach aside and keep it warm.

In a medium large skillet place the 2 teaspoons of sesame oil and heat it on medium high until it is hot. Add the leeks, yellow and red bell peppers, and haricots vert. Sauté the ingredients for 2 to 3 minutes, or until they are just tender. Set the vegetables aside and keep them warm.

Season the salmon fillets with the salt and black pepper. Grill them for 2 to 3 minutes on each side, or until they are half done.

In a small bowl place the Chinese mustard, soy sauce, and honey. Stir the ingredients together.

Brush the Chinese mustard glaze on top of each salmon fillet. Grill them for 3 to 4 minutes on each side, or until they are just done.

On each of 4 individual serving plates place the wilted spinach with the salmon on top. Arrange the sautéed leeks, yellow bell peppers, and red bell peppers around the edge of the plate. Add the new boiled potatoes and a sprig of parsley.

serves 4

"Here is a dish that is healthy, light, flavorful, with a beautiful presentation. It is a variation on a recipe from the regent in Hong Kong. I like to do this on an outside barbecue so that the grill marks show on the fish. The Chinese mustard glaze is hot and sweet, and it adds a wonderful Oriental zip to the flavor of the salmon."

"When I was at the Beverly Wilshire the sous chef and I would go to all of the best restaurants in town to see what other chefs were doing. We would get their menus, figure out the cost per plate to the restaurant, study the presentations, and so on. Then we would sit down with our pencils and figure out our own menu so that it came out better than all of our competition, including cost, flavor, and presentation. This may sound unethical, but it was an excellent method for keeping one step ahead of our competition."

Jim Makinson
Bishop's Lodge

Grilled Swordfish Rolls Sicilian Style

2	tablespoons capers
2	tablespoons green Sicilian olives, pitted and chopped
2	tablespoons fresh Italian parsley, chopped
2	cloves garlic, chopped
¼	cup olive oil
½	cup bread crumbs
2	pounds swordfish, sliced horizontally into 16 thin pieces
¼	cup olive oil
½	cup bread crumbs *(or as needed)*

In a medium bowl place the capers, olives, parsley, garlic, the first ¼ cup of olive oil, and the first ½ cup of bread crumbs. Mix the ingredients together.

Dredge the swordfish pieces in the second ¼ cup of olive oil.

Across the center of each piece of swordfish place a finger-sized portion of the filling. Roll the swordfish up so that is the shape of a cigar.

Press the rolled fish into the second ½ cup of bread crumbs so that it is coated all over.

On each of 4 skewers place 4 of the swordfish rolls. Grill them for 5 to 7 minutes on each side, or until they are done.

serves 4

Grilled Tuna with Black Bean Coulis and Spicy Tomato Peanut Sauce

Grilled Tuna with Black Bean Coulis

1   **cup cooked black beans** *(recipe on page 285)*
1   **jalapeño chile pepper, minced**
1   **teaspoon ground cumin**
4   **6-ounce tuna steaks**
1   **tablespoon olive oil**
     salt *(to taste)*
     black pepper *(to taste)*
     Spicy Tomato Peanut Sauce *(recipe on next page)*

In a food processor place the black beans, jalapeño chile peppers, and cumin. Purée the ingredients so that they are smooth *(add enough water so that it is the consistency of a thick, heavy cream)*. Set the coulis aside.

Brush both sides of the tuna steaks with the olive oil. Sprinkle on the salt and black pepper. Grill the tuna for 3 to 4 minutes on each side, or until it is just done.

On each of 4 individual serving plates spread the black bean coulis. Place a grilled tuna steak on top. Spoon on the Spicy Tomato Peanut Sauce.

serves 4

"The black bean coulis goes really well with the tuna and the Spicy Tomato Peanut Sauce. The colors are very striking and it makes an impressive dish to serve to guests."

"I believe that there is a natural talent in good cooking. Some people can go to culinary school for years and yet they never quite get the knack. Others look like they are born to a kitchen. A lot of people who are chefs do a lot of moaning and groaning, because the hours are long, it's hot and noisy, and the work is hard. Other people look like they are having a ball, and these are the ones who make the best cooks. To be good, you have to love what you are doing."

Paul Hunsicker
Paul's Restaurant of Santa Fe

Spicy Tomato Peanut Sauce

4	tomatoes, chopped medium
1	large green bell pepper, seeded and chopped medium
1	medium onion, chopped medium
1	lime, juiced
1	cup water
⅛	teaspoon cayenne pepper
2	tablespoons peanut butter
	salt *(to taste)*
	black pepper *(to taste)*

In a medium saucepan place the tomatoes, green bell peppers, onions, lime juice, water, and cayenne pepper. Stir the ingredients on medium heat for 8 to 10 minutes, or until the tomatoes come apart.

Add the peanut butter, salt, and black pepper, and stir them in. Cook the mixture for 5 minutes more.

Pour the mixture into a food processor and purée it *(the sauce should be the consistency of a thick, heavy cream).*

makes approximately 1½ cups

"I once saw a recipe for this in a cookbook. I tried to re-create it in the restaurant, only I goofed and forgot what several of the ingredients were. Luckily, it came out just great.....maybe even better than the original. You can make the sauce into a wonderful soup by thinning it out with more water."

Paul Hunsicker
Paul's Restaurant of Santa Fe

Spicy Seared Tuna Loin with Smoked Chile Papaya Relish

Spicy Seared Tuna Loin

½ tablespoon paprika
½ tablespoon Cajun spice mix
1 pinch cayenne pepper
½ tablespoon salt
½ tablespoon black pepper
6 6-ounce tuna loins
2 tablespoons olive oil
   Smoked Chile Papaya Relish (recipe on next page)

Preheat the oven to 350°.

In a small bowl place the paprika, Cajun spice mix, cayenne pepper, salt, and black pepper. Mix the spices together.

Roll the tuna loins in the spice mixture so that they are well coated.

In a large sauté pan place the olive oil and heat it on high until it is hot. Add the tuna loins and quickly sear them on all sides.

Place the seared tuna loins in a baking dish and bake them for 5 to 7 minutes, or until they are medium rare.

Slice the tuna loins. Serve them with the Smoked Chile Papaya Relish.

serves 6

"Recently there has been a large promotion by Hawaii to get their seafood into the continental states, and that is the inspiration for this recipe. The seasonings on the tuna are spicy, especially because of the cayenne pepper. I say to use a 'pinch', because this gives you freedom in controlling the heat. So, how hot it comes out depends on how big your 'pinch' is. If you don't know about pinches, then use ⅛ teaspoon. When you sear the fish you are just sealing it so that the juices stay inside. Be careful not to overcook it, because tuna has a tendency to get very dry. Chefs learn how to tell the doneness of meat or fish by pressing down on the flesh with their fingers. The softer the flesh the more rare it is. If you see white specks leaching out, it's done for sure!"

John Davis
Old House

Smoked Chile Papaya Relish

2	chipotle chile peppers *(canned in adobo sauce)*, **stem and veins removed, and minced**
2	papayas, peeled, seeded, and diced
1	small red onion, minced
1	small red bell pepper, seeded and minced
1	small green bell pepper, seeded and minced
1	tablespoon fresh chives, minced
1	tablespoon fresh cilantro, minced
1¼	cups papaya nectar
¼	cup rice vinegar
	salt *(to taste)*
	white pepper *(to taste)*

In a medium bowl place all of the ingredients and mix them together.

makes approximately 2 cups

"This is a hot, spicy relish, but then hot is always relative.....what is hot to me may be mild to you. So, as always when cooking, keep tasting what you are making till you get it right."

"When I was a little boy I used to sneak down to the kitchen at night, when everyone was asleep, and cook all sorts of food for myself. I always cleaned everything up perfectly, so no one ever knew. Maybe my mom suspected, but she never said anything."

John Davis
Old House

Francisco's Grilled Tuna with Cool Cucumber Relish

Francisco's Grilled Tuna

4   6-ounce tuna steaks
½   lemon
2   teaspoons olive oil
     salt *(to taste)*
     black pepper *(to taste)*
     Cool Cucumber Relish *(recipe follows)*

Rub both sides of the tuna steaks with the lemon half. Brush the olive oil on both sides. Sprinkle on the salt and black pepper. Grill the tuna steaks for 4 to 5 minutes on each side, or until they are just done *(do not overcook them)*.

On each of 4 individual serving plates place the tuna steaks. Spoon the Cool Cucumber Relish on top.

serves 4

Cool Cucumber Relish

2   jalapeño chile peppers, seeded and finely diced
1   red bell pepper, seeded and finely diced
1   yellow bell pepper, seeded and finely diced
1   medium tomato, finely diced
½   medium red onion, finely diced
½   English cucumber, peeled, seeded, and finely diced
4   cloves garlic, finely diced
1   tablespoon red wine vinegar
½   bunch fresh cilantro, finely chopped
     salt *(to taste)*

In a medium bowl place the jalapeño chile peppers, red and yellow bell peppers, tomatoes, red onions, cucumbers, garlic, and red wine vinegar. Mix the ingredients together and then let them sit for 10 minutes. Add the cilantro and salt, and stir them in.

Refrigerate the relish for 1 hour before serving it.

makes approximately 2 cups

"I like this dish, especially for the summer, because it's so nice and light. You can use any kind of fish that is good and fresh."

"In our restaurant we design a new menu each week. This is a lot of work, but it keeps us original and creative in the kitchen. Our ingredients are absolutely fresh, and we try to borrow from lots of different cuisines and ethnic groups."

"If you are short of time and don't want to dice all of these vegetables, then you can run them in the food processor. The consistency won't be the same because it won't be chunky, but the flavor will still be great."

"This relish goes very well with grilled chicken, or even with corn chips. The flavors are well balanced so that no one thing is dominant."

Don Fortel
Francisco's

Wayne Gustafson
Julian's

"This is a classic, southern Italian-style dish that means squid with 'hot devil sauce'. It's very simple and it tastes wonderful. There are a few ingredients you cook together, you add the calamari, and then BOOM, you're done in 3 minutes and eating. If you don't like squid, then use shrimp instead."

"The trick is not to overcook the squid. If you cook it over 3 to 4 minutes, then it will toughen. If you are in a restaurant and you eat squid that is chewy, then you know the kitchen blew it and left it on the stove too long. The rule for cooking squid is generally under 3 minutes or over 15. In between these times something chemical happens to the squid and an enzyme builds up to make it tough. You have to cook it for a while in order to break the enzyme down."

"Although this dish is spicy, it does not overpower the taste of squid. Something to realize is that in Italy, a dish that is called 'spicy' pales in comparison to the New Mexican food that we are used to here. To Italians 'hot' means a little burn to your tongue, which to us in Santa Fe is NOTHING!"

Calamari Fra Diavolo

4	tablespoons olive oil
1	small red onion, chopped
4	cloves garlic, chopped
1	pound tomatoes, peeled, seeded and coarsely chopped
1	teaspoon chile caribe *(crushed red chile peppers)*
1	tablespoon fresh oregano leaves *(or 1 teaspoon dried)*
	salt *(to taste)*
	black pepper *(to taste)*
2	pounds squid, cleaned and cut into rings

In a large sauté pan place the olive oil and heat it on high until it is hot. Add the red onions and garlic, and sauté them for 5 to 7 minutes, or until the onions are translucent.

Add the tomatoes, chile caribe, oregano, salt, and black pepper. Cook the ingredients *(while breaking the tomatoes up with a spoon)* for 20 minutes, or until the tomatoes are soft.

Add the squid and cook it for 3 minutes *(don't overcook it or it will be tough)*.

serves 4 to 6

Halibut Bomba with
Avocado Pepita Salsa

Halibut Bomba

4   6" squares of puff pastry
1   mango, peeled and flesh puréed
4   6-ounce halibut fillets
    Avocado Pepita Salsa *(recipe on next page)*
2   fresh red chile peppers, roasted, peeled, seeded, and cut
    into thin strips *(see chef's comments on page 159)*
1   egg, lightly beaten with 1 tablespoon water

Preheat the oven to 400°.

In the center of each of the puff pastry squares spread on the mango purée.

Place a halibut fillet on top, at a diagonal *(flesh side down)*.

Spread the Avocado Pepita Salsa on top of the fish.

Lay the roasted red chile strips on top.

Brush the egg wash on the exposed part of the puff pastry. Fold the corners over and seal them so the fish is tightly wrapped. Pierce a sharp knife into each side so that two small air holes are formed.

Place the wrapped fish fillets on top of an oiled tray. Bake them for 20 minutes, or until the dough is golden brown.

serves 4

"Rather than just grilling or baking a piece of fish, which anyone can do, I tried to come up with a presentation that was really special. This idea is a spin-off from a classic salmon en croûte, which I've always liked to experiment around with. I would put fresh fruits and different little sauces and condiments inside, and come up with some very nice combinations. In this recipe the flavors really work well together.....the mangos are fresh and sweet, the avocados are rich and smooth, the roasted chiles are mildly hot, and the flavor of the fish still comes through."

"The fish needs to be sealed so that it steams inside the dough. Make sure that you wrap it very tight. The little knife holes in the sides are necessary so that the whole thing won't explode, and really go off like a bomba!"

Marc Greene
Old Mexico Grill

Avocado Pepita Salsa

4	medium, ripe avocados, peeled, pitted, and coarsely chopped
2	tomatillos, husked and coarsely chopped
2	small yellow onions, peeled and coarsely chopped
4	cloves garlic
2	jalapeño chile peppers, coarsely chopped
4	ounces pepitas *(roasted pumpkin seeds)*
2	tablespoons fresh oregano
¼	cup celery leaves
½	cup chicken stock *(recipe on page 295)*
¼	cup lime juice, freshly squeezed
3	tablespoons olive oil
2	teaspoons sugar
⅛	teaspoon cayenne pepper
1	teaspoon salt *(or to taste)*
1	teaspoon black pepper *(or to taste)*

In a blender place all of the ingredients and purée them together.

makes approximately 1 quart

"Everyone who tries this salsa raves about it. There are a lot of ingredients and the flavors are complex, but they meld together to make a really dynamite taste. Use this instead of guacamole with chips, or as an accompaniment to lamb or fish."

"I really enjoy my job. It's fun for me to dabble with the different flavors of Mexican cooking. I also like to mix with the guys in the kitchen. I speak a little Spanish, but I'm not great. It's amazing, because the closer I work my way over to the dishwasher, the better I speak it. By the time I get over there and start washing some dishes, I'm talking like a native!"

Marc Greene
Old Mexico Grill

Spicy Sautéed Mahi Mahi
with Avocado and Jicama Salsa

Spicy Sautéed Mahi Mahi

½   cup flour
2   teaspoons fresh oregano, chopped
1   tablespoon red chile powder
1   tablespoon garlic powder
½   teaspoon cayenne pepper
4   8-ounce mahi mahi fillets
¼   cup olive oil
     Avocado and Jicama Salsa *(recipe on next page)*

In a medium bowl place the flour, oregano, chile powder, garlic powder, and cayenne pepper. Mix the ingredients together so that they are well combined.

Dredge the mahi mahi fillets in the flour mixture.

In a large skillet place the olive oil and heat it on medium high until it is hot. Sauté the fish fillets for 3 to 5 minutes on each side, or until they are just done.

In the center of 4 individual serving plates spoon on the Avocado and Jicama Salsa. Place the fish fillets on top.

serves 4

"There's no trick to making this recipe. Just make sure the fish is fresh. Other kinds of nice fish to use are sole or pompano. If you want to grill the fish instead of sautéing it, you have to use a firm fleshed fish like halibut, swordfish, tuna, or mahi mahi. Rub the fish with oil and then sprinkle on the spices (don't use the flour)."

"I got my love of cooking from my grandfather. He wasn't a professional, but he was a great cook! When I was a little boy I used to watch him in the kitchen, and sometimes he would let me help him. Usually he was pretty weird about people being in the kitchen and he would scream and yell at them to get out of his way. But I was his little grandson, so he tolerated my presence."

"I love coming to work. Things are always happening in the kitchen.....there's never a dull moment!"

Anthony Carpenter
Garfield Grill

"I would call this a Southwestern salsa with a Mexican flair. It's very tasty and has a lot of contrasting textures, with the avocado, jicama, peppers, and onions. The poblano chile pepper has a really nice flavor and it isn't too spicy. It's the jalapeños that are hot."

"This salsa is great with shrimp, chicken, and chips. Just make sure that the avocados don't turn brown. You must serve it right after you chill it."

Anthony Carpenter
Garfield Grill

Avocado and Jicama Salsa

2	cups avocados, diced medium
1	cup jicama, peeled and diced medium
½	cup red bell peppers, seeded and diced medium
¼	cup poblano chile peppers, diced medium
2	tablespoons jalapeño chile peppers, minced
¼	cup fresh cilantro, chopped
¼	cup onions, thinly sliced
1	tablespoon fresh garlic, minced
⅛	cup lime juice, freshly squeezed
2	teaspoons salt *(or to taste)*
1	teaspoon black pepper, freshly ground

In a medium bowl place all of the ingredients and gently toss them together. Cover the salsa and place it in the refrigerator for 30 minutes before serving it.

makes approximately 1 quart

Spicy Grilled Swordfish with Warm Pineapple Salsa

Spicy Grilled Swordfish

3	tablespoons red chile powder *(hot)*
2	teaspoons cayenne pepper
1	tablespoon Hungarian paprika
1	teaspoon garlic powder
1	teaspoon onion powder
1	teaspoon kosher salt
1	teaspoon black pepper, freshly ground
4	8-ounce swordfish steaks
	Warm Pineapple Salsa *(recipe on next page)*
4	sprigs fresh cilantro

In a small bowl place the red chile powder, cayenne pepper, Hungarian paprika, garlic powder, onion powder, kosher salt, and black pepper. Mix the spices together.

Dust the swordfish steaks with the spice mixture. Grill them *(oil the grill first)* for 3 to 5 minutes on each side, or until they are medium rare.

On each of 4 individual serving plates place a swordfish steak. Spoon the Warm Pineapple Salsa on top. Garnish the dish with a cilantro sprig.

serves 4

"John Egan, the owner of Rancho Encantado, went on a diet where he lost about 70 pounds. Whenever we had this dish on the menu he would eat it. It was his very favorite thing because it was full of flavor, and yet it was very light."

"There is a huge ego in this industry, not only with men, but with women as well. Cooking is a form of art, and if you criticize someone's culinary creation, then you are attacking them and what they are. A lot of chefs won't share their recipes, or they will leave out an important ingredient. I hate this, but sometimes I find myself doing the same thing!"

Karen Woods
Rancho Encantado

Warm Pineapple Salsa

1	large ripe pineapple, peeled, cored, and diced large
1/3	cup pineapple juice
1	lime, juiced
2	tablespoons red wine vinegar
1/4	cup brown sugar
2	jalapeño chile peppers, stems removed
1/4	cup fresh cilantro, chopped

In a medium saucepan place the pineapple pieces, pineapple juice, lime juice, red wine vinegar, and brown sugar. Bring the ingredients to a boil over high heat.

Add the jalapeño chile peppers. Reduce the heat to medium and cook the ingredients on a low simmer for 20 minutes. Add the cilantro and stir it in.

Serve the salsa warm.

makes approximately 3 cups

"Fruit salsas are all the rage these days. This recipe is a little different because it is served warm, instead of cold. We leave the jalapeño chile peppers in the salsa whole, and they become pickled. The heat leaks out from them, so the longer they are in the salsa, the hotter it gets. If it gets too hot, you can always take them out."

Karen Woods
Rancho Encantado

Breaded Sesame Seed Cod with Sweet and Spicy Sautéed Bananas

Breaded Sesame Seed Cod

4	**6-ounce cod fillets**
	salt *(to taste)*
	black pepper *(to taste)*
¼	**cup lime juice, freshly squeezed**
¾	**cup bread crumbs**
½	**cup sesame seeds**
½	**cup flour** *(or as needed)*
2	**eggs, lightly beaten**
½	**cup vegetable oil**
	Sweet and Spicy Sautéed Bananas *(recipe on next page)*
1	**lime, quartered**

Sprinkle the cod with the salt and black pepper.

Pour the lime juice over the cod fillets and let them marinate for 15 minutes at room temperature.

Preheat the oven to 350°.

In a small bowl place the bread crumbs and sesame seeds, and mix them together.

Dip the fillets first in the flour, next in the beaten eggs, and then in the bread crumb-sesame seed mixture.

In a large skillet place the vegetable oil and heat it on medium high until it is hot. Add the breaded fish fillets and sauté them for 2 minutes on each side, or until they are a light, golden brown.

Place the breaded, sautéed cod fillets in a pan and bake them for 10 minutes, or until they are just done *(turn them over once)*.

On each of 4 individual serving plates place a cod fillet. Place one Sweet and Spicy Sautéed Banana on top. Pour on some of the sauce from the bananas. Garnish the plate with a lime wedge.

serves 4

"Here is a wonderful fish recipe that everyone will love.....even those people who aren't fish fans. It may sound strange to serve the fish with the sautéed bananas, but trust me..... the combination of flavors and textures is fantastic! For a really nice presentation you can put the sauce from the bananas on the plate, place the fish on the sauce, and then top it with a sautéed banana."

"I am Swiss and received most of my training in Europe. When I eventually moved to Santa Fe, I had absolutely no idea of what chile or northern New Mexican cuisine was. My first job was at La Fonda, and right away my boss asked me to make a great big pot of red chile. I told him I didn't know how, so he asked if I could make a meat sauce. I said, 'Sure', so he told me to make a meat sauce and then throw a bunch of red chile powder in it. So that's what I did, and everyone just loved it! Since then I have grown to love the food of the Southwest. And, I am also pretty good at cooking it."

Ernie Bolleter
Inn at Loretto

Sweet and Spicy Sautéed Bananas

3	**tablespoons sweet butter**
2	**bananas** *(ripe but firm)*, **peeled and sliced in half both ways**
2	**teaspoons chile caribe** *(crushed red chile peppers)*
2	**tablespoons honey**
½	**lime, freshly squeezed**

In a medium skillet place the butter and heat it on medium high until it has melted and is hot. Add the bananas and sauté them for 20 seconds on each side.

Add the chile caribe, honey, and lime juice. Remove the pan from the heat and swirl it around *(without breaking the bananas)* so that the honey, butter, and lime juice bind to form a smooth mixture.

serves 4

"When you cook the bananas you must be careful not to break them when you turn them over. And, don't let them get mushy or they won't look good (but they will still taste good). The sauce is really delicious because some of the bananas will get into it, and then it gets nice and creamy."

Ernie Bolleter
Inn at Loretto

Grilled Alaskan Halibut with Roasted Pepper and Chile Caribe Vinaigrette

Grilled Alaskan Halibut

4   8-ounce halibut steaks
1   tablespoon vegetable oil
      salt and black pepper *(to taste)*
      Roasted Pepper and Chile Caribe Vinaigrette
        (recipe follows)

Lightly brush the halibut steaks with the vegetable oil. Season them with the salt and black pepper. Grill them for 4 to 6 minutes on each side, or until they are just done. Spoon the Roasted Pepper and Chile Caribe Vinaigrette on top.

serves 4

Roasted Pepper and Chile Caribe Vinaigrette

4   red bell peppers, roasted, peeled, and seeded *(see chef's comments on page 159)*
4   shallots, peeled and coarsely chopped
4   cloves garlic, coarsely chopped
½   cup sherry vinegar
1½   cups extra virgin olive oil
¼   cup fresh oregano, chopped
¼   cup chile caribe *(crushed red chile peppers)*
      salt and black pepper *(to taste)*
¼   cup fresh chives, chopped

In a food processor place 2 of the roasted red bell peppers, the shallots, and garlic, and purée them. With the processor running on high speed, slowly dribble in the vinegar and oil.

Add the other 2 roasted red bell peppers, the oregano, chile caribe, salt, and black pepper. Pulse the processor on and off so that the ingredients are coarsely chopped. Add the chives and stir them in.

makes approximately 1 quart

"American cooking and dining are undergoing a transformation. Fine dining, which was once available only to the wealthy, is now accessible to most people. There are a growing number of chefs like myself who are trying to be creative and improve upon the quality and freshness of food that is prepared in restaurants."

"This vinaigrette is not for salads.....rather, it is a sauce that goes well with mild, flaky fish like halibut or grouper. To me, it is not overly spicy, so you could add more chile if you wish."

"There most definitely is a talent to cooking, which I think is a combination of an innate gift, exposure to good food, and learned skills. Also, a certain type of temperament is required to be a chef. You need to be strong willed and to have a good sense of yourself. You must have opinions about food, and you must know what you like and don't like."

David Jones
Casa Sena

Sautéed "Baquetta" Sea Bass with Roma Tomatoes and Fried Leeks

"Baquetta is a type of sea bass that is very similar to golden sea bass. You can use any kind of sea bass that is fresh, or a monkfish. The Baquetta has a slightly different texture and flavor from other kinds. Try to cook the fish to medium rare so that it is medium by the time you eat. People tend to overcook both fish and pork, and this is a big mistake, because it ruins them."

"I diet all of the time. I eat anything that I want, but I limit my caloric intake. Also, I eat 7 times a day, but in small amounts only. You have to trick your body into losing weight because often it will do the opposite of what you want it to do. If you eat only once a day, and the rest of the time you are hungry, then your metabolism slows down and burns calories a lot slower. But if you eat small portions all day long your metabolism speeds up, and your stomach feels full and it shrinks."

Martin Lackner
The Palace Restaurant

1   cup vegetable oil
3   leeks, tops cut off, washed and julienned
3   pounds "Baquetta" sea bass, cut into 6 portions
    salt (to taste)
    black pepper (to taste)
3   tablespoons extra virgin olive oil
3   cloves garlic, chopped
6   ripe Roma tomatoes, halved, seeded, sliced, and julienned
2   tablespoons fresh basil, chopped

In a small saucepan place the 1 cup of vegetable oil and heat it on medium high until it is hot. Add the leeks and fry them for 1 to 2 minutes, or until they are a golden brown. Remove them with a slotted spoon and drain them on paper towels.

Season the sea bass with the salt and black pepper.

In a large sauté pan place the 3 tablespoons of extra virgin olive oil and heat it on high until it is hot. Add the sea bass pieces and quickly sear them on each side. Reduce the heat to medium low and sauté them for 2 minutes on each side, or until they are barely done.

Remove the sea bass from the pan. Add the garlic and cook it for 1 minute. Add the Roma tomatoes and basil, and stir them in.

On each of 6 individual serving plates place the sea bass. Spoon the tomatoes on top. Sprinkle on the fried leeks.

serves 6

Baked in Parchment Sole with Chile Ginger Mayonnaise

Baked in Parchment Sole

8   **fillets of sole** *(all the same size)*
       salt *(to taste)*
       white pepper *(to taste)*
       Chile Ginger Mayonnaise *(recipe on next page)*
1   **small leek** *(white part only)*, **washed, thinly sliced, and
          separated into rings**
1   **small carrot, thinly julienned**

Preheat the oven to 450°.

Season both sides of the fillets of sole with the salt and white pepper.

For each serving lay 1 piece of sole down flat in the center of a lightly buttered piece of parchment paper *(cut the paper 2" longer than the length of the sole, and 3 times as wide)*. Spread the Chile Ginger Mayonnaise over the sole *(leave a ½" margin on all sides)*. Lay another piece of sole on top. Sprinkle on the leek rings and carrots.

Bring the two lengthwise edges of the parchment paper together. Fold them over together into several, tiny ¼" wide folds. Fold the ends over underneath, and then fold them into tiny ¼" wide folds, so that the fish is tightly sealed by the paper *(and the steam will be contained)*.

Place the wrapped fillets on a cookie sheet and bake them for 7½ minutes. Serve the fish in the parchment paper.

serves 4

"You can't stuff sole because it is too thin, so I thought of using two pieces, one on top of the other, with the mayonnaise spread in between. It's a really nice, light dish, and by cooking it in parchment paper the fish steams in its own juices. The trick is to wrap the parchment paper really tight, so that no steam can escape. If the fish isn't done when you take it out of the oven, then finish it off in the microwave. It's nice to serve the fish wrapped up in the paper, so that when it is opened on the plate all of the aromas flood out."

"For the first two-thirds of my life I was a composer. Music and cooking are similar in that they are both creative, and you are putting different ingredients or notes together in a pleasing way. But, music is very abstract and does not usually imitate or relate to your environment, whereas cooking and food are your environment. Cooking has been very good for me because it has forced me to become aware of and enjoy all of my senses, instead of just living in my head."

Tom Wright
Galisteo Inn

Chile Ginger Mayonnaise

1	egg
2	limes, juiced and strained
1	teaspoon salt
1	cup canola oil
½	cup olive oil
1½	tablespoons red chile powder *(or to taste)*
2	teaspoons fresh ginger root, peeled and finely grated

In a food processor place the egg, lime juice, and salt. Process the ingredients for 30 seconds.

With the processor still running, slowly dribble in the canola oil and olive oil.

Add the red chile powder and ginger, and process them.

makes approximately 2 cups

This is just a basic mayonnaise to which I have added fresh ginger and red chile powder. Instead of making your own mayonnaise you can use a good store bought one, although it will have more in it than just the basic mayonnaise ingredients. If you have a food processor, then homemade mayonnaise is a snap to make."

Tom Wright
Galisteo Inn

Drunken Blue Corn Fried Trout with Granny Apple Jack Compote

Drunken Blue Corn Fried Trout

4	egg whites
⅛	teaspoon ground cumin
⅛	teaspoon dried basil, ground
⅛	teaspoon granulated garlic
¼	teaspoon baking soda
1	12-ounce bottle pale ale
3	cups blue cornmeal
¼	cup olive oil
4	10-ounce trout fillets
1	cup Granny Apple Jack Compote *(recipe on next page)*

In a medium bowl place the egg whites, and lightly beat them. Add the cumin, basil, and granulated garlic, and whisk them in.

Add the baking soda and mix it in.

Add the pale ale and mix it in well.

Add the blue cornmeal and mix it in.

In a large skillet place the olive oil and heat it on medium until it is hot. Dip each trout fillet in the batter. Sauté it with the meat side down for 1 to 2 minutes, or until that side is golden brown. Turn the trout over and cook the other side for 1 to 2 minutes more, or until it is just done.

Serve the trout with the Granny Apple Jack Compote spooned on top.

serves 4

"It seems that everyone is using blue cornmeal in Santa Fe, and I wanted to come up with my own idea. I've always loved to batter-fry fish, and trout is one of my favorites, so this recipe seemed to be a natural."

"I like for people to eat my food and enjoy it. A lot of times I will try a new creation out on the other cooks or waitpeople. When they hear what's in it they think I'm out of my gourd. But, usually, if they have the guts to try it, then they really enjoy it. I guess my imagination is a little wild, but through trial and error I have developed a taste for what most people like. Sometimes, though, what I make is a total disaster. When this happens my fellow guinea pigs will scrunch up their faces and say, 'Yuk! What in the world is this stuff!?' I don't view these experiences as failures. Rather, I see them as opportunities for learning what flavors don't work together, and I am a better cook for it."

Jonathan Coady
Piñon Grill

Granny Apple Jack Compote

1	tablespoon walnut oil
2	large Granny Smith apples, peeled, cored, and diced
¼	cup Jack Daniels whisky
½	lemon, juiced
⅛	teaspoon mace
1	tablespoon honey *(locally made, if possible)*
2	sprigs fresh mint, chopped

In a medium sauté pan place the walnut oil and heat it on medium until it is barely hot. Add the apples and sauté them for 6 to 8 minutes, or until they are halfway tender.

Add the Jack Daniels and flambé it *(see chef's comments on page 35 for instructions)*.

Add the lemon juice and mace, and stir them in. Add the honey and stir it in. Simmer the ingredients for 5 minutes, or until the apples are cooked al dente. Add the mint and toss it in for 30 seconds.

makes approximately 2 cups

"You can serve this as soon as you make it, or you can let it sit overnight, in which case the flavors will be stronger and richer. It has a neat, sweet taste, and it's wonderful with all kinds of fish, chicken, or wild game."

" I was never exposed to cooking until I was a teenager and got my first job as a dishwasher in a restaurant. I remember being very impressed by the amount of work involved in preparing the food. And, I loved the fast pace and excitement in the kitchen."

Jonathan Coady
Piñon Grill

Trout Propellers with Yellow Bell Pepper Mole and Chipotle Tomato Butter

Trout Propellers

1	**cup cornmeal**
1	**tablespoon red chile powder**
½	**teaspoon salt**
¼	**teaspoon black pepper**
4	**trout, head and bones removed, and split down the middle lengthwise** *(to make 8 fillets)*
¼	**cup peanut oil**
1	**cup Yellow Bell Pepper Mole** *(recipe on next page)*
4	**tablespoons Chipotle Tomato Butter** *(recipe on next page)*

In a medium bowl place the cornmeal, red chile powder, salt, and black pepper. Dredge the trout fillets in the mixture.

In a large skillet place the peanut oil and heat it on high until it is hot. Add the trout fillets and sauté them for 2 minutes on one side. Reduce the heat to medium. Turn fillets over and sauté them for 3 to 4 minutes more, or until they are just done.

On each of 4 individual serving plates place the Yellow Bell Pepper Mole. Spread the sauce over the plate so that it is completely covered.

Place one trout fillet across the center of the plate. Place the other fillet on top, so that a cross is formed. Put a dollop of the Chipotle Tomato Butter on top.

serves 4

"When you have one trout fillet placed perpendicular on top of the other one, they look like airplane propellers. We place a small mound of cooked grain right between two of the 'propellers', so that it looks like a little cockpit. I love to take ordinary items like this, and present them in a way that is visually different. Once in Paris I saw a work by Picasso which I found to be very inspirational. He had taken an old bicycle seat and a set of handlebars, and he had placed them in such a way that they looked like the skeleton of a cow's head. I loved the way he took two simple, dull items and transformed them into something marvelous."

Lawrence McGrael
Geronimo Lodge

"Our customers never know what to expect, because our food is on the cutting edge. Lawrence, the chef, is just wonderful. I like to think of his creations as inspired by LSD flashbacks. Many times I see the waitpeople coming out of the kitchen with raised eyebrows, looking very dubious because of some new wild thing he's doing."

Cliff Skoglund
Geronimo Lodge

Yellow Bell Pepper Mole

3   yellow bell peppers, seeded and coarsely chopped
1   medium onion, coarsely chopped
1   teaspoon fresh garlic, chopped
2   jalapeño chile peppers, cut in half
2   cinnamon sticks
¼   cup almond slivers
3   corn tortillas, cut into pieces
¼   teaspoon salt
¼   teaspoon black pepper
1   cup water *(or as needed)*

In a medium saucepan place all of the ingredients *(use just enough water to cover them)*. Simmer them on low heat for 45 minutes, or until the yellow bell peppers are very tender.

Remove the pan from the heat, strain out the liquid, and reserve it. Remove the jalapeño chile peppers and cinnamon sticks, and discard them.

Place the remaining ingredients in a food processor and purée them. Add enough of the reserved liquid so that a slow-running sauce is achieved.

serves 4

"I like this recipe because it's fun and easy to make, and it has a beautiful, vibrant color. You must pay attention to the amount of liquid that you add, because this controls the consistency. When I cook, I always am careful to watch what happens to the food. Even with the best written recipes there are many uncontrollable variables, such as the water content of the vegetables, how hot your stove is, and the size of your pan. Pay attention and use common sense!"

Chipotle Tomato Butter

2   chipotle chile peppers
1   tablespoon tomato paste
1   pound sweet butter
   salt *(to taste)*
   black pepper *(to taste)*

In a food processor place the chipotle chile peppers and tomato paste, and blend them together.

With the food processor constantly running, add the sweet butter in small amounts. Blend the ingredients until the butter is smooth, and the chile peppers and tomato paste are well incorporated. Season the butter with the salt and black pepper, and blend them in.

makes 1 pound

"This is a fairly straightforward compound butter recipe. The chipotle peppers are hot, and they will give you a pretty good hit. When you make this in a food processor it may be difficult to get everything well blended, so stop every so often and stir the butter with a spoon. If there are little bits that never get blended, you can remove them. This butter is wonderful with all kinds of fish and meat. And, you can freeze it."

Lawrence McGrael
Geronimo Lodge

LP CALDWELL

Fowl

Marinated Spicy Chicken Breasts

2	serrano chile peppers, minced
2	cloves garlic, minced
⅓	cup lime juice, freshly squeezed
½	teaspoon ground cumin
½	teaspoon red chile powder *(mild)*
¼	teaspoon cayenne pepper
¼	teaspoon salt
4	chicken breasts, skin and bones removed, and lightly pounded
½	teaspoon paprika
1	lime, quartered
4	fresh cilantro sprigs

In a medium bowl place the serrano chile peppers, garlic, lime juice, cumin, red chile powder, cayenne pepper, and salt. Mix the ingredients together.

Add the chicken breasts and chill them in the refrigerator overnight.

Grill the chicken for 3 to 5 minutes on each side, or until it is done.

Sprinkle on the paprika. Garnish each chicken breast with a piece of lime and a sprig of cilantro.

serves 4

"Here is a mildly spicy chicken dish with a real Southwestern flair. The recipe was developed by Shelley Smith, who has one of the most finely developed palates I have ever known. You also can use the marinade with beef or pork. When you grill the chicken let it get grate marks on it. Then grill it at a 90° angle on the same side, so that you get crisscross marks on it. Do this on both sides of the chicken."
Michael Nelsen
Zia Diner

"When I was growing up in the Bay Area of California my parents were very interested in the new California cuisine. We went to a lot of excellent restaurants, and so I developed an appreciation for fine food at a young age. Also, at the age of 17 I was fortunate enough to be an exchange student in Japan. My host mother was a fantastic cook, and she taught me how to look at food and think the flavors through in my head. From her I learned the artfulness of putting food together in simple ways that are both beautiful and savory."
Sarah Alvord
Zia Diner

Mediterranean Grilled Chicken Breast with Sun-Dried Tomato Pesto

"A lot of people complain that chicken is too bland. Here is a wonderful way to both tenderize and infuse a great flavor into your chicken. If possible, try to use free-range chicken that is hormone free. But, just a word to the wise.....never assume that just because chicken or meat is sold in a health food store that it is hormone free. I have heard stories of how regular chickens are sold right next to organic ones, and unless you read the label carefully you never would know the difference. The rule is, always ask before you buy."

Sarah Alvord
Zia Diner

"When I was a little boy I used to try to cook, and I was just terrible at it. My first attempt at baking was to make a 3-layer cake which came out ¾ inches high!"

"One of my favorite things to do is to eat late at night until I get very full, and then to fall asleep. I know this sounds very bad, and I don't do it all of the time, but I really do enjoy it. Often I don't get home from work until 10 or 11 o'clock at night. I have been watching people all day long enjoying their food, and I think about and plan what I am going to eat when I get home."

Michael Nelsen
Zia Diner

Mediterranean Grilled Chicken Breast

1	cup lemon juice, freshly squeezed
½	cup olive oil
4	cloves garlic, finely minced
¼	cup fresh basil leaves, minced
½	teaspoon salt
6	whole chicken breasts, skin and bones removed
1	cup Sun-Dried Tomato Pesto *(recipe follows)*

In a large bowl place the lemon juice, olive oil, garlic, basil, and salt. Mix the ingredients together well. Add the chicken breasts and let them marinate for 1 hour at room temperature.

Grill the chicken breasts for 3 to 5 minutes on each side, or until they are just cooked through.

Serve each chicken breast with a dollop of the Sun-Dried Tomato Pesto.

serves 6

Sun-Dried Tomato Pesto

4	ounces sun-dried tomatoes *(dried, not packed in olive oil)*, **reconstituted** *(simmer in water until tender)*, **and drained**
¼	cup pine nuts
¼	cup Parmesan cheese, freshly grated
2	tablespoons fresh basil, chopped
2	cloves garlic, chopped
¼	cup olive oil
¼	teaspoon salt

In a food processor place the sun-dried tomatoes and roughly purée them. Add the remainder of the ingredients and purée them so that a smooth paste is formed.

makes 1 cup

Chicken Fajitas

2   pounds chicken breasts, skin removed
1   teaspoon fresh ginger root, peeled and grated
1   teaspoon fresh garlic, minced
1   cup soy sauce
¼   cup orange juice, freshly squeezed
¼   cup lime juice, freshly squeezed
2   tablespoons honey
1   tablespoon vegetable oil
1½   red bell peppers, seeded and julienned
1½   green bell peppers, seeded and julienned
½   large red onion, thinly sliced
½   large yellow onion, thinly sliced
12   flour tortillas, warmed
6   dollops sour cream
1   cup Monterey Jack cheese, grated
        Guacamole *(recipe on page 171, or see chef's comments on this page)*
        Pico de Gallo *(recipe on page 171)*

In a medium large bowl place the chicken, ginger, garlic, soy sauce, orange juice, lime juice, and honey. Let the chicken marinate for 3 to 6 hours.

Grill the chicken. Remove it from the bones and cut it into thin strips.

In a large, cast iron skillet place the oil and heat it on high until it is very hot. Add the red and green bell peppers and the red and yellow onions, and sauté them for 2 minutes.

Add the chicken and sauté it for 1 minute, or until it is hot.

Serve the chicken with the flour tortillas, sour cream, cheese, Guacamole, and Pico de Gallo on the side.

serves 6

"People tell us that our fajitas are the best they have ever tasted. The marinade is especially tangy and good. We serve the chicken in a sizzling hot, cast iron skillet, so the presentation really gets your attention. People seem to get a big kick out of it."

Patricia Helmick
Peppers Restaurant

"We make an excellent guacamole to go with our New Mexican dishes. It consists of avocados, fresh green chile, tomatoes, onions, finely minced garlic, lemon juice, and salt. Guacamole is so delicious that no matter how you prepare it, it's always good."

Dan Kelley
Peppers Restaurant

"My wife Patricia and I love to dine out. We go out primarily to have a good time, but we always keep our ears and eyes open so that we know what our competition is up to. We want our restaurant to be the very best. If another restaurant serves the same item that we do, we want to make sure that ours is equally as good, if not better."

Rick Helmick
Peppers Restaurant

Greek Chicken Breast Sauté

4	whole chicken breasts, skin and bones removed
1	cup flour, seasoned with salt and black pepper
¼	cup olive oil
1½	cups dry white wine
1	cup fresh tomatoes, peeled, seeded, and chopped
½	cup capers
½	cup black olives, pitted and sliced
½	cup green olives, pitted and sliced
1	tablespoon fresh rosemary

Dredge the chicken in the seasoned flour (shake off any excess).

In a large skillet place the olive oil and heat it on medium high until it is hot. Carefully place the floured chicken in the skillet. Sauté it for 2 to 3 minutes on each side, or until it is golden brown but not done.

Add the white wine and simmer it for 5 minutes.

Add the tomatoes, capers, black olives, green olives, and rosemary. Simmer the ingredients for 3 to 4 minutes more, or until the sauce is slightly thickened and the chicken is just done (be very careful not to overcook the chicken or it will be tough).

On each of 4 individual heated plates place the chicken. Spoon the sauce on top.

serves 4

"When I was 10 years old I became ill and was out of school for 8 weeks. I felt okay and wasn't bed-ridden, but I was pretty bored. One day I got the bright idea to make banana bread, because I had always loved bananas. I followed the recipe right out of 'Joy of Cooking', and it came out really good. So every day I made 2 or 3 loaves, and my big entertainment was to sit in front of the oven (it had a glass window in the door) and watch the bread for 45 minutes while it rose up and got brown. I would stare at it in fascination until the timer went off. It was kind of like watching grass grow, but I loved it, and it gave me something to do. After a while our freezer was full of banana bread loaves, all wrapped in foil. So my mom started taking them to her bridge club, and pretty soon I was being commissioned by her friends to bake them banana bread. It was a great deal! They paid me 25 cents a loaf, and the ingredients were free because my mom bought them."

Walt McDowell
423

Radicchio Tacos with Grilled Chicken and Fresh Basil Aioli

Radicchio Tacos with Grilled Chicken

4   **7-ounce chicken breasts, skin and bones removed**
4   **shallots, finely chopped**
2   **tablespoons fresh thyme, chopped**
3   **juniper berries, crushed in a mortar**
1   **lemon, juiced**
2   **large heads radicchio, washed, dried, and leaves separated**
       Fresh Basil Aioli *(recipe follows)*

In a medium bowl place the chicken, shallots, thyme, juniper berries, and lemon juice. Marinate the chicken for 2 to 4 hours in the refrigerator.

Grill the chicken for 3 to 5 minutes on each side, or until it is just done. Cut the chicken into thin strips *(across the grain)*.

On each of 4 individual serving plates place 4 radicchio leaves. Place the chicken on top of each leaf. Spoon on the Fresh Basil Aioli.

serves 4

Fresh Basil Aioli

3   **cloves garlic**
1   **egg yolk**
20   **fresh basil leaves, stacked and cut into thin strips**
½   **lemon, juiced**
½   **cup olive oil**
½   **cup vegetable oil**
       salt and black pepper *(to taste)*

In a food processor place the garlic, egg yolk, basil, and lemon juice. Blend the ingredients together.

With the food processor constantly running, slowly dribble in the two oils so that a mayonnaise consistency is achieved. Season the aioli with the salt and black pepper.

makes 1¼ cups

"When you buy the radicchio try to get large heads that have tight leaves, like a head of cabbage. Cut the root end off, and then peel off the outer leaves. They will be too thin for this recipe, but you can use them in a salad. You need to use the leaves that are firm and cup shaped, so that they will stand up on a plate and hold the chicken mixture."

"I like to cook because I like to eat. Unfortunately, I am approaching 30, and I can feel myself spreading out. It happens when you reach 30.....you just get wide. I eat less now than I have ever eaten in my life, and I am still getting wide!"

"A lot of people are afraid to make mayonnaise (aioli), but it really is quite easy to do as long as you follow the directions. Be sure to add the oil drop by drop, or else the mayonnaise will separate, and then you will have to start all over. I love this aioli. It tastes good with almost everything you can think of.....kind of like butter does."

Jonathan Horst
Adobo Catering

Sautéed Breast of Chicken in a Sweet and Sour Red Wine Sauce

"This dish is based on an ancient Roman recipe. People love it and it is one of our most popular chicken dishes. When you are cooking the chicken in the sauce you are going to have to use your head. You may have to add more sauce, or you may have to remove the chicken so that it doesn't overcook and then continue to cook the sauce without it. To make a dark chicken stock takes some time in the home kitchen, and most people won't want to go to the trouble. You can use regular chicken stock that is reduced. However, if you want the real thing, then roast some chicken carcasses in the oven so that they are dark. Caramelize some tomato paste in a large pot with some oil, and then add the roasted bones, herbs, water, and red wine. Cook the ingredients for 2 hours or more, and strain the liquid."

"When you are caramelizing the sugar you will stand there and stir it, and nothing will happen for a long time. All of a sudden it will melt, turn brown, and burn. It happens fast, so be careful! If this is too stressful for you, then just use brown sugar. The sugar will harden when the liquids are added, but then it remelts."

Wayne Gustafson
Julian's

Sautéed Breast of Chicken

2   tablespoons olive oil
4   whole chicken breasts, skin and bones removed, and split in half
⅓   cup dark and white raisins *(mixed)*, soaked in warm water to soften them
1   tablespoon capers
2   shallots, minced
   salt and black pepper *(to taste)*
   Sweet and Sour Red Wine Sauce *(recipe follows)*

In a large sauté pan place the olive oil and heat it on high until it is hot. Add the chicken breasts and sauté them for 1 to 2 minutes on both sides, or until they are brown.

Add the raisins, capers, shallots, salt, black pepper, and the Sweet and Sour Red Wine Sauce. Reduce the heat to medium and cook the chicken on a high simmer for 3 to 4 minutes, or until it is just done and the sauce has a nice sheen.

serves 4

Sweet and Sour Red Wine Sauce

½   cup powdered sugar
¼   cup red wine vinegar
1   cup red wine
1   cup dark chicken stock *(see chef's comments on this page)*
   salt and black pepper *(to taste)*

In a medium saucepan place the powdered sugar and cook it on high heat for 3 to 5 minutes, or until it is melted and slightly darkened *(stir it constantly and do not let it burn)*.

Add the red wine vinegar, red wine, and chicken stock. Boil the sauce for 6 to 10 minutes, or until it is reduced and slightly thickened. Season the sauce with the salt and black pepper.

makes approximately 2½ cups

Chicken Makhani

¼ cup plain yogurt
½ teaspoon fresh garlic, minced
½ teaspoon fresh ginger root, peeled and minced
2 teaspoons lemon juice, freshly squeezed
¼ cup vegetable oil
½ teaspoon garam masala *(see chef's comments on page 230)*
½ teaspoon ground cumin
½ teaspoon ground coriander
1 teaspoon salt
4 whole chicken breasts, skin and bones removed, and cut into 1" squares
1 cup fresh tomatoes, blended
¼ teaspoon fresh garlic, minced
¼ teaspoon fresh ginger root, peeled and minced
1 tablespoon butter
1 teaspoon salt *(or to taste)*
½ cup cream
½ teaspoon fenugreek powder
2 tablespoons fresh cilantro, chopped

In a medium bowl place the yogurt, the ½ teaspoon of garlic, the ½ teaspoon of ginger, lemon juice, vegetable oil, garam masala, cumin, coriander, and the first 1 teaspoon of salt. Stir the ingredients together. Add the chicken and marinate it for 24 hours in the refrigerator.

Place the marinated chicken pieces on long skewers. Grill them for 4 to 5 minutes *(turn the skewers)*, or until the chicken is just done.

In a medium large saucepan place the blended tomatoes, the ¼ teaspoon of garlic, the ¼ teaspoon of ginger, butter, and the second 1 teaspoon of salt. Bring the ingredients to a boil and then simmer them for ½ hour.

Remove the chicken from the skewers. Add it to the saucepan, and cook it for 3 minutes, or until it is heated.

Add the cream and bring the sauce to a boil.

Add the fenugreek powder and stir it in.

Serve the chicken with the chopped cilantro sprinkled on top.

serves 4

"In India every mother has a different recipe for the same dish. If you put 4 mothers together and had them cook this Chicken Makhani, each dish would come out differently."

"Our chef, Baldev Singh, has very high standards in the kitchen. He will not serve anything that he would not eat himself, and he must be completely satisfied with the integrity of the dish before it goes out of the kitchen. One day we had a customer who wanted all of her food put in a blender and puréed together.....including the bread and rice. Baldev got a little bit upset and considered the request to be an insult, because he had put so much devotion into making each dish unique and perfect. He offered to blend the different items separately and serve them that way, but she insisted that everything be ground together. My job is to do whatever is necessary to satisfy the customer, so I went into the kitchen and blended the food for her. She loved it, and ate every single bite!"

Nitin Bhakta
India Palace

Cau-Cau Spearmint Chicken Stew

¼   **cup salad oil**
1   **medium red onion, chopped medium**
2   **cloves garlic, finely chopped**
1   **teaspoon ground cumin**
1   **teaspoon ground turmeric**
¼   **teaspoon salt**
¼   **teaspoon black pepper, freshly ground**
2   **pounds chicken breasts, skin and bones removed, and cut into 1" squares**
2   **cups chicken stock** *(recipe on page 295)*
6   **medium red potatoes, washed and cut in ½" cubes**
½   **cup fresh spearmint, chopped**
2   **cups cooked white rice, heated**

In a large saucepot place the salad oil and heat it on medium high until it is hot. Add the onions, garlic, cumin, turmeric, salt, and black pepper. Sauté the ingredients for 5 minutes, or until the onions are tender.

Add the chicken pieces and sauté them for 5 minutes.

Add the chicken stock, red potatoes, and spearmint. Reduce the heat to low and simmer the ingredients for 20 to 25 minutes, or until the potatoes are tender.

Serve the stew over the cooked white rice.

serves 4

Hot Shredded Chicken

3	jalapeño chile peppers, coarsely chopped
1½	cups evaporated milk
4	slices fresh white bread, coarsely torn
½	cup walnuts
3	tablespoons salad oil
1	small red onion, finely diced
1	teaspoon fresh garlic, minced
1	teaspoon fresh oregano, chopped
¼	teaspoon salt *(or to taste)*
¼	teaspoon black pepper, freshly ground
1	whole chicken, cooked, skin and bones removed, and shredded
½	cup Parmesan cheese, freshly grated

In a blender place the jalapeño chile peppers, evaporated milk, bread, and walnuts. Purée the ingredients until they are smooth. Set the mixture aside.

In a large saucepan place the oil and heat it on medium high until it is hot. Add the red onions, garlic, oregano, salt, and black pepper. Sauté the ingredients for 4 to 6 minutes, or until the onions are tender.

Lower the heat to medium. Add the puréed mixture to the onions and stir it in well. Cook the mixture *(stir it occasionally)* for 5 to 7 minutes, or until it is thick and creamy.

Add the shredded chicken and stir it in.

Add the Parmesan cheese and stir it in.

Note: This dish may be served hot or cold.

serves 4

"This is something that many families make in Peru. It is fairly spicy, so you may want to cut back on the jalapeño peppers. In the restaurant we import the peppers from Peru, so the dish is very authentic. They taste different from New Mexican chile peppers, and their heat is more subtle. Here, you eat a bowl of local green chile, and BAM, the heat hits you immediately. With the Peruvian chiles, the heat kind of creeps up on you and you start to burn later on. You might say they are not quite as straightforward in their hotness!"

Brad Lyon
Alfredo's Restaurant

"In Peru the people go to the big market every day to buy their food. This includes the restaurant chefs as well, because there is no food delivery service. You may think this sounds like a lot of work, but think how fresh everything is when we cook it!"

Alfredo Miranda
Alfredo's Restaurant

Seven Aroma Roasted Chicken with Spicy Peppers

"These spices would be good on a turkey, roast beef, pork loin, or roasted potatoes. In the summer you should be able to get most of the fresh herbs. It is okay to use dried herbs and often you can buy a good commercial herb mixture in the grocery store. If you do substitute dried herbs, then use only 1 teaspoon of each."

"People come to our restaurant for this dish only. The peppers make it spicy, and we try to use free-range chicken."

"I don't like to cook on my days off. I am around food for 60 to 70 hours a week, and when I am home I don't want to have to deal with it, much less the clean up. Also, I am spoiled, because in the restaurant I have all of the ingredients at hand, and at home there is hardly anything in my cupboards. In the restaurant I can cook a meal for five people in 10 minutes, but at home I would have to go shopping for everything and it would take me 2 hours."

Martin Lackner
The Palace Restaurant

1	tablespoon fresh garlic, finely chopped
1	tablespoon fresh rosemary, chopped
1	tablespoon fresh thyme, chopped
1	tablespoon fresh parsley, chopped
1	tablespoon fresh oregano, chopped
1	tablespoon fresh sage, chopped
1	teaspoon ground coriander
2	teaspoons salt *(or to taste)*
1	teaspoon black pepper *(or to taste)*
3	whole chickens, washed and dried
½	cup white wine
1	red bell pepper, seeded and julienned
1	green bell pepper, seeded and julienned
1	yellow bell pepper, seeded and julienned
2	Anaheim chile peppers, seeded and julienned
2	poblano chile peppers, seeded and julienned
	salt *(to taste)*
	black pepper *(to taste)*

Preheat the oven to 375°.

In a small bowl place the garlic, rosemary, thyme, parsley, oregano, sage, coriander, and the 2 teaspoons of salt. Mix the ingredients together.

Rub the herb mixture into the chickens, inside and out.

Place the chickens in a roasting pan and bake them for 50 minutes, or until they are done. Remove the chickens from the pan, cut them in half, and set them aside.

Pour the excess fat out of the roasting pan.

Place the roasting pan on the stove and heat it on high until it is hot. Add the white wine and deglaze the pan.

Add all of the peppers and sauté them for 1 to 2 minutes, or until they are cooked al dente. Add the salt and black pepper, and stir them in.

On each of 6 individual serving plates place a roasted chicken half. Spoon on the peppers and any sauce that is in the roasting pan.

serves 6

Piñon Breaded Chicken with Ancho Chile-Lingonberry Sauce

Piñon Breaded Chicken

¾   cup piñon nuts *(pine nuts)*, coarsely chopped
⅓   cup bread crumbs
3   cloves garlic, minced
3   tablespoons fresh parsley, finely chopped
3   tablespoons fresh herbs, finely chopped
½   teaspoon salt
¼   teaspoon white pepper
2   whole chicken breasts *(free-range)*, halved
½   cup flour *(or as needed)*
2   eggs, beaten
¼   cup olive oil
     Ancho Chile-Lingonberry Sauce *(recipe on next page)*

In a small bowl place the piñon nuts, bread crumbs, garlic, parsley, fresh herbs, salt, and white pepper. Mix the ingredients together.

In this order, dip the chicken breasts first into the flour, then the beaten eggs, and then the bread crumb mixture.

In a large skillet place the olive oil and heat it on medium high, or until it is hot. Add the breaded chicken breasts and sauté them for 4 to 5 minutes on each side, or until they are golden brown and just done.

On each of 4 individual serving plates place the Ancho Chile-Lingonberry Sauce. Place a chicken breast on top.

serves 4

"This is one of our signature dishes and it is very popular with our customers. People like the idea of getting some of the flavors of the Southwest without the item being in the enchilada and burrito crowd. It's not overly spicy, and because the chicken is hormone free, it is quite plump and juicy."

"I get my ideas for recipes from a number of areas. I read extensively the writings by other chefs, I dine out frequently, I travel as much as I can and taste the food along the way, and I am constantly seeking out new and exotic ingredients."

"Criticism is an important part of the creative process. You need to accept self criticism as well as criticism from your peers. A chef needs to hear other opinions and take some of them to heart, while rejecting others. Ultimately, however, a chef needs to have his own opinions and make his own decisions."

David Jones
Casa Sena

Ancho Chile-Lingonberry Sauce

2	tablespoons olive oil
2	shallots, minced
2	cloves garlic, minced
½	cup Madeira wine
2	cups chicken stock *(recipe on page 295)*
2	ancho chile peppers, softened in boiling water for 2 minutes, and drained
1	4-ounce jar lingonberries in syrup
¼	cup fresh thyme, chopped
	salt *(to taste)*
	black pepper *(to taste)*

In a medium saucepan place the olive oil and heat it on medium high until it is hot. Add the shallots and garlic, and sauté them for 2 minutes, or until the garlic is brown.

Add the Madeira, chicken stock, and ancho chile peppers. Cook the ingredients over high heat for 5 minutes, or until the liquid is reduced by ½ and the chile peppers are soft.

Remove the peppers from the liquid. Remove the seeds and stems, and discard them. Purée the peppers in a food processor. Add the purée back to the liquid.

Add the lingonberries and thyme. Cook the sauce for 5 minutes more, or until it is the consistency of heavy cream. Add the salt and black pepper.

makes approximately 1½ cups

"Lingonberries are wild berries that are found in northern Europe. You can buy them in jars, and they usually come packed in a syrup. I like them because they have a fairly tart flavor, but at the same time the syrup gives them a sweetness. The fruit works very well with the spiciness of the chiles, and tones their heat down somewhat. If you can't find lingonberries, you can use cranberries."

"I have done extensive traveling throughout the world, and so I have tasted the flavors of many traditional cuisines in their native environments. I like to experiment with these different ethnic cuisines, and mix and match them together with our own local New Mexican ingredients."

"To be a good chef you have to constantly grow, expand your knowledge, and challenge yourself."

David Jones
Casa Sena

Rotisserie Chicken

½   tablespoon garlic salt
½   tablespoon garlic powder
1   teaspoon chile pequin *(hot red chile flakes)*
½   tablespoon whole black peppercorns
2   bay leaves, broken in half
1   chicken, well washed and dried
1   lemon, cut ⅓ of the way through at the end, in a crisscross pattern

In a small bowl place the garlic salt, garlic powder, chile pequin, black peppercorns, and bay leaves. Mix the ingredients together.

Rub the spice mixture all over the inside of the chicken. Place the lemon inside.

Place the chicken on the rotisserie skewer so that the bar goes through the lemon. Tie the chicken up tightly at both ends so that the ingredients will stay inside. Grill the chicken on the rotisserie over medium heat for 1 to 1½ hours, or until it is done.

serves 2

Lemon Chicken

1   tablespoon fresh cilantro, chopped
1   tablespoon fresh garlic, chopped
1   teaspoon fresh oregano, chopped
2   bay leaves
1   lemon, zested *(outer yellow part grated off)*
3   tablespoons lemon juice, freshly squeezed
1   cup olive oil
4   6-ounce chicken breasts, skin and bones removed

In a medium large bowl place all of the ingredients *(except for the chicken breasts)* and mix them together. Add the chicken breasts and marinate them in the refrigerator *(covered)* overnight.

Grill the chicken for 4 to 5 minutes on each side, or until it is just done.

serves 4

Fowl

> "When you bake this chicken with the lemon and spices inside, they move around and really baste it. The meat is kept moist and all of the flavors seep in."

> "The Mexican women who work here are extremely talented. They are close to the earth, very family oriented, and their cooking stems back countless generations. There is a consistency to their recipes, and when you eat their food you know that this is how it was prepared 300 years ago, from daughter to mother to grandmother to great-grandmother. I find this continuity very appealing."
>
> Marc Greene
> Old Mexico Grill

> "This is a simple version of lemon chicken that really tastes good grilled. Chicken must be cooked to a certain degree before it is edible. There is nothing worse than biting into chicken that has a cold, clammy, undercooked center.....it's very unpleasant and can ruin your whole meal! On the other hand, you don't want to cook it so much that it is dried out."
>
> Mark Hawrylak
> The Evergreen

Raspberry-Plum Glazed Grilled Chicken

"This dish came into being one late summer day when we had lots of raspberries, and my neighbor had just given us a huge bag of delicious purple plums. When you are taking the pits out of the plums, check to see if any of them look strange. If one does, then don't use that plum. Don't brush the glaze on the side of the chicken that you are grilling, because it will caramelize and tend to burn."

"I am writing my own cookbook called 'The Natural Cafe Cookbook'. It's being published by The Crossing Press and will be out soon."

"At one point in my life when I was a child my father was very over-weight. My mother was worried about him and finally convinced him to see a doctor. When he was told that he had high blood pressure he became extremely health conscious and completely changed his lifestyle. He exercised every day, made his own yogurt, and lost 80 pounds in 6 months."

Lynn Walters
The Natural Cafe

2	cups ripe plums *(red or purple)*, **pitted**
1	cup red wine
1	cup fresh raspberries
⅛	teaspoon salt
¼	teaspoon black pepper
2	small chickens, halved and skin removed
1	tablespoon vegetable oil
1	lemon, halved

In a medium saucepan place the plums and red wine. Simmer the plums on low heat for 15 to 20 minutes, or until they are soft and the skins are loose. Remove the skins and discard them.

Add ½ of the raspberries, the salt, and black pepper, and stir them in. Keep the glaze warm.

Rub both sides of each chicken half with the vegetable oil. Grill the chicken for 5 to 8 minutes on one side. Turn the chicken over and squeeze on the juice from one of the lemon halves. Brush on some of the glaze. Grill the chicken for 5 to 8 minutes more, or until it just done.

On each of 4 individual serving plates place one chicken half, glazed side down. Squeeze on the juice from the other lemon half. Pour the remaining glaze on top. Sprinkle on the remaining raspberries.

serves 4

Chicken Breasts with Zucchini Stuffing and Lemon Basil Butter

Chicken Breasts with Zucchini Stuffing

½   large zucchini, washed and coarsely chopped
2   cloves garlic, finely chopped
1   teaspoon fresh basil, chopped
¼   cup Parmesan cheese, freshly grated
¼   cup walnuts, toasted and chopped
¼   cup bread crumbs
1   egg
½   teaspoon salt
¼   teaspoon black pepper
4   whole chicken breasts, bones removed
4   teaspoons olive oil
     salt *(to taste)*
     black pepper *(to taste)*
     Lemon Basil Butter *(recipe on next page)*

Preheat the oven to 350°.

In a food processor place the zucchini, garlic, basil, Parmesan cheese, toasted walnuts, bread crumbs, egg, the ½ teaspoon of salt, and the ¼ teaspoon of black pepper. Purée the ingredients so that a smooth paste is formed.

Lay the chicken breasts on a flat surface with the skin side down. In the center of each breast place the zucchini stuffing. Roll the breasts up. Secure them with a toothpick.

In a small roasting pan place the rolled, stuffed chicken breasts with the skin side up and the seam down. Brush on the olive oil, and sprinkle on the salt and black pepper. Bake the chicken for 20 minutes, or until the skin is golden brown.

On each of 4 individual serving plates place one of the rolled chicken breasts. Spoon the Lemon Basil Butter on top.

serves 4

"This recipe was created one day when we had a whole lot of zucchinis to use up. It's simple to make, healthy, and has a wonderful flavor. If you want, you can quickly sear the chicken in some hot olive oil before you bake it."

"If you don't mind the extra calories, you can add 2 ounces of cream to the dressing. This makes it creamier and smoother. However, the cream, as well as the egg, will make the dressing expand when you bake it. I use only about 2 tablespoons of stuffing for each breast. People look at it and say 'Jeez! That's not nearly enough!' But it really puffs up in the oven."

"The toasted walnuts give this a really neat flavor. I know they are fattening, so you can eliminate them, depending on how hard core you want to be about your calorie intake. The walnuts and zucchini contrast with the lemons and wine in the sauce, so all the taste buds of your tongue are hit."

Paul Constantine
Chez What

Lemon Basil Butter

1	**lemon, zested** *(outer yellow part grated off)* **and juiced**
¼	**cup white wine**
1	**teaspoon shallots, finely chopped**
2	**tablespoons heavy cream**
4	**tablespoons sweet butter, softened**
¼	**cup fresh basil, chopped**
	salt *(to taste)*
	black pepper *(to taste)*

In a small saucepan place the lemon zest and juice, white wine, and shallots. Heat the ingredients on medium high for 3 to 4 minutes, or until the liquid is reduced by ⅔. Add the heavy cream and boil it for 2 minutes.

Remove the pan from the heat. Quickly add the butter and whisk it in. Add the basil, salt, and black pepper.

makes ½ *cup*

"This is a basic sauce that has infinite uses. It goes well with fish, chicken, and vegetables. It's even good with beef."

"In cooking you want to hit all areas of the tongue.....the salty, sweet, bitter, and sour. In this recipe we were trying to appeal to all of your taste buds, and I think we definitely succeeded!"

Paul Constantine
Chez What

Lime-Curry Chicken Breast

½   **tablespoon black pepper**
1½   **tablespoons curry powder, toasted** *(see chef's comments on this page)*
¼   **cup olive oil**
¼   **cup honey**
2   **limes, juiced**
2   **large whole chicken breasts, split**

In a medium bowl place all of the ingredients *(except for the chicken breasts)* and mix them together. Add the chicken breasts and dredge them in the marinade. Let them sit in the refrigerator for 12 hours.

Grill the chicken for 5 to 7 minutes on each side, or until it is done.

serves 4

"To toast the curry powder you just heat and stir it in a dry pan for several minutes, until the flavors are released."

"The chicken will taste like all of the flavors in the marinade.....sweet, citrus, curry, and olive oil. This dish is one of our most popular."

Laszlo Gyermek
Santacafe

"New Mexico goat cheese is my very most favorite kind in the whole world. It's so creamy, and not at all salty, and I use it in many of our dishes. Be careful not to put too much of the filling in the chicken breasts.....the goat cheese will ooze out and burn, the skin won't get crispy, and it will be a disaster!"

"I think that many women chefs have been given a bad rap because men feel that women are overly emotional. There is a saying that when you hire a staff you hire people that reflect aspects of your-self.....and one thing I can say about my staff is that we are all highly emotional! However, this aspect of our personalities in no way hinders our ability to function efficiently and creatively in the kitchen. We all have a lot of respect for each other, and there is no problem with my being a young woman who oversees men who are older than myself. We all exchange ideas for new menus and there is a real communal effort in making our restaurant as excellent as it is.....from the top position right on down to the dishwasher."

Karen Woods
Rancho Encantado

Baked Chicken Breast with Herbed New Mexico Goat Cheese

1½	cups Coon Ridge Blanc goat cheese *(or French goat cheese)*
1	tablespoon fresh garlic, chopped
1	teaspoon fresh rosemary, chopped
1	tablespoon fresh basil, chopped
1	tablespoon fresh marjoram, chopped
1	tablespoon fresh thyme, chopped
⅛	teaspoon black pepper
6	10-ounce double chicken breasts, bones removed

Preheat the oven to 350°.

In a small bowl place all of the ingredients *(except for the chicken)* and mix them together well. Stuff 2 tablespoons of the herbed cheese under the skin.

Grill the chicken for 3 to 5 minutes *(start with the skin side down)* on each side, or until grill marks appear.

Place the chicken breasts in a pan and bake them for 8 to 10 minutes, or until they are just done.

serves 6

Chicken Curry

½	cup vegetable oil
2	onions, finely chopped
1	tablespoon cumin seeds
5	whole cloves
5	green cardamom pods
1	stick cinnamon
2	bay leaves
2	teaspoons fresh garlic, finely chopped
2	teaspoons fresh ginger root, peeled and chopped
½	cup yogurt
2	tomatoes, chopped
1	teaspoon turmeric
1	teaspoon garam masala *(see chef's comments on this page)*
1	teaspoon ground cumin
1	teaspoon ground coriander
1	teaspoon cayenne pepper
2	teaspoons paprika
2½	teaspoons salt
¼	cup water
1	chicken, skin removed, and chopped into 2" pieces *(meat left on the bones)*

In a medium large saucepan place the vegetable oil and heat it on medium until it is hot. Add the onions, cumin seeds, cloves, green cardamom, cinnamon stick, and bay leaves. Sauté the ingredients for 8 to 10 minutes, or until the onions are brown. Add the garlic and ginger, and stir them in.

In a food processor place the yogurt and tomatoes, and blend them together. Add the yogurt-tomato mixture to the onion mixture, and stir it in.

While stirring constantly, one at a time add the remaining ingredients *(except for the water and the chicken)*. Cook the mixture for 5 minutes.

Add the water and thoroughly mix it in.

Add the chicken and mix it in. Cover the pan and cook the chicken for 30 minutes, or until it is done.

serves 4

"This is a classic recipe that everyone in India makes. Each family prepares it in their own particular way, and no two curries ever taste the same. It can be made hot or mild, depending upon individual taste.....or, in some cases, according to doctors' orders."

"Use your own judgment when you add your spices. Garam masala is a mixture of different spices, and can be purchased in most good markets. It has a very strong flavor, and should be used with care."

"All of the Indian restaurant owners in America have a network connection with each other. We all know each other, stick together, and help each other out. This way we have a good source for locating chefs and waitpeople as needed."

Nitin Bhakta
India Palace

Honey Chicken with Roasted Tomato Relish

Honey Chicken

6   **chicken breasts, skin and bones removed**
1½   **tablespoons fresh garlic, finely minced**
½   **cup scallions, finely chopped**
2   **tablespoons chile pequin** *(hot red chile flakes)*
1   **tablespoon red chile powder**
1   **cup honey**
1   **bottle Chinese beer**
¾   **cup olive oil**
½   **cup soy sauce**
1½   **teaspoons salt**
½   **teaspoon black pepper**
   Roasted Tomato Relish *(recipe follows)*

In a medium large bowl place all of the ingredients *(except for the Roasted Tomato Relish)*. Let the chicken marinate for 24 hours.

Grill the chicken for 4 to 6 minutes on each side, or until it is just done. Serve the chicken with the Roasted Tomato Relish on top.

serves 6

Roasted Tomato Relish

12   **medium tomatoes, grilled until black and finely chopped**
2   **cups white onions, minced, rinsed, and gently squeezed in a colander**
1   **tablespoon fresh garlic, minced**
1   **tablespoon serrano chile peppers, seeded and minced**
¼   **cup fresh cilantro, coarsely chopped**
½   **tablespoon red chile powder**
1   **teaspoon salt** *(or to taste)*
1   **tablespoon lemon juice, freshly squeezed**

In a medium bowl place all of the ingredients and mix them together.

makes approximately 6 cups

Marinated Chicken Enchiladas with Green Chile Sauce and Melon Pepper Salsa

Marinated Chicken Enchiladas

1	cup light Mexican beer
¼	cup red wine
1	tablespoon Worcestershire sauce
½	cup olive oil
½	cup orange juice
½	teaspoon dried tarragon
¾	teaspoon dried thyme
¾	teaspoon salt
4	6-ounce chicken breasts, skin and bones removed
2	tablespoons olive oil *(or as needed)*
8	corn tortillas
3	cups Green Chile Sauce *(recipe on next page),* **heated**
1	cup Monterey Jack cheese, grated
1	cup cheddar cheese, grated
2	cups Melon Pepper Salsa *(recipe on page 234)*

In a medium bowl place the beer, red wine, Worcestershire sauce, the ½ cup of olive oil, orange juice, tarragon, thyme, and salt. Stir the ingredients together. Add the chicken breasts and marinate them for 2 hours in the refrigerator.

Remove the chicken and grill it for 3 to 4 minutes on each side, or until it is just done. Cut the chicken into thin, 1" long strips.

In a medium sauté pan place the 2 tablespoons of olive oil and heat it on high until it is hot. Flash fry the tortillas so that they are soft, and then drain them on paper towels.

Preheat the oven to 400°.

On each of 4 individual oven-proof serving plates, place one of the tortillas. Place the chicken strips on top. Spoon on ¼ cup of the Green Chile Sauce. Sprinkle on ⅛ cup each of the Monterey Jack cheese and the cheddar cheese. Place another tortilla on top. Ladle on ½ cup more of the Green Chile Sauce. Sprinkle another ⅛ cup of each of the two cheeses on top.

(continued on next page)

"Usually chicken enchiladas are made with chicken that is either boiled or baked, and to me it has no flavor at all. We wanted to do something that was tastier, so we decided to marinate it. Although the recipe says to grill the chicken, a nice alternative is to roast it. Also, this is a great recipe for chicken to be eaten plain, without putting it in the enchiladas."

"I don't consider myself to be a chef. However, I am fortunate in that I have been able to eat at fine restaurants all over the world, so I have developed a taste for good food. I get ideas for dishes and then let my chefs develop them. I give my feedback on what they are doing, until they get it right according to my taste. I encourage their creativity, but no new dish or sauce is supposed to come out of the kitchen without my prior approval. Once in a while something might slip by, and then I get really upset."

Herb Cohen
Steaksmith

Place the enchiladas in the oven for 10 minutes, or until the cheese is hot and bubbly.

Place a serving of the Melon Pepper Salsa next to each enchilada.

serves 4

Green Chile Sauce

5	pounds frozen green chile peppers *(medium hot)*, **defrosted and chopped**
1	yellow onion, diced medium
8	cups water
2	tablespoons fresh oregano, chopped
1	tablespoon fresh garlic, minced
1	tablespoon chicken base
2	tablespoons salt
½	cup cornstarch, well mixed with 1¼ cups cold water *(no lumps)*

In a large saucepan place the green chile peppers, onions, and water. Over medium low heat bring the ingredients to a simmer.

Add the oregano, garlic, chicken base, and salt. Simmer the ingredients for 10 minutes, or until the onions are tender.

While stirring constantly, slowly add the cornstarch mixture. Continue to stir the mixture over low heat for 10 minutes more, or until the sauce has thickened.

Note: You may freeze this sauce in smaller amounts.

makes approximately 1 gallon

Melon Pepper Salsa

1	red bell pepper, seeded and diced medium
1	green bell pepper, seeded and diced medium
1	yellow bell pepper, seeded and diced medium
1	cup cantaloupe, diced medium
⅓	cup fresh fresh cilantro, finely minced
⅓	cup fresh parsley, finely minced

In a medium bowl place all of the ingredients and toss them together. Cover the bowl and refrigerate the salsa for 1 hour before serving it.

makes approximately 3 cups

"There is no trick to making this. Just make sure that everything is very fresh, and try to cut the ingredients into uniform sizes."

"My partner, Ralph Balding, and I have another Steaksmith in Colorado Springs. His wife, Jeanie, is an excellent cook and she has helped to create many items on our menu."

Herb Cohen
Steaksmith

"Turkey is a wonderful, wonderful meat. When cooked correctly it is very moist and flavorful, and it is far better for you than chicken. Many of us have a bad attitude toward it because we grew up on turkey that was cooked for a very long time, and the meat was dry and lifeless. But, if you follow this recipe and don't overcook it, the meat will be so delicious that you won't even recognize it as turkey."

"If you are cooking a whole turkey, the night before you should rub it all over with a marinade consisting of low sodium soy sauce or tamari, garlic purée, turmeric, and cumin. The next day when you roast it there will be a wonderful, exotic aroma in the kitchen. Your nose buds will be stimulated and excited. Cover the breast with foil, because it will cook faster."

"I love the smokiness of chipotle chile peppers. To me, the chipotle is one of the hottest chile peppers in the world. But, rather than searing you with its heat it slowly encompasses you. I compare it to a bass note in music as opposed to a high note. The former emanates out and gradually envelops you with its presence, whereas the latter pierces you sharply."

Robert Goodfriend
ek mas

Grilled Turkey Breast with Chipotle-Tomatillo Salsa

Grilled Turkey Breast

½   whole turkey breast, sliced against the grain into ½" wide strips
1   tablespoon olive oil
  salt *(to taste)*
  black pepper *(to taste)*
  Chipotle-Tomatillo Salsa *(recipe follows)*

Brush the turkey strips with the olive oil. Season them with the salt and black pepper.

Grill the turkey strips on medium high heat for 3 to 5 minutes on each side, or until they are barely done.

Serve the turkey with the Chipotle-Tomatillo Salsa on the side.

serves 4

Chipotle-Tomatillo Salsa

2½   pounds tomatillos, husks removed
3   chipotle chile peppers, soaked in warm water until pliable, seeds removed, and finely diced
1   medium onion, finely chopped
1   tablespoon ground cumin
  salt *(to taste)*
  black pepper *(to taste)*

In a medium saucepan place the tomatillos and cover them with water. Bring the water to a boil, and then simmer the tomatillos for 30 minutes, or until they are tender. Strain the tomatillos in a colander so that most of the liquid drains off. Place them in a food processor and purée them.

In a medium bowl place the puréed tomatillos and the remainder of the ingredients, and mix them together. Refrigerate the salsa for 2 hours before serving it.

makes approximately 3 cups

Breast of Turkey Stuffed with Peach Cornbread Dressing and Maple Port Gravy

Breast of Turkey Stuffed with Peach Cornbread Dressing

1	tablespoon olive oil
1	medium yellow onion, chopped
1	cup peach wedges *(fresh or frozen)*, **peeled and chopped**
1	cup cornbread stuffing
1	egg, lightly beaten
1	teaspoon dried rosemary, finely ground
	salt *(to taste)*
	black pepper *(to taste)*
2	turkey breasts
	Maple Port Gravy *(recipe on next page)*

In a large sauté pan place the olive oil and heat it on medium until it is hot. Add the onions and gently sauté them for 5 minutes, or until they are translucent. Add the peaches and cook them on low heat for 5 minutes.

In a medium large bowl place the cornbread stuffing. Add the onion-peach mixture, the egg, rosemary, salt, and black pepper. Mix the ingredients together with your hands.

Preheat the oven to 350°.

For each turkey breast lift up the skin, peel it back, and slice the meat across so that the knife goes halfway through the meat. Put the knife down into the bottom of the cut, and cut the meat sideways on each side, so that a pocket is formed *(don't cut through the sides)*. Season the meat, inside and out, with the salt and black pepper.

Place the stuffing inside evenly. Bring the incisions together and pull the skin back over the top. Gently push and knead the meat so that the stuffing is distributed out evenly.

Roast the turkey breasts for 1 hour, or until a meat thermometer reaches 155° *(or roast them in a Weber, using the indirect method – see chef's comments on this page for instructions)*.

(continued on next page)

"If you own an outdoor Weber grill, then I would highly recommend cooking the turkey in it, using the indirect method. This is a way to cook things slowly without burning them. Place the turkey in the middle of the grill, with a pan underneath, and put the coals on each side of the pan. The meat will acquire a wonderful smoky flavor. This method really works wonders on all poultry."

"When you cut the pocket in the turkey breast be careful that you don't poke the blade through the breast. Use a sharp paring knife with a very short blade."

"Cooking is a fun thing to do, and it is something that can be enjoyed by all people, at any level of skill."

Tom Wright
Galisteo Inn

Starting from the center, slice the turkey into ½" wide pieces *(don't use the very ends)*.

On each of 4 individual serving plates place the Maple Port Gravy. Artfully arrange the turkey slices on top.

serves 4

Maple Port Gravy

¼   **cup flour**
¼   **cup canola oil**
3   **cups chicken stock** *(recipe on page 295)*
⅜   **cup port wine** *(ruby, if possible)*
   salt *(to taste)*
   white pepper *(to taste)*
2   **tablespoons maple syrup** *(or to taste)*

In a medium saucepan place the flour and canola oil. Mix them together and cook them for 5 minutes on medium low heat.

Add the chicken stock. While stirring constantly, cook the mixture on medium high heat for 5 minutes, or until it boils and thickens.

Add the port wine, salt, white pepper, and maple syrup.

makes 4 cups

Marinated Duck Breast with Raspberry Chile Puya and Guajon Sauce

Marinated Duck Breast

4	duck breasts, split and skin removed
2	cups balsamic vinegar
4	fresh rosemary sprigs
3	large cloves garlic, thinly sliced
1	tablespoon black peppercorns
	Raspberry Chile Puya and Guajon Sauce *(recipe on next page)*

In a medium large bowl place the duck breasts, balsamic vinegar, rosemary, garlic, and black peppercorns. Marinate the duck for 1 hour.

Grill the duck over flavored wood *(apple, mesquite, etc.)* for 3 to 5 minutes on each side, or until it is medium rare.

In the center of each of 4 individual serving plates spread on the Raspberry Chile Puya and Guajon Sauce. Cut each duck breast in half and place one piece on top of the sauce. Slice the other half into medallions and fan them out on the plate.

serves 4

"I have been cooking duck for many years, and have prepared it in a hundred different sauces.....pear sauce, mandarin orange sauce, blueberry sauce. Basically I used anything fresh that I could get my hands on. In this recipe the fruitiness of the raspberries goes really well with the heat and flavor of the chiles. A lot of hot peppers don't blend well with fruit, but this is the exception."

"Cooking to me has always been very rewarding. There is no limit to what you can do, and no matter how skilled or artistic you become, there is always further to go and more to achieve."

"I love working with the people in our kitchen. Most of our staff is from Mexico, and they have been exposed to this kind of cooking all of their lives, where their grandmothers and mothers did it. Everybody in the kitchen has a hand in what we do, and each day I learn something new."

Marc Greene
Old Mexico Grill

Raspberry Chile Puya and Guajon Sauce

1	pint raspberries
5	puya chile peppers, washed, stems and seeds removed
4	guajon chile peppers, washed, stems and seeds removed
½	cup sugar
1½	cups water
2	cups duck stock *(or rich chicken stock)*

In a medium saucepan place the raspberries, puya and guajon chile peppers, sugar, and water. Cook the ingredients on a high simmer for 30 to 45 minutes, or until the chile peppers are soft.

Place the ingredients in a food processor and purée them.

Place the purée in a fine sieve and whisk it so that it pushes through. Place the strained mixture back into the saucepan. Add the duck stock and stir it in. Cook the sauce on medium heat for ½ hour, or until it is thickened.

makes approximately 3 cups

"I love to experiment around with different varieties of peppers. One day I combined the puya and guajon peppers, and discovered that they go together very well. By themselves they are not too hot, but when you mix them together they produce a really nice heat with an excellent flavor. Be sure that you strain the sauce through a sieve so that the skins are removed, because they are very waxy and you can't digest them."

Marc Greene
Old Mexico Grill

Ballotine Duck with Celery Sauce and Blackberry Sauce

Ballotine Duck

1	**pound Italian sausage** (hot), **removed from casing**
1	**egg yolk**
¼	**cup heavy cream**
½	**pound spinach, washed, dried, stems removed, steamed** (to wilt it), **and cooled**
¼	**cup walnuts, finely chopped and roasted**
4	**duck legs with thighs**
	salt (to taste)
	black pepper (to taste)
	Celery Sauce (recipe on next page)
	Blackberry Sauce (recipe on page 242)

Place your food processor bowl and metal blade in the freezer for ½ hour. Assemble it together. Add the Italian sausage and pulse it so that it becomes a paste (scrape down the sides). Add the egg yolk and process it in. With the food processor running, slowly dribble in the heavy cream. Add the steamed spinach and process it in.

Place the mixture in a medium bowl. Add the walnuts and mix them in. Set the stuffing aside.

Preheat the oven to 450°.

For each duck leg piece, starting at the thigh end, carefully scrape and cut the meat away from the bone, so that it is as intact as possible. When you get to the bottom of the leg, pull the meat back, and, using a cleaver, chop the bone off so that only ½" of it remains. Season the inside of the duck with the salt and black pepper.

Thread a large needle with 2 feet of dental floss (unwaxed and unflavored). Tie a toothpick to one end. Starting at the bottom of the leg sew up the duck, so that a small opening remains at the other end. Place the stuffing in a pastry bag and pipe it inside the meat so that it is slightly puffed up (don't overstuff it). Sew up the open end of the duck. Make a 1" loop as close to the meat as possible. Pull the loop and put it over the bone at the other end.

(continued on next page)

"Ballotine is a process of removing the bones from a fowl, and then stuffing it with a mixture of ground meat and various other ingredients. The most difficult thing in this recipe is getting the meat off the bone, especially around the knee joint. You need to use a combination of scraping the meat and cutting the tendons. This takes some time and practice, but it is something that anyone can do. The other tricky thing is stuffing the duck. When I first made this dish I spooned the stuffing in and it took me forever. Now I use a pastry bag to pipe it in, and this works great. After the duck is sewn up (and dental floss is definitely the way to go), then all you have to do is cook it. Because there is a lot of fat in the duck, the cooking time isn't so crucial. With lean meat like chicken or fish, a few minutes too long or too short can make all the difference."

Tom Wright
Galisteo Inn

"I don't know what Tom does to his duck to make it taste so good, but this is the best duck that I have ever eaten. And, the presentation with the two sauces is absolutely beautiful."

Joanna Kaufman
Galisteo Inn

"The purpose of the tooth-pick tied to the end of the dental floss is to keep it from unthreading. Also, it gives you something to hold on to when you take the string off."

"To properly serve this dish you need a large plate for each person. When I serve entrées with sauces, most dinner plates seem to be too small for the correct presenation. At home I have over-sized plates and they work well."

Tom Wright
Galisteo Inn

"The Galisteo Inn is located 30 minutes outside of Santa Fe, and it is in a very serene, restful, and comfortable environment. When people come here they can kick back and relax, without having to worry about a thing. Some people use this as a home base while visiting Santa Fe, and others lie by the pool all day without ever leaving the grounds at all. We also have some men who relax at the inn while their wives go shopping in Santa Fe."

Joanna Kaufman
Galisteo Inn

Season the outside of the duck with more of the salt and black pepper. Place the duck on a rack in a baking pan and roast it for 25 minutes. Prick each side 4 times with a pin. Turn the duck over and roast it for another 20 minutes.

Cut off the loop and pull the toothpick so that the floss is removed. Slice each piece of duck into 5 pieces.

On each of 4 individual serving plates spread on the Celery Sauce. Drizzle the Blackberry Sauce on ½ of the plate so that random patterns are formed *(similar to Japanese writing)*. Artfully arrange the duck pieces on the other half of the plate.

serves 4

Celery Sauce

3	**tablespoons olive oil**
6	**celery stalks, diced small**
2	**tablespoons flour**
1⅓	**cups milk**
1	**teaspoon duck base** *(or chicken base)*
	salt *(to taste)*
	white pepper *(to taste)*

In a medium saucepan place the olive oil and heat it on medium low until it is hot. Add the celery and sauté it for 8 to 10 minutes, or until it is tender.

Add the flour and stir it for 5 minutes.

Add the milk and stir it for 5 minutes, or until the sauce boils and thickens. Add the duck base and stir it in. Season the sauce with the salt and white pepper.

makes approximately 2 cups

Blackberry Sauce

1   **pint blackberries, cleaned**
¼   **cup corn syrup**
       sugar *(to taste)*

In a small saucepan place the blackberries. Simmer them on low heat for 10 minutes, or until they can be mashed.

Place the blackberries in a blender and purée them. Strain them through a chinois *(a very fine sieve)* or several pieces of cheesecloth, so that the seeds are removed.

In the same small saucepan place the strained blackberries and corn syrup, and simmer them on low heat for 10 minutes. Adjust the sweetness with the sugar.

makes 2 cups

"This sauce is very easy to make. It's important that you get every single black-berry seed out, because they are very bitter, and even one seed in the sauce will spoil it. The sauce should be very smooth and satiny."

Tom Wright
Galisteo Inn

Cornish Hen Stuffed with Pears and Chorizo

"This recipe works well with blue cornbread stuffing. You can't buy it pre-made, so you will first have to make some blue cornbread, dry it out, and then crumble it up. This goes really well with the chorizo sausage and pears. When people eat this they can't figure out what exactly is in the stuffing, although they love it.....it's the pears that fool them!"

"Cooking is like chess. You can learn the moves in chess very quickly, and right off you can play the game and enjoy it. It's complex and rich enough so that you can continue to improve for the rest of your life. Similarly, with cooking you can easily learn the basics and enjoy making recipes from day one. As with chess, cooking can be enjoyed on any level and you can take it as far as you want to go."

Tom Wright
Galisteo Inn

2	pears, peeled, cored, and cut into 8 pieces
1	egg
3	cups dry cornbread stuffing mix
½	pound chorizo, casing removed, sautéed, and drained of grease
4	Cornish hens, washed and dried
¼	cup clarified butter

Preheat the oven to 350°.

Place the pears in a food processor and chop them. Add the egg and process it for 30 seconds.

In a medium bowl place the pear mixture, cornbread stuffing, and chorizo. Mix the ingredients together well.

Stuff the Cornish hens with the mixture. Cross the legs and tie up the opening so that the stuffing stays inside. Tuck the wings under.

Place the hens on a rack in a baking pan. Brush them with the clarified butter. Roast them for 1 hour *(baste them frequently)*, or until they are done.

serves 4

Roasted Marinated Quail with Papaya Salsa

Roasted Marinated Quail

1	cup orange juice, freshly squeezed
5	teaspoons rice vinegar
½	cup fresh cilantro, chopped
¼	teaspoon salt
¼	teaspoon black pepper
¾	cup olive oil
8	8-ounce quail, semi-boneless
2	cups Papaya Salsa *(recipe on next page)*

In a food processor place the orange juice, rice vinegar, cilantro, salt, and black pepper. Blend the ingredients together.

With the food processor running slowly, dribble in the olive oil.

In a medium bowl place the quail and then pour on the marinade. Refrigerate the quail for 2 hours.

Broil *(or grill)* the quail for 30 to 60 seconds on each side, or until the skin is lightly browned *(do not burn them)*.

Preheat the oven to 350°.

In a small baking pan place the quail and roast them for 8 to 10 minutes, or until they are done.

On each of 4 individual serving plates place 2 of the quail. Spoon the Papaya Salsa on top.

serves 4

"When you buy the quail they are always semi-boneless. I call for two 8-ounce quail per person, which may seem like a lot. But you have to remember that when you cook the quail they shrink to about half their original size."

"The marinade for the quail makes an outstanding salad dressing. I've also marinated fish in it, and it was wonderful. The citrus and cilantro flavors come through, and the vinegar flavor isn't that strong."

"I want our customers to love every bite of their food. And, if they don't, then I want to hear about it! A lot of people are reluctant to report to the chef that something on their plate is not good. But, there is nothing we chefs hate more than hearing about a complaint after the check has been paid. We want to know about the problem immediately so that we can fix it. People should realize that chefs appreciate the bad comments as well as the good comments."

Adrienne Sussman
Chez What

Papaya Salsa

2	**large ripe papayas, peeled, seeded, and finely diced**
1	**medium red onion, finely diced**
2	**serrano chile peppers, seeded and finely chopped**
¼	**cup fresh cilantro, chopped**
2	**tablespoons lime juice, freshly squeezed**
2	**tablespoons peanut oil** *(or vegetable oil)*
1	**tablespoon water**
½	**teaspoon salt**
¼	**teaspoon black pepper, freshly ground**

In a medium bowl place all of the ingredients and toss them together well. Refrigerate the salsa for at least 1 hour before serving it.

makes approximately 2 cups

"It's important that you use nice, ripe papayas. They might disintegrate after they have been marinating for awhile, but that's okay. The sweet in the salsa brings out the sweet in the quail. And, there is a touch of 'hot' to clean out the mouth. This is a nice, light dish that's especially good in the summer."

Adrienne Sussman
Chez What

Meat

Mesquite Grilled Pork with Spicy Chile Citrus Sauce

Mesquite Grilled Pork

2   **pork tenderloins, well cleaned**
      salt and black pepper *(to taste)*
      Spicy Chile Citrus Sauce *(recipe follows)*

Season the pork with the salt and black pepper. Grill it over mesquite wood for 2 minutes on each side, or until grill marks are made.

Preheat the oven to 350°. In a baking dish place the pork and cover it with the Spicy Chile Citrus Sauce. Bake the pork for 30 minutes, or until the desired doneness is achieved. Slice the pork into medallions and serve them with more of the Spicy Chile Citrus Sauce spooned on top.

serves 4

Spicy Chile Citrus Sauce

10   **dried puya chile peppers, grilled until brown, stems and seeds removed**
8   **dried arbol chile peppers, grilled until brown, stems and seeds removed**
10   **cloves garlic, roasted** *(see chef's comments on page 37)*
½   **bunch fresh oregano**
2   **tablespoons whole black peppercorns**
2   **quarts rich chicken stock** *(recipe on page 295)*
1   **cup orange juice, freshly squeezed**
1   **lime, juiced**
¾   **cup tamarind nectar**

In a medium large saucepan place the grilled chile peppers, roasted garlic, oregano, black peppercorns, and chicken stock. Bring the ingredients to a boil and then simmer them for 1 hour.

Place the mixture in a food processor and purée it. Strain the purée through a fine sieve, and return it to the saucepan. Add the orange juice, lime juice, and tamarind nectar. Simmer the sauce for ½ hour, or until it is the consistency of heavy cream.

makes approximately 4 cups

Meat

"This is a classical northern Mexican dish, and it is very rich and delicious. Be sure that the pork is completely covered with the sauce when you are baking it. If you don't have enough sauce to cover the pork, then baste it with what sauce there is."

"Our cuisine is classical Mexican, but it is much more sophisticated than your basic Mexican enchiladas, tacos, rice, and beans. It's fun for me to dabble with the different flavors, and to come up with a subtle twist to a traditional recipe. We may stray from the classical a little bit, but not too far."

"In my job I like to share things and have everybody get along with each other, so that we have a happy, harmonious kitchen. Also, I enjoy the hands-on creativity of cooking and the one-on-one interaction with my staff."

Marc Greene
Old Mexico Grill

Grilled Marinated Pork Tenderloin with Chipotle Orange Tomato Sauce

Grilled Marinated Pork Tenderloin

4	6-ounce pork tenderloins, sliced at a diagonal into 2" wide pieces
½	cup shallots, chopped
1	cup white wine
2	tablespoons olive oil
½	teaspoon salt
¼	teaspoon black pepper
	Chipotle Orange Tomato Sauce *(recipe follows)*

In a medium bowl place the pork, shallots, white wine, olive oil, salt, and black pepper. Marinate the pork in the refrigerator for 6 hours.

Grill the pork for 2 to 3 minutes on each side, or until it is done.

In the center of 4 individual serving plates spread on the Chipotle Orange Tomato Sauce. Fan out the sliced pork medallions on top.

serves 4

Chipotle Orange Tomato Sauce

2	tablespoons olive oil
1	small onion, finely chopped
4	medium tomatoes, chopped medium
⅓	cup chipotle chile peppers *(canned in adobo sauce)*
1	large orange, peeled, seeds and membranes removed, and sectioned

In a medium sauté pan place the olive oil and heat it on medium high until it is hot. Add the onions and sauté them for 4 to 6 minutes, or until they are translucent.

Add the tomatoes, chipotle chile peppers, and orange sections. Sauté the ingredients on medium heat for 10 minutes, or until the sauce thickens.

makes 1 cup

"This dish is not for the weak-hearted, because it's definitely spicy. The pork marinated with the wine really tastes nice, and it complements the flavors in the Chipotle Orange Tomato Sauce. I like to cook the pork so that it is medium done, with just a little bit of pink inside. I know that most people disagree with my taste, so in the restaurant we serve it with no pink. Still, we try not to kill it, so that it doesn't get too dry."

"I really get disappointed when I go to a restaurant and the flavors are so bland that I have to add something extra to the food, like hot sauce or a spice. When I eat I want the flavors to explode in my mouth, and that's the kind of food I like to cook."

Paul Hunsicker
Paul's Restaurant of Santa Fe

Sirloin Chile

¼	cup olive oil
2	pounds New York strip steak, diced into 1" cubes
1	cup cooked black beans
2	cups cooked posole *(or canned hominy)*
1	cup tomatoes, chopped
2	serrano chile peppers, thinly julienned
½	cup ancho chile peppers, thinly julienned
1	cup fresh corn kernels
1	tablespoon fresh garlic, finely chopped
1½	cups chicken broth *(recipe on page 295)*
1	tablespoon red chile powder
½	tablespoon ground cumin
	Hot Desert Seasonings Mix *(recipe on page 297)*, **to taste**
8	corn tortillas, warmed

In a medium large saucepan place the olive oil and heat it on high until it is hot. Add the meat and sear it for 5 seconds.

Add the remainder of the ingredients *(except for the Hot Desert Seasoning Mix and the corn tortillas)* and cook them for 3 to 5 minutes, or until they are hot.

Season the chile with the Hot Desert Seasoning Mix. Serve it with the corn tortillas.

serves 4

"Although I love chile, I don't think that it normally looks too appetizing. In this recipe I use a very high quality cut of beef, and cut it into large chunks so that you can definitely see them. The whole dish can be prepared in 10 minutes (after the beans and posole are cooked), but it looks like you have been cooking all day. The recipe is fairly spicy, but you can control the heat by adding fewer or more chile peppers."

"I am a fanatic about tasting food along the way. I am constantly tasting, adjusting, and changing things, depending upon what's going on with the products. And, I believe that when tasting you always should use a spoon, and not your hands. The other chefs think I'm crazy when I tell them this, but I have an extremely sensitive palate, and I definitely can tell the difference."

Pete Zimmer
Inn of the Anasazi

"When I am around Peter, I feel the creative energy he exudes towards food. I have seen him do things that I never would have thought of myself, and I have been in the business for a long time. His energy level is phenomenal!"

Dolly Nevada Hand
Inn of the Anasazi

Carne Adovada

1½	medium onions, chopped
2	cloves garlic, minced
½	teaspoon dried oregano
1½	teaspoons ground coriander
4	tablespoons red chile powder
1	tablespoon chile caribe *(crushed red chile peppers)*
½	teaspoon ground cloves
½	teaspoon salt
1	tablespoon honey
2	tablespoons sherry vinegar
1	cup chicken stock *(or as needed), (recipe on page 295)*
4	pounds pork, fat and bones removed, and thinly sliced

In a food processor place the onions, garlic, oregano, coriander, red chile powder, chile caribe, cloves, salt, honey, and sherry vinegar. Purée the ingredients together. Add the chicken stock as needed so that a thick sauce is achieved.

In a medium large bowl place the sauce and pork, and mix them together well. Cover the bowl and marinate the pork in the refrigerator for 24 hours.

In a medium large saucepan place the sauce and meat. Simmer the ingredients for 2 hours, or until the pork is tender.

serves 6 to 8

Osso Bucco Milanaise

4	**veal shanks**
	salt *(to taste)*
	black pepper *(to taste)*
½	**cup flour** *(or as needed)*
2	**tablespoons olive oil**
½	**cup white wine**
1	**tablespoon olive oil**
1	**yellow onion, chopped**
4	**cloves garlic, chopped**
1	**cup carrots, shredded**
4	**large tomatoes, diced**
1	**tablespoon dried basil**
	salt *(to taste)*
	black pepper *(to taste)*
2	**cups water** *(or as needed)*

Season the veal with the salt and black pepper. Press the veal into the flour so that it is well coated on all sides.

In a large, heavy stockpot place the 2 tablespoons of olive oil and heat it on high until it is hot. Add the flour-coated veal shanks, cover the pot, and reduce the heat to medium. Cook the shanks on each side for a total of 15 minutes, or until they are nicely browned. Add ½ of the white wine and simmer the meat *(covered)* for 15 minutes more.

Meanwhile, in a large sauté pan place the 1 tablespoon of olive oil and heat it on medium high until it is hot. Add the onions and garlic, and sauté them for 5 minutes. Add the carrots, tomatoes, basil, salt, and black pepper. Simmer the ingredients for 15 minutes. Add the rest of the white wine and simmer the sauce for 15 minutes more.

Add the sauce and the water to the veal. Cover the pot and simmer the ingredients for 2 hours *(add more water if necessary)*, or until the meat is very tender.

serves 4

"Although this is an Italian recipe, I spell it in the French way because this is how I knew it when I was growing up in Switzerland (the French part). It takes some time to cook, although it's not at all hard to make. Once everything is prepared, then the meat cooks by itself. You must make sure that there is enough liquid toward the end of the cooking time. The meat should be very tender, but not falling off the bone. Serve this with some noodles, Caesar salad, bread, and red wine."

"What I really love the most about osso bucco is the marrow in the middle of the bone. I pick it out with a fork, put lots of pepper on it, and then eat it.....it's delicious!"

"In Switzerland there is an obligatory school for young girls, where we had to learn how to cook and sew, to prepare us for marriage. This is when I first learned about cooking, and I started making meals for my grandparents. They weren't anything fancy or special.....just the basic, simple things that my family cooked."

Marie Jeanne Chaney
Swiss Bakery

Sautéed Lamb Chops in Marsala Sauce

"One day I wanted to prepare a rack of lamb, but I didn't want to roast it because that seemed too ordinary. I had always enjoyed sautéing little veal chops, which I did from an Italian recipe whose translation means 'burn your finger chops' (I love the Italian language because it is so descriptive of its food), and so I decided to sauté the lamb as well. The sauce is not a cream sauce. The cream is used only as a binder and an emulsifier.....it helps to thicken the sauce and hold it together. When the sauce is done (there will be very little) it should be a very dark brown. When you add the pine nuts the pan will be very hot, so shake it and add the wine right away. At the worst the nuts won't get toasted, but this is no big deal.....better not toasted than burned!"

"Veal demi-glace is a dark veal stock that has been reduced to a very thick consistency. You can use canned beef bouillon that has been reduced. I like to use things like demi-glace. They enrich a sauce and make it taste wonderful without using a lot of fat."

Wayne Gustafson
Julian's

4	tablespoons olive oil
12	lamb chops, cut from the rack and trimmed
¼	cup pine nuts
2	sprigs fresh rosemary
½	cup Marsala wine
¼	cup veal demi-glace *(see chef's comments on this page)*
¼	cup heavy cream

In an extra large sauté pan place the olive oil and heat it on high until it is hot. Add the lamb chops and cook them for 3 to 5 minutes *(turn them frequently)*, or until the desired doneness is achieved. Remove the lamb chops from the pan, arrange them on a platter, and place it in a warm place.

Pour out the grease from the sauté pan. Add the pine nuts and a few leaves of the rosemary. Toss the pine nuts for 15 seconds, or until they are lightly toasted.

Add the Marsala and boil it rapidly for 1 minute so that the alcohol is removed.

Add the veal demi-glace and the heavy cream. Simmer the sauce for 3 to 4 minutes, or until it thickens.

Top the chops with the sauce *(there will not be much left)*, and garnish them with the remaining rosemary.

serves 4

Grilled Dijon Marinated Pork Tenderloin with Ginger Applesauce

Grilled Dijon Marinated Pork Tenderloin

½   cup Dijon mustard
1   teaspoon fresh garlic, minced
¼   teaspoon white pepper
4   small pork tenderloins, cleaned
    Ginger Applesauce *(recipe on next page)*

In a medium size glass baking dish place the Dijon mustard, garlic, and white pepper. Mix the ingredients together. Add the pork tenderloins and coat them with the mixture. Let the pork marinate in the refrigerator for 6 to 12 hours.

Grill the pork on a medium hot grill for 7 to 9 minutes *(keep the pork on the cooler part of the grill and rotate it frequently)*, or until the desired doneness is achieved.

Let the grilled pork tenderloins sit for several minutes. Slice them into medallions that are ½" thick.

On each of 4 individual serving plates place the medallions in an overlapping, curved pattern. Place the Ginger Applesauce next to the medallions.

serves 4

"This recipe is a takeoff on grandma's pork with applesauce. It's a very homey, warming dish that can be served in a casual setting, or in an extremely elegant setting. The only trick is to be gentle with the meat and don't cook it too quickly or on too high a heat. It should be very soft and tender, with no crust on the outside."

"I guess that the ad campaign stating that pork is the 'other white meat' has had an effect on me, because I believe that pork is much healthier and more flavorful than beef. Also, pork is so much more versatile in the ways that you can prepare it, and the wines that you can serve with it."

"Many of us who live in Santa Fe have solar homes and we understand the principle of a thermal mass, where the adobe bricks hold the heat and release it later. The same theory applies to cooking meat or fish, because the mass retains the heat, which emanates out to continue cooking. A good rule is to remove the item from the heat when you think it is slightly underdone. By the time you serve it on a warm platter the cooking will have reached another level and it will be just perfect."

Robert Goodfriend
ek mas

"This is not a dessert applesauce, so I don't like to use too much sugar. Rather, it is a savory applesauce, and I like to emphasize the flavor of the ginger and onions. Also, the crystallized ginger is coated with sugar and this adds a bit more sweetness. Taste it after it is made and then use your own judgment. Take my recipe and make it your recipe!"

"When I was younger I lived in Spain for several years. For awhile I stayed on a beautiful beach in the northern part of the country. As with most European beaches, clothing was optional. Eventually I decided that I should do something to make money, so I got a 55 gallon drum and made a barbeque grill. There was a little hut-like structure on the beach where coffee and drinks were served, and I approached the owner with a business proposition.....if he would let me share his space I would sell grilled fish and encourage my customers buy his drinks, and he would do the same for me. He said 'Sure!', so every morning I bought fresh fish at the market and then grilled it and sold it with a salad. But, the whole time I was running my barbecue joint I was stark naked! This was my first commercial endeavor in the food business."

Robert Goodfriend
ek mas

Ginger Applesauce

5	**large Granny Smith apples, peeled, cored, and quartered**
8	**½" thick pieces fresh ginger root, peeled**
	water *(as needed)*
3	**ounces crystallized ginger, minced**
1	**tablespoon olive oil**
1	**onion, thinly sliced**
1	**tablespoon sugar** *(or to taste)*
	salt *(to taste)*
	black pepper *(to taste)*

In a medium saucepot place the apples and the fresh ginger. Add enough water so that the ingredients are covered. Simmer them for 10 minutes, or until the apples are tender *(but not mushy)*.

Remove the pieces of fresh ginger. Strain out the liquid. Place the cooked apples and crystallized ginger in a food processor, and blend them so that the desired consistency is achieved *(smooth or chunky)*.

In a small saucepan place the olive oil and heat it on medium low until it is hot. Add the onions and sauté them for 20 minutes, or until they are very soft and caramelized.

Add the sautéed onions, sugar, salt, and black pepper to the apple mixture. Stir everything together well.

makes 3 cups

Marinated Lamb Brochette

2	**red bell peppers, seeded and cut into 1" squares**
1	**onion, cut into 1" squares**
1	**leg of lamb, tender portions only cut into 1" cubes** *(see chef's comments on this page)*
½	**cup olive oil**
3	**cloves garlic, coarsely chopped**
¼	**onion, coarsely chopped**
2	**bay leaves**
1	**fresh rosemary sprig**

On each of 8 small wooden skewers place, in this order, a piece of red bell pepper, onion, lamb, onion, lamb, onion, lamb, onion, and red bell pepper.

In a medium bowl place the olive oil, garlic, chopped onion, bay leaves, and rosemary. Mix the ingredients together.

Add the brochettes, cover the bowl, and place it in the refrigerator overnight.

Grill the brochettes for 3 to 5 minutes, or until the desired doneness is achieved *(rotate them periodically)*.

serves 4

"Preferably you should buy a domestic, spring leg of lamb. Have the butcher cut out the tender portions for you, and then clean them of all fat and sinew. Use this tender part for the brochette cubes. The tougher parts can be used for a lamb stew. We make a lamb stew here by sautéing onions, celery, carrots, and thyme, and then adding sautéed lamb pieces along with some wine and stock. Let the stew simmer for 1 to 2 hours, and then thicken it with a purée of sweet red bell peppers."

"When I was seven years old my mother became ill and I had to take over a lot of the cooking. I knew how to thicken sauces, steam vegetables, and cook meat. Another chore I had was to put the food away and clean up the pots and pans. I remember once we had a big pot roast for company. As I was cleaning up, I saw that the roast was too big to fit in the refrigerator, so I decided to store it in the oven overnight. Needless to say, the next day it was completely inedible. My family was not pleased."

Ned Laventall
El Farol

Sautéed Veal Chops with Belgian Endive

4	veal chops, well trimmed
	salt *(to taste)*
	black pepper *(to taste)*
1	tablespoon extra virgin olive oil
4	Belgian endives, cored, leaves separated, washed, and dried
3	tablespoons dry sherry
1	cup cream
2	tablespoons butter *(cold)*, cut into pieces
1	tablespoon fresh tarragon, chopped
	salt *(to taste)*
	black pepper *(to taste)*

Season the veal chops with the salt and black pepper.

In a large sauté pan place the olive oil and heat it on medium high until it is hot. Add the veal chops and sauté them for 5 minutes on each side, or until they are medium rare. Remove the chops from the pan, put them on a warm platter, and keep them warm in the oven.

To the sauté pan add the Belgian endive leaves and sauté them for 1 minute, or until they are softened. Add the endive to the warm platter in the oven.

Add the dry sherry to the sauté pan and deglaze it. Add the cream and cook the sauce for 5 minutes, or until it is reduced by ½ and thickened.

Remove the pan from the heat. Add the pieces of butter one at a time, and stir them in.

Add the tarragon, salt, and black pepper.

On each of 4 individual serving plates place a veal chop and the endive. Pour a small amount of the sauce on top.

serves 4

"This is a classical dish from Belgium and the northeastern part of France, where they cook a lot of salad greens. The recipe calls for cream and butter, and I believe that they are needed for the success of this dish. You could reduce the amounts used, but I wouldn't leave them out altogether. Just remember that you are going to eat only a very small amount of the sauce, so the total fat consumed will be minimal. This is back to my old theory about food, where I believe that what you eat is not nearly as important as how much of it you eat."

"Be careful not to overcook the Belgian endive. It should be softened, but not too much. Its flavor is slightly bitter, which goes really well with the sweetness of the sherry and the richness of the butter and cream. The whole dish tastes fantastic!"

"Whenever you put butter in a dish the flavors will be more developed. If you have to be extremely careful with your fat intake, then cut the amounts down to ¼ of what the recipe calls for..... and exercise more!"

Martin Lackner
The Palace Restaurant

Meat

Blue and Gold Corn Flake Pork

1	cup yellow tortilla chips *(unsalted)*, **crumbled**
1	cup blue tortilla chips *(unsalted)*, **crumbled**
1	cup corn flakes, crumbled
½	teaspoon salt
¼	teaspoon black pepper
12	4-ounce pieces pork loin, fat removed
4	eggs *(or as needed)*, **beaten**
¼	cup peanut oil

Preheat the oven to 450°.

In a food processor place the crumbled yellow and blue tortilla chips, corn flakes, salt, and black pepper. Blend the ingredients so that they are finely ground.

Dip the pork loin pieces into the beaten eggs. Dredge them in the ground crumb mixture.

In a large skillet place the peanut oil and heat it on high until it is very hot. Add the breaded pork loins and sauté them for 1 minute on each side.

Place the sautéed pork loins in a baking pan and roast them for 5 to 6 minutes, or until they are done.

serves 4

"This is a variation of a basic breaded pork cutlet, the way your mom used to make it. Be sure to get the oil good and hot so that it quickly sears the meat. This way the crust will absorb very little oil. It will be nice and crispy on the outside, and the meat will be moist and tender on the inside."

Lawrence McGrael
Geronimo Lodge

"Our restaurant is in a very old adobe home, and it has a wonderful energy to it. However, I must mention that we do have a ghost who lives here. He's a benign ghost, but he does enjoy playing tricks on us and messing with our minds. One of his favorite torments is to back up our plumbing 10 minutes before we are scheduled to open for dinner. On the other hand, he helps us all to stay calm in a crisis situation. When something goes wrong we just look at each other and say 'Oh, no problem. It's just the ghost acting up again.' This way we mentally take a step away from the situation and we maintain a healthier attitude."

Cliff Skoglund
Geronimo Lodge

Red Chile Grilled Pork Tenderloin with Tomatillo and Roasted Piñon Pesto

> "I try to greet my customers with a real Southern hospitality. I work hard to make certain that the waitpeople are very cordial, but also that they do not overpower the customers with their personalities. I want each customer to feel really welcome, respected, and appreciated for being here."
>
> *Phillip Howell*
> *Garfield Grill*

Red Chile Grilled Pork Tenderloin

3   tablespoons olive oil
2   pounds pork tenderloin, fat and silver skin removed
2   tablespoons red chile powder
     Tomatillo and Roasted Piñon Pesto (recipe follows)

Brush the olive oil on the pork tenderloin. Sprinkle on the red chile powder.

Grill the pork on each side for 3 to 5 minutes, or until it is done. Let it sit for 5 minutes and then slice it into medallions.

On each of 4 individual serving plates place the pork medallions in a fan-like pattern. Spread the Tomatillo and Roasted Piñon Pesto on top.

serves 4

> "You can use this pesto with a lot of other things. It's excellent with pasta, shrimp, and rack of lamb. I can't describe the flavor, but it's really delicious. Plus, it's quick and easy to make.....a main priority of mine!"

Tomatillo and Roasted Piñon Pesto

2   cups tomatillos, husked and coarsely chopped
1   cup piñon nuts (pine nuts), roasted (see chef's comments on this page)
½   cup fresh cilantro sprigs
2   cloves garlic
¼   cup white wine
⅛   cup lime juice, freshly squeezed
1   teaspoon cayenne pepper
½   teaspoon ground cumin
1   teaspoon salt (or to taste)
½   teaspoon white pepper

> "Roast the piñon nuts in a 350° oven for about 10 minutes and watch them carefully. They are very expensive, so don't let them burn."
>
> *Anthony Carpenter*
> *Garfield Grill*

Place all of the ingredients in a food processor and purée them.

makes approximately 2 cups

Pork Brochettes with Pasta Pillows and Grilled Marinated Vegetables

Pork Brochettes

¾	**cup sugar**
¼	**cup cornstarch**
2	**cups soy sauce**
1½	**cups dry sherry**
¼	**cup sesame oil**
1	**cup water**
3½	**pounds pork loin, cleaned and cut into 1" cubes**
½	**cup peanuts**
1	**teaspoon red chile powder**
2	**tablespoons olive oil**
	Pasta Pillows *(recipe on next page)*
	Grilled Marinated Vegetables *(recipe on next page)*
	Oriental Sauce *(recipe on page 119)*
¼	**cup scallions, thinly sliced**

In a large bowl place the sugar, cornstarch, soy sauce, sherry, sesame oil, and water. Mix the ingredients together so that the cornstarch is dissolved.

On each of 8 bamboo skewers place the cubes of pork. Place the skewers in the marinade and refrigerate them for 24 hours.

Preheat the oven to 350°.

In a small bowl place the peanuts, red chile powder, and olive oil. Mix the ingredients together. Spread the peanut mixture out on a flat sheet. Bake it for 25 minutes, or until it is a chestnut color. Set it aside.

Grill the pork for 4 to 6 minutes, or until the desired doneness is achieved.

In the center of each of 4 individual serving plates place 2 of the skewers so that they form a wide "V". Place a Pasta Pillow in the center of the "V". Place the Grilled Marinated Vegetables along the outside of both sides of the "V". Pour some of the Oriental Sauce over the pork and the pasta. Sprinkle on the scallions and the hot peanuts.

serves 4

"This is a beautiful dish. Pork is an excellent meat, and, contrary to popular belief, it is very lean compared to beef. The marinade seeps right into the meat, and when you grill it, it tastes fantastic!"

Eric Sanders
Ogelvies

"I used to work at the Santacafe with Michael Fennelly, where I learned a lot about combining Asian ingredients with other types of cooking. The flavor of this dish is sweet and sour, and it is very popular in the restaurant."

Frank Peña
Ogelvies

Pasta Pillows

1	pound angel hair pasta, cooked al dente and drained
2½	tablespoons peanut oil
1	teaspoon fresh mint, chopped
	salt *(to taste)*
	black pepper *(to taste)*

Divide the pasta into 4 parts, and twirl each one with a fork so that it forms a "pillow". Chill the pasta pillows in the refrigerator for 30 minutes, or until they are firm.

In a large sauté pan place the peanut oil and heat it on medium high until it is hot. Sauté the pasta pillows for 2 minutes on each side, or until they are golden brown. Sprinkle on the mint, salt, and black pepper.

serves 4

"These pasta pillows are fun to serve as an alternative to more traditional starch dishes. When you fry them they get a crispy crust, and the flavor is delicious."

Frank Peña
Ogelvies

Grilled Marinated Vegetables

½	head red cabbage, quartered
½	head green cabbage, quartered
2	heads radicchio, quartered
1½	red onions, thickly sliced
1	teaspoon fresh garlic, chopped
1	cup olive oil
⅓	cup rice wine vinegar
1	teaspoon salt
1	teaspoon black pepper

Grill the red and green cabbage, radicchio, and red onions for 3 minutes, or until they are blackened *(turn them as necessary)*.

In a large bowl place the garlic, olive oil, rice wine vinegar, salt, and black pepper. Add the grilled vegetables and marinate them at room temperature for 1 hour.

serves 4

"My wife Kate and I have a lot of fun cooking at home. We love to try new recipes and experiment with different cuisines. She likes to follow directions to a 'T' the first time she tries a recipe. After that the two of us will alter it as we see fit. We have a tradition which we like to call 'experimenting on the neighbors'. When we find a new recipe or wine that we want to try out we invite our neighbors over to serve as 'tasters'. Usually the experiment is a success, and no matter what, we always have a good time!"

Eric Sanders
Ogelvies

Sunburnt Ribeye Steak with Broiled Tomatillo Salsa

Sunburnt Ribeye Steak

6   **12-ounce ribeye steaks**
      Blackening Spices *(recipe on page 285)*
      Broiled Tomatillo Salsa *(recipe on next page)*

Dredge the steaks in the Blackening Spices so that they are well coated on each side.

Place a heavy, seasoned, cast iron skillet on high heat for 10 minutes, or until it is very hot. Add the steaks and cook them for 3 to 6 minutes on each side, or until the desired doneness is achieved.

Serve the steaks with the Broiled Tomatillo Salsa on top.

serves 6

"When you make blackened dishes you need a good ventilation system because there is a lot of smoke in the process. Another good way to cook them is to put your cast iron skillet on an outdoor grill. Just make sure that the pan gets really, really hot. The spices should cook very fast and they should not really burn. If huge billows of black smoke come up then you probably have cooked it too much."

Isaac Modivah
Ore House

Broiled Tomatillo Salsa

3	cups tomatillos, husks removed
2	cups tomatoes, cored and quartered
8	cloves garlic
1	small red onion, peeled and quartered
3	pickled jalapeño chile peppers
1	bunch scallions, coarsely chopped
2	tablespoons fresh cilantro
½	cup red wine vinegar
¼	cup lime juice, freshly squeezed
1	teaspoon ground cumin
1	teaspoon dried oregano
	salt *(to taste)*
	black pepper *(to taste)*, coarsely ground

In a metal pan place the tomatillos and tomatoes. Place the garlic cloves on top. Broil the ingredients for 5 minutes, or until the skins are charred and the garlic is roasted.

In a food processor place the broiled tomatillos, tomatoes, and garlic, and purée them. Remove the mixture and set it aside in a medium bowl.

In a food processor place the red onions, pickled jalapeño chile peppers, scallions, and cilantro. Roughly chop the ingredients together. Add them to the tomato purée mixture. Add the red wine vinegar, lime juice, cumin, oregano, salt, and black pepper. Stir the ingredients together so that they are well mixed.

makes approximately 1½ quarts

"I think that we have the best tomatillo salsa around town. By first broiling the tomatillos and tomatoes, their flavors are really enhanced. This salsa has a rich and powerful flavor, and it stands up well to blackened dishes. You should serve it with a wine that has a strong character, so that all aspects of the meal relate well together, with no one item overpowering the others."

"Our executive chef, Isaac Modivah, has a wonderful, even temperament, and he is very easy to work with. If I tell him that I don't like something he listens to me, and doesn't become upset. A lot of chefs are so touchy that if you criticize them once, knives fly!"

Daniela Croce
Ore House

"When you are charring the tomatillos, tomatoes, and garlic, you should keep a close eye on them. You want the skins to get black all over, but you don't want the insides to get charred. This can happen pretty quickly under a home broiler."

Isaac Modivah
Ore House

Braised Lamb Shanks

4	**small lamb shanks** *(14 to 18 ounces each, with bone in)*
2	**cups flour, seasoned with salt and pepper**
½	**cup olive oil**
10	**cloves garlic, smashed and coarsely chopped**
5	**large yellow onions, diced large**
1	**cup dry red wine**
1	**cup dry white wine**
½	**cup chicken stock** *(recipe on page 295)*

Preheat the oven to 275°.

Roll the lamb shanks in the seasoned flour *(shake off the excess)*.

In a large, heavy Dutch oven with a tight lid place the olive oil and heat it on medium high until it is hot. Add the flour-dusted lamb shanks and brown them for 5 minutes on each of their 4 sides, or until they are a dark, golden brown. Remove the shanks and set them aside.

Add the garlic and sauté it for 20 to 30 seconds, or until it turns a golden brown. Add the onions and sauté them for 5 to 7 minutes, or until they are translucent.

Add the red and white wines, the chicken stock, and the browned lamb shanks.

Cover the pot and place it in the oven. Braise the lamb for 3 to 4 hours, or until it is so tender that it falls off the bone.

serves 4

"This is my grandmother's recipe. When I was growing up we would go over to her house every Sunday afternoon for dinner, and it was always a real big deal. She would make her own noodles and serve them on a big platter with butter, parsley, and these braised lamb shanks on top. This recipe appeared in 'Gourmet' magazine, which I think would tickle my grandmother pink if she were alive to know."

"Garlic is one of the oldest domesticated foods in history. It has been revered for thousands of years for its flavor, medicinal qualities, and supernatural powers. Garlic in its raw form is very difficult to digest, and if you eat too much you can get stomach cramps. But, if you brown it or cook it for a long time, then you can eat large amounts with no ill effects. Once I got a recipe from Gilroy, California, which is called the Garlic Capital of the World. It called for 100 cloves of garlic to be put in a chicken that you roasted. I thought that 100 cloves sounded pretty excessive, but I went ahead and made it anyway, and it was excellent!"

Walt McDowell
423

Peruvian Lamb Stew

¼   **cup salad oil**
1   **medium red onion, finely diced**
1   **teaspoon fresh garlic, minced**
½   **teaspoon chile pequin** *(hot red chile flakes)*
½   **teaspoon ground cumin**
¼   **teaspoon salt**
¼   **teaspoon black pepper, freshly ground**
1   **pound boneless leg of lamb, fat removed, and cut into**
       ½" cubes
6   **medium red potatoes, cut into ½" cubes**
½   **cup carrots, diced medium**
½   **cup frozen peas**
¼   **cup fresh cilantro, chopped**
½   **cup beer**
1   **cup chicken stock** *(recipe on page 295)*
4   **cups cooked white rice, heated**

In a large saucepan place the salad oil and heat it on medium high until it is hot. Add the red onions, garlic, chile pequin, cumin, salt, and black pepper. Sauté the ingredients for 3 to 4 minutes, or until the onions are tender.

Add the lamb and sauté it for 3 to 4 minutes, or until it is lightly browned.

Add the remaining ingredients. Bring the liquid to a boil and then simmer the stew for 30 minutes, or until the potatoes are tender.

Serve the stew over the white rice.

serves 4

"All of the dishes I feature in my restaurant were cooked by my mother when I was growing up. It's funny, because Peruvian people are like the Mexican people who work for me here. They bring burritos to eat for lunch, and when I see them in the shopping mall they are eating burritos there, too. We both like to eat the same food out that we eat at home."

"It's important to me that people learn about Peruvian food, because no one in this country really knows what it is. They know about Chinese, Mexican, Italian, French, Japanese, Indian.....but not Peruvian! I hope that the people who buy this book will try my recipes, because the food is really delicious, with lots of strong, spicy flavors. At the same time, it is well-balanced and nutritious."

Alfredo Miranda
Alfredo's Restaurant

Mixed Grill with Field Greens and Sun-Dried Tomato Vinaigrette

Mixed Grill with Field Greens

4	lamb chops, trimmed
1	chicken breast, skin and bones removed, and cut into 4 pieces
4	2-ounce beef tenderloins
2	tablespoons extra virgin olive oil
2	cups baby field greens *(frisee, arugula, red oak, etc.)*
1	Belgian endive, washed, dried, cored, and separated
1	head radicchio, cored and leaves separated
2	Roma tomatoes, peeled, quartered, and seeded
1	yellow bell pepper, roasted, peeled, seeded, and julienned *(see chef's comments on page 159)*
	Sun-Dried Tomato Vinaigrette *(recipe on next page)*
1½	cups yams, peeled, julienned, and fried till crispy *(1 to 2 minutes)*
12	calamata olives, pitted

Brush the lamb chops, chicken, and beef tenderloins with the olive oil. Grill them on a high heat for 2 to 4 minutes, or until the desired doneness is achieved.

On each of 4 individual serving plates artfully place the baby field greens, Belgian endive, radicchio, Roma tomatoes, roasted yellow bell peppers, and grilled meats. Dribble on the Sun-Dried Tomato Vinaigrette. Garnish the plate with the fried yams and the calamata olives.

serves 4

"I put this recipe together for the summer. It's light, yet flavorful, and takes no time at all to put together. I like to combine grilled meats with greens because they make a good, low calorie meal, and yet they leave you feeling satisfied."

"In my opinion there is no recipe that comes out of the sky and is completely original. Cooking is many thousands of years old, and during this time almost everything possible has been done. Sometimes a chef can come up with a recipe that is almost original, but this is rare."

"My parents always owned a hotel restaurant in Austria, and I will never forget the wonderful aromas that were in the kitchen. By the time I was fourteen years old, I knew that I wanted to be a chef."

Martin Lackner
The Palace Restaurant

Sun-Dried Tomato Vinaigrette

8	tablespoons sun-dried tomatoes, minced
3	cloves garlic, minced
1	tablespoon fresh basil, chopped
½	tablespoon black cracked peppercorns
3	tablespoons balsamic vinegar
¾	cup extra virgin olive oil
	salt *(to taste)*

In a food processor place all of the ingredients *(except for the olive oil and salt)* and blend them together. With the processor still running, slowly dribble in the olive oil. Season the dressing with the salt.

makes approximately 1½ cups

"The sun-dried tomatoes have a strong flavor which is a good contrast to the grilled meats. Anchovies could be used as well. This dressing is wonderful with grilled fish, and it also should work as a marinade."

Martin Lackner
The Palace Restaurant

L.P. CALDWELL

Side Dishes

Southwestern Potato Pancakes

1	cup sweet potatoes, peeled, shredded, and drained for 1 hour
1	cup white potatoes, peeled, shredded, and drained for 1 hour
¼	cup green bell peppers, seeded and diced small
¼	cup red bell peppers, seeded and diced small
¼	cup yellow bell peppers, seeded and diced small
½	cup green chile peppers, diced small
1	tablespoon fresh garlic, minced
2	teaspoons fresh oregano, chopped
2	teaspoons ground cumin
1	teaspoon cayenne pepper
1	teaspoon black pepper, freshly ground
1	teaspoon salt
2	whole eggs, lightly beaten
¾	cup flour
½	cup olive oil

In a medium large bowl place all of the ingredients *(except for the olive oil)*. Mix them together so that they are well combined. Place the mixture in the refrigerator for 1 hour.

Form the mixture into 12 patties *(squeeze out the liquid)*.

In a large skillet place the olive oil and heat it on medium until it is hot. Sauté the patties for 2 to 3 minutes on each side, or until they are golden brown and heated through.

serves 6

"I developed this recipe because I wanted to have a more exotic side dish. It's slightly spicy, and really colorful, with the orange, white, green, and red ingredients."

"I love being a chef. It's very gratifying to create something that gives people so much pleasure."

Anthony Carpenter
Garfield Grill

Frijoles Refritos

4	tablespoons peanut oil
1	medium onion, diced medium
2	cloves garlic, minced
3	cups cooked pinto beans *(recipe on page 276)*, **drained** *(reserve the cooking liquid)*
1	tablespoon jalapeño chile peppers, minced
2	tablespoons fresh cilantro, chopped
¼	cup queso fresca *(see chef's comments on this page)*, **crumbled**

In a large sauté pan place the peanut oil and heat it on medium high until it is hot. Add the onions and garlic, and sauté them for 6 to 8 minutes, or until the onions are translucent.

In a food processor place ⅔ of the cooked beans and a small amount of the reserved cooking liquid, and purée them.

To the sauté pan with the onions add the puréed beans, the rest of the cooked beans, and the jalapeño chile peppers. Stir everything together well. Add enough of the reserved cooking liquid from the pinto beans so that a soupy consistency is achieved.

While stirring constantly, cook the beans on medium heat for 10 to 15 minutes, or until a thick paste is formed.

Serve the beans with the cilantro and queso fresca cheese sprinkled on top.

serves 6 to 8

"Queso fresca is a young, white Mexican cheese that is very soft. You may have difficulty in finding it. If so, use Monterey Jack cheese instead. A traditional recipe for refried beans would call for lard, but I find that peanut oil is a good substitute and will get the job done. Lard has a much richer flavor, but it is not too good for you. While you are stirring and frying the beans, use a flat wooden spatula. You want to scrape the toasted starch from the beans off the bottom of the pan and then incorporate it back into the beans. This is what develops the flavor and makes refried beans taste like nothing else."

"Whenever possible I like to use fresh produce, especially organic, and free-range meats. I appreciate the low fat approach to cooking, although it is not always possible to eliminate the dairy and still achieve the desired result. So, you have to balance things, and do the best that you can."

Peter Raub
Santa Fe School of Cooking

Sautéed Summer Squash Ratatouille

⅓   **cup olive oil**
2   **large yellow onions, sliced**
3   **cloves garlic, chopped**
6   **medium yellow squash, cut lengthwise and sliced into half circles, ¼" thick**
6   **medium zucchinis, cut lengthwise and sliced into half circles, ¼" thick**
½   **cup fresh cilantro, chopped**
4   **tablespoons red chile powder** *(medium hot)*
      salt *(to taste)*
      black pepper *(to taste)*

In a large, heavy sauté pan place the olive oil and heat it on medium high until it is hot. Add the onions and garlic, and sauté them for 6 to 8 minutes, or until the onions are translucent.

Add the remainder of the ingredients and cook them on medium low heat for 30 minutes, or until a thick stew is formed *(stir it frequently)*.

serves 6

"The origin of this recipe is a native northern New Mexican dish called calabacitas. It has a very earthy, almost primitive kind of flavor."

"The first thing that I ever cooked on my own was a birthday cake for my mother. I was only 5 years old, and I got the recipe out of our Betty Crocker cookbook. The recipe called for a pinch of salt, so I reached into the salt can, took out a fist full of salt, and threw it in the batter. The cake looked beautiful (for a 5-year-old) and we had the party at my sister-in-law's house. My grandmother took the first bite and she spit it right out. Everyone started laughing when they tasted the cake, and I was chagrined. My sister-in-law, being as conservative as the Pennsylvania Dutch all are, took the cake and threw it out for the birds to eat. The next day there were dead birds everywhere."

"When I was little and had a headache, my grand-mother would press an aspirin into a gummy mint leaf, and give it to me to eat. I would bite into it, not knowing the aspirin was there, and it would taste like bitter mint. The funny thing is, to this day I still kind of crave them."

Jonathan Horst
Adobo Catering

Potato Chapatis

"This recipe was given to
me by an East Indian man
who is a very good friend.
He's a wizard of a cook!
Chapatis are a traditional
Indian flatbread. They are
good with meals, or as
snacks."

3	large white potatoes, boiled, peeled, mashed, and cooled
2	tablespoons sesame oil
1	teaspoon cumin seeds, roasted
1	teaspoon salt
1	cup whole wheat pastry flour
½	cup unbleached white flour
½	cup whole wheat bread flour
¼	cup unsalted butter, melted and clarified

In a medium bowl place the cooled, mashed potatoes. Add the
sesame oil and mix it in.

Add the roasted cumin seeds and salt, and stir them in.

Slowly add the three flours, and mix them in with your hands
until the dough is soft, but holds its shape. (You may not need to
use all of the flour. See chef's comments on this page.) Cover the
dough and let it sit for 2 hours.

Divide the dough into 12 pieces. On a floured board (unbleached
white flour is best), very gently roll out each chapati until it is ¹⁄₁₆"
thick and in a round shape.

Heat a seasoned griddle (or cast iron skillet) on medium until it is
hot. Place the chapatis on top and cook them on one side for 1
to 2 minutes, or until they are slightly puffed and golden brown
on the bottom. Brush them with the clarified butter and then flip
them over. Cook the other side until they are golden brown.
Brush on the rest of the butter.

serves 6

"When you are making the
dough you may not have
to use all of the flour
because the size of the
potatoes will vary. The
dough should be very soft
and pliable. If you make it
too stiff the chapatis will
be tough. Rolling out the
dough may take some
practice.....use gentle, even
pressure."

Lynn Walters
The Natural Cafe

Fried Zucchini Flowers

1   **cup ricotta cheese, crumbled**
½   **cup Parmesan cheese, freshly grated**
2   **red bell peppers, roasted, peeled, seeded, and diced** *(see
         chef's comments on page 159)*
2   **ounces sun-dried tomatoes, reconstituted and diced**
2   **tablespoons fresh basil, chopped**
         salt *(to taste)*
         black pepper *(to taste)*
12   **large zucchini flowers** *(tightly closed)*
½   **cup Parmesan cheese, freshly grated**
½   **cup flour**
         salt *(to taste)*
         black pepper *(to taste)*
2   **eggs, whisked together with 2 tablespoons water**
½   **cup peanut oil**

In a medium bowl place the ricotta cheese, the first ½ cup of
Parmesan cheese, red bell peppers, sun-dried tomatoes, basil,
salt, and black pepper. Mix the ingredients together so that they
are well combined.

Stuff each zucchini flower with the cheese mixture. Close the
flower around the filling.

In another bowl place the second ½ cup of Parmesan cheese,
flour, salt, and black pepper. Mix the ingredients together.

Dip the flowers in the egg wash and then in the flour mixture.

In a large sauté pan place the peanut oil and heat it on medium
high until it is hot. Add the stuffed flowers and sauté them for 1
minute, or until they are golden brown. Drain them on paper
towels.

serves 4

*"Another name for
zucchini flowers is squash
blossoms. They are
available from June to the
middle of August before
any freezing weather
comes. A lot of good
produce stores carry them,
and they can be specially
ordered. They don't really
taste like squash.....rather,
they have a light, fresh
green flavor. This recipe
will work with any kind of
squash flowers, and they
can be served as an
appetizer or side dish."*

Steven Lemon
Pranzo Italian Grill

*"I think that the secret of
being a good manager is to
be a good listener. Here at
Pranzo we all take our jobs
very seriously, and yet at
the same time we try to
have fun."*

Judy Seymour
Pranzo Italian Grill

"Calabacitas is a squash dish, and it is very traditional in northern New Mexico. There are as many recipes for this as there are recipes for spaghetti sauce in Italy. Everybody who was involved in the Santa Fe School of Cooking researched into old recipes, and finally we came up with this version as being the best. The recipe here is a side dish, but if you added some cooked and shredded chicken, then it could be an entrée. My only caution is not to overcook the vegetables. Just let them steam enough so that they are heated through and somewhat soft, but still crisp."

"When I am teaching the cooking classes I crack jokes and go off on different tangents, depending upon what the audience is like, and what their demands are. We get a lot of Europeans and people from different cultural backgrounds, which always makes it interesting. The English hate hot food, and they tell me that immediately, so I have to kind of re-route myself and approach the class from their perspective. All in all, everybody comes together and has a good time."

Peter Raub
Santa Fe School of Cooking

Calabacitas

2	**tablespoons butter**
1	**tablespoon olive oil**
4	**cups calabacitas** (yellow and green squash), **diced**
2	**cloves garlic, minced**
1	**medium white onion, halved and sliced**
6	**scallions, finely chopped**
1	**cup green chile peppers, roasted, peeled, seeded and chopped** (see chef's comments on page 159)
1	**cup corn kernels**
2	**cups chicken stock** (recipe on page 295)
	salt (to taste)
	black pepper (to taste)
½	**cup Monterey Jack cheese, grated**
½	**cup tomatoes, diced**
2	**tablespoons fresh cilantro, chopped**

In a large sauté pan place the butter and olive oil, and heat them on medium high until they are hot. Add the calabacitas, garlic, and white onions, and sauté them for 5 minutes.

Add the scallions and sauté them for 1 minute.

Add the green chile peppers, corn, and chicken stock. Simmer the ingredients for 20 minutes. Add the salt and black pepper.

Add the Monterey Jack cheese, tomatoes, and cilantro. Simmer the ingredients for 5 minutes.

serves 4 to 6

Pinto Beans

2	cups pinto beans, well cleaned
2	quarts cold water
4	quarts chicken stock *(recipe on page 295)*
1	chipotle chile pepper
1	medium onion, diced
1	clove garlic, minced
2	bay leaves
1	teaspoon epazote *(see chef's comments on this page)*
1	teaspoon ground cumin
1	teaspoon dried oregano
	salt *(to taste)*

In a large saucepan place the pinto beans and water. Simmer the ingredients for 1 hour. Strain and rinse the beans, and then return them to the pot.

Add the remainder of the ingredients and simmer them for 3 hours, or until the beans are tender and infused with flavor *(remove the chipotle pepper and bay leaves before serving).*

serves 10

"Epazote is an herb that is used throughout Mexico. When it is cooked with beans it reduces their gaseousness and makes them easier to digest. The flavor is very pronounced, and it has a slightly resinous taste. I really love it, but a lot of people don't feel the same way. The great thing is that when you purée it with the pinto beans you can barely detect that it is there. This is true for most beans, except black beans, where the flavor comes through very strongly. You can find the herb in Mexican specialty shops or in good supermarkets. Actually, if you know what to look for you can find it wild. It's a common backyard weed and it grows all over the United States."

"Some optional seasonings that you can add to the beans are salt pork, bacon, sage, thyme, oregano, or coriander. My own feeling is that beans have such a wonderful flavor all by themselves, that you shouldn't add too many other ingredients.....just 1 or 2 at the most. Eat these beans with posole and you will have a perfect protein."

Peter Raub
Santa Fe School of Cooking

Spicy Mixed Vegetables

¼	cup vegetable oil
1	teaspoon ground cumin
1	potato, peeled and diced small
2	carrots, peeled and diced small
¼	cauliflower, cut into florets
1	teaspoon fresh garlic, minced
1	teaspoon fresh ginger root, peeled and minced
⅛	teaspoon cayenne pepper
½	teaspoon turmeric
1	teaspoon salt
½	cup green beans, strings removed, and cut into 1" long pieces
½	cup frozen green peas
½	cup garam masala *(see chef's comments on page 230)*
1	tablespoon fresh cilantro, chopped

In a large skillet place the vegetable oil and heat it on medium high until it is hot. Add the cumin and stir it for 1 minute, or until it browns.

Add the potatoes, carrots, and cauliflower. Sauté the ingredients for 1 minute.

Add the garlic, ginger, cayenne pepper, turmeric, and salt. Stir the ingredients together. Cover the pan and cook the vegetables on low heat for 10 minutes *(stir them occasionally so that they do not stick)*.

Add the green beans, peas, and garam masala. Stir the ingredients together. Cover the pan and cook the vegetables for 5 minutes more, or until they are done.

Garnish the vegetables with the chopped cilantro.

serves 4

"With this recipe you can add whatever vegetables you want, or you can eliminate what you don't like. People are strange about vegetables. Sometimes there is one kind that you hate, for no apparent reason. Myself, I can't stand baby corn."

Baldev Singh
India Palace

"Every day for lunch we serve a buffet that includes many different Indian dishes. Some of the items, like Tandoori chicken, are never varied, but most of them are. We decide what we are going to serve each day by what side we get out of the bed on that morning!"

Nitin Bhakta
India Palace

Allogobi

¼	**cup vegetable oil**
½	**onion, finely chopped**
1	**teaspoon fresh garlic, finely minced**
1	**teaspoon fresh ginger root, peeled and finely minced**
½	**teaspoon cumin seeds**
1	**tomato, thinly sliced**
1	**potato, diced small**
2½	**cups cauliflower, cut into florets**
1	**teaspoon turmeric**
½	**teaspoon cayenne pepper**
½	**teaspoon garam masala** *(see chef's comments on page 230)*

In a large skillet place the vegetable oil and heat it on medium until it is hot. Add the onions, garlic, ginger, and cumin seeds. Sauté the ingredients for 8 to 10 minutes, or until the onions are brown.

Add the tomatoes and potatoes, and sauté them for 5 minutes.

While stirring constantly, slowly add the remaining ingredients, one at a time.

Reduce the heat to medium low. Cover the pan and cook the vegetables for 5 minutes, or until they are tender.

serves 4

"In India we don't eat a lot of chicken or meat, and beef is never consumed. We do eat a lot of vegetables, though, and this is a great recipe that is very popular in our country. It is a mildly spicy dish.....on a scale of 1 to 10 (with 10 being the hottest), I would say that it is a 3 or 4."

Nitin Bhakta
India Palace

"This dish is very simple to make, although it would be helpful if you could watch me make it first. There are a lot of subtle things in Indian cooking that cannot be communicated in recipes."

Baldev Singh
India Palace

Quinoa

¼	**cup olive oil**
1	**cup quinoa** *(uncooked), (see chef's comments on this page)*
1	**bay leaf**
1½	**cups water**
2	**tablespoons olive oil**
½	**red bell pepper, seeds removed, and diced**
½	**bunch scallions, diced**
½	**teaspoon fresh garlic, finely chopped**
¼	**cup carrots, grated**
	salt *(to taste)*

In a heavy, medium saucepan place the ¼ cup of olive oil and heat it on high until it is hot. Add the quinoa and stir it so that the grains are well coated with the oil.

Add the bay leaf. Stir the ingredients for 5 minutes, or until the quinoa is lightly toasted.

Carefully add the water *(it will sizzle)*, cover the pan, and bring it to a boil. Reduce the heat to low. Simmer the ingredients for 20 minutes, or until the quinoa is cooked. Remove the pan from the heat and let it cool.

In a large sauté pan place the 2 tablespoons of olive oil and heat it on medium high until it is hot. Add the red bell peppers, scallions, and garlic. Sauté the ingredients for 2 minutes.

Add the grated carrots and cooked quinoa. Sauté the ingredients for 2 minutes more. Add the salt and stir it in.

serves 4 to 6

"Quinoa is a protein-rich grain that only grows at high altitudes. The flavor is nutty, especially when the grains are first heated in oil. It has similar properties to rice in that if you overcook it, it will be gloppy, and if you undercook it, it will be hard. As with rice, it is very versatile, and you can prepare it in many different ways."

"My grandmother used to live in a hotel, and our family would frequently eat with her in the hotel restaurant. The waitresses knew me and liked me, and they would take me around with them for entertainment. I was fascinated by the kitchen.....I loved the smells, the yelling, and watching the chefs bang all those pots and pans around. But my favorite place to hang out was at the hotel newsstand, where every so often I got to sneak a look at the 'Police Gazette'."

Ned Laventall
El Farol

Posole

4	**cups posole, rinsed and cleaned twice**
1	**pound pork bones**
2	**quarts cold water**
2	**tablespoons vegetable oil**
1½	**large onions, diced**
2	**cloves garlic, minced**
2	**quarts chicken stock** *(recipe on page 295)*
1	**teaspoon dried Mexican oregano**
1	**teaspoon coriander seeds, crushed**
1	**tablespoon chile caribe** *(crushed red chile peppers)*
2	**bay leaves**
12	**flour tortillas** *(recipe on page 290),* **warmed**

In a large stockpot place the posole, pork bones, and cold water. Cover the pot and simmer the posole for 2 hours, or until the kernels begin to burst. Strain and rinse the posole, and return it to the pot *(along with the pork bones)*.

In a medium sauté pan place the vegetable oil and heat it on medium high until it is hot. Add the onions and garlic, and sauté them for 6 to 8 minutes, or until they are tender.

Add the sautéed onions and garlic to the posole. Add the chicken stock, Mexican oregano, coriander seeds, chile caribe, and bay leaves.

Simmer the ingredients for 1 to 2 hours, or until the posole is soft. Serve the posole with the tortillas.

serves 12

"Posole has been popular with Native Americans all over the country for centuries. Depending on where you are it will be prepared different ways and have different names. For instance, in the South it is called hominy. Traditional folks in New Mexico will almost always add pork.....it is a given. So, if you wish to prepare this in the more classical way, then add some lean pork that is cut into bite size pieces. For additional flavoring you can add pork bones, bay leaves, fresh cilantro, red or green chile, lime juice, or azafran, which is a Mexican saffron. There are so many variations to posole that you can pretty much add whatever you want. I like it to be fairly firm with a clear broth, which is what you will get with this recipe. If you want a softer posole with a more starchy broth, then cook it for another hour or so."

"On Christmas Eve every traditional family has a big pot of posole simmering on their stove, and each recipe is the very best in the whole world! Friends and family will go around visiting each other, and everyone samples a steaming hot bowl of the soup, along with flour tortillas."

Peter Raub
Santa Fe School of Cooking

Escabeche

1½	cups salad oil
½	cup white vinegar
1	tablespoon Dijon mustard
2	tablespoons fresh oregano
2	teaspoons salt *(or to taste)*
1	teaspoon black pepper *(or to taste)*
1	cup broccoli florets, cooked al dente
1	cup cauliflower florets, cooked al dente
1	red bell pepper, seeded and julienned
1	green bell pepper, seeded and julienned
1	cup carrots, sliced and cooked al dente
1	small red onion, julienned
1	small yellow onion, julienned
1	cup baby corn
1	cup pickled jalapeño chile peppers *(whole)*, **drained** *(reserve the juice)*
1	cup pickled jalapeño chile peppers, sliced and drained *(reserve the juice)*

In a food processor place the salad oil, white vinegar, Dijon mustard, oregano, salt, and black pepper. Blend the ingredients for 5 minutes.

In a large bowl place the vinaigrette and the remainder of the ingredients. Mix them together with your hands so that the vegetables are well coated. Add some of the reserved jalapeño juice to taste. Marinate the vegetables in the refrigerator for 2 to 8 hours.

makes approximately 10 cups

"This is a pickled vegetable mixture that we serve as a condiment with all meals. You can vary the vegetables any way you want, but this is the exact recipe we have been using since day one at the restaurant. The jalapeños are hot, and their heat seeps into all of the other vegetables. Some of you may want to reduce the amounts."

"There is a myth that all Mexicans love food that is spicy. We have some guys in our kitchen who come from Chihuahua and Durango, and they think that we Americans are crazy! Once in a while they may use a few jalapeños, but very sparingly."

Marc Greene
Old Mexico Grill

Crispy Matchstick Leeks

3   **leeks** (*white parts only*), **sliced into thin matchsticks, washed, and dried**
2   **tablespoons cornstarch**
2   **cups peanut oil** (*or as needed*)
     salt (*to taste*)

Toss the leeks with the cornstarch.

In a medium large sauté pan place the peanut oil (*it should be 3" deep*) and heat it on medium high heat until it is hot. Add the leeks and cook them for 5 minutes, or until they are barely a golden color.

Remove them with a slotted spoon and then drain them on paper towels. Sprinkle on the salt.

serves 6

"These fried leeks are wonderfully fun and delicious. You can sprinkle them on salads, soups, or noodles (or should I say PASTA, since that's the current 'in' term for noodles), and they make a beautiful garnish. They are so good that you can't stop eating them.....kind of like potato chips."

Katharine Kagel
Cafe Pasqual's

Salami Sandwich

½   **tablespoon aioli** (*see chef's comments on this page*)
½   **loaf focaccia bread** (*recipe on page 291*), **sliced in half horizontally and toasted**
6   **slices Finochio salami**
2   **ounces pickled vegetables** (*or pickled peppers*), **chopped**
2   **slices Fontina cheese**

Spread the aioli on each slice of the bread.

On the bottom slice place the salami, pickled vegetables, and cheese.

Heat the bottom part on the sandwich in the oven until the cheese is melted. Place the other slice of focaccia on top. Slice the sandwich diagonally.

serves 1

"Aioli is a roasted garlic mayonnaise. In your food processor put 3 egg yolks, 2 whole eggs, 1 ounce of lemon juice, and ⅛ teaspoon of salt. Blend everything, and then, with the processor still running, slowly dribble in about 3 cups of corn oil. Add 12 cloves of roasted garlic that are finely minced."

Steven Lemon
Pranzo Italian Grill

Salsify and Wild Mushrooms

2	**tablespoons butter**
¼	**pound wild mushrooms** (oyster, trumpet, shiitake, inoki, etc.), **washed, thick ends trimmed off, and cut into bite size pieces**
1	**small can salsify, drained** (see chef's comments on this page)
¼	**cup fresh Italian parsley, chopped**
	salt (to taste)

In a medium sauté pan place the butter and heat it on medium until it has melted and is hot. Add the mushrooms and sauté them for 3 to 4 minutes, or until they are slightly wilted.

Add the salsify and toss it in for 1 minute, or until it is heated.

Add the parsley and salt, and toss them in.

serves 4 to 6

Red Cabbage and Brown Rice Sauté

2	**tablespoons canola oil**
2	**cups red cabbage, finely chopped**
½	**package Lundberg Wahini Brown Rice, cooked**
	salt (to taste)

In a large sauté pan place the canola oil and heat it on medium until it is hot. Add the red cabbage and sauté it for 20 to 30 minutes, or until it is tender.

Add the brown rice to the cabbage and stir it in. Season the dish with the salt.

serves 4

Griddled Japanese Eggplant

5   tablespoons fresh garlic, chopped
2   serrano chile peppers, seeded and finely minced
1   tablespoon red chile powder
⅓   cup soy sauce
½   cup toasted sesame oil
5   Japanese eggplants, sliced lengthwise into ⅛" thick pieces

In a medium bowl place the garlic, serrano chile peppers, red chile powder, soy sauce, and toasted sesame oil. Whisk the ingredients together.

Add the eggplant pieces and let them marinate for 2 to 6 hours.

On a seasoned, hot griddle *(or a large, hot, nonstick sauté pan)* place the marinated eggplant pieces. Cook them for 3 minutes on each side, or until they are lightly browned.

serves 6 to 8

> "Japanese eggplants are wonderful. They require no preparation with salt in order to drain out the bitterness, as with regular eggplants. In the restaurant we serve the eggplant with fried leeks and marinated scallops (the recipes are on pages 282 and 176)."
>
> "I love to cook because it is a total experience.....it is life feeding life. Cooking keeps me aware of how precious it is to be alive. I am humbled to be able to give nourishment and pleasure to others."
>
> *Katharine Kagel*
> Cafe Pasqual's

Barley Tabbouleh

1   cup barley, roasted *(see chef's comments on this page)* **and cooked**
½   cup onions, chopped
½   cup scallions, chopped
1   cup fresh parsley, chopped
¼   cup fresh basil, chopped
¼   cup fresh mint, chopped
½   cup olive oil
2   tablespoons balsamic vinegar
      salt and black pepper *(to taste)*
1   tomato, skinned, seeded, and chopped

In a large bowl place all of the ingredients *(except for the chopped tomatoes)* and mix them together with a wooden spoon. Garnish each serving with the chopped tomatoes.

serves 4

> "Spread the barley on top of some wax paper that is on a baking sheet, so that there is just one layer. Roast it in the oven at 325° for 10 to 15 minutes, or until it turns a light brown color."
>
> "This is a very healthy Middle Eastern dish that you can serve with anything. It would be great to serve at a potluck dinner, along with little pieces of pita bread, or sliced up baguettes. Stir it with a wooden spoon, rather than a metal one, so that the acids don't interact with the metal and give it a funny taste."
>
> *Mark Hawrylak*
> The Evergreen

Black Beans

2	cups black beans, washed and cleaned
6	cups water *(or as needed)*
1	medium onion, chopped
1	tablespoon granulated garlic
2	tablespoons salt

In a medium large stockpot place all of the ingredients. Bring them to a boil and then reduce the heat to low. Simmer the beans for 2 to 3 hours or until they are very tender *(add more water as needed and skim the foam off the top)*.

serves 4 to 6

Sugar Snap Peas with Mint Raita

2	cups plain yogurt
2	tablespoons fresh mint, minced
¼	teaspoon salt
¾	cup water
1	pound fresh sugar snap peas, strings removed
1	teaspoon butter
	salt *(to taste)*

In a medium bowl place the yogurt, mint, and salt. Mix the ingredients together well. Cover the raita and let it chill in the refrigerator for 1 hour.

In a medium saucepan *(covered)* place the water and bring it to a boil over high heat. Add the sugar snap peas and boil them for 2 to 4 minutes, or only until they turn bright green.

Drain the peas. Add the butter and salt, and stir them to coat the peas. Serve the peas with the chilled raita on the side.

serves 4 to 6

"When I was growing up my mother and father both worked, so I usually tried to have something on the stove when they came home. I have always loved to cook and I have always known that I was going to be a chef. My dream is to one day have my own restaurant in the Pacific Northwest."

Sean McKim
Guadalupe Cafe

"Sugar snap peas may be difficult to find in the grocery store. You can substitute snowpeas, but they won't be as crunchy or flavorful. We grow these peas in my garden. They are beautiful plants that are good for the soil, and children love to pick and eat them."

Lynn Walters
The Natural Cafe

Potpourri

Jalapeño Cheese Baguette

2	cups unbleached white flour
1	package dry yeast
2	tablespoons honey
1¼	cups water
1	teaspoon salt
¼	cup unbleached white flour
¼	cup unbleached white flour
¼	cup blue cornmeal
¼	cup unbleached white flour
2	cups jalapeño cheese, grated

In a medium large mixing bowl place the 2 cups of unbleached white flour, yeast, honey, and water. Using the main beater, beat the ingredients with a heavy duty electric mixer (preferably a Kitchen Aid) on slow speed until the flour is incorporated. Increase the speed to medium high and beat the mixture until the dough balls up onto the beater. Switch the main beater for the dough hook, and knead the dough for 10 minutes.

Add the salt and mix it in for 1 minute.

One at a time, add in this order, and mix on low speed, the first ¼ cup of flour, the second ¼ cup of flour, the blue cornmeal, and the third ¼ cup of flour. Knead the dough for 5 minutes.

Cover the dough in the bowl with a towel and place a plate on top. Let the dough rise for 1 to 2 hours, or until it doubles in size *(the length of time it takes for the dough to double in size will vary, depending on the altitude)*. Punch down the dough, and let it rise for 1 hour, or until it again doubles in size.

Place the dough on a floured board and divide it in half. Cover the dough with a towel and let it sit for 5 minutes.

Form the dough into two 6" by 8" rectangles. On top of each rectangle sprinkle on ½ cup of the jalapeño cheese so that it forms a lengthwise strip approximately ⅓ of the distance from the top of the dough. Fold the top ⅓ of the dough over so that the cheese is encased. Fold the dough over the bottom ⅓, so that the original rectangle has been folded over twice, lengthwise, with the cheese inside.

(continued on next page)

"This is a classic French bread recipe to which I added blue cornmeal for texture, honey for sweetness, and jalapeño cheese for flavor. The cheese oozes out and the bread doesn't rise much, so it is not a perfect, pristine looking loaf. It's more like peasant food, and it looks good in an earthy, organic way. People love this bread.....it's really delicious!"

"It's difficult to explain in words how to form the baguettes with the cheese inside. If possible, refer to a baking cookbook with pictures."

"If you aren't a baker and have never made bread before, I would still encourage you to make this recipe. If you follow the instructions it should come out well, especially if you have a heavy duty electric mixer. If not, you can knead the dough by hand, but you have to do it correctly. Fold the dough, push it down with your knuckles, turn the dough a quarter of a turn, and keep repeating this process for as long as you would mix it with an electric mixer. The gluten in the dough needs to develop so that it will rise."

Tom Wright
Galisteo Inn

Pound the dough with your hands so that the length is increased by ½.

Sprinkle the other ½ cup of the cheese down the center of the dough. Fold the dough over the cheese, lengthwise. Pinch the crease together. Pound out the dough so that it is 18" long.

Fold the top ½ of the dough over. Pinch the crease together so that it is well sealed. Roll the dough with your hands so that a tube shape is formed. Smooth out the seam.

Place a pan of water in the oven. Preheat the oven to 425°.

Place the two loaves in a baguette pan (or on a flat baking sheet covered with a piece of lightly buttered parchment paper). Cover them with a towel and let them rise until they are doubled in size.

Bake the baguettes for 25 minutes, or until they are golden brown (if you thump them with your finger they should sound hollow).

makes 2 loaves

Mini Blue Corn Muffins

½	cup brown sugar
½	cup white sugar
½	cup margarine, softened
½	cup shortening, softened
2¼	cups blue cornmeal
3	cups white flour
1	teaspoon baking powder
1½	cups milk
5	eggs

Preheat the oven to 350°.

In a medium bowl place the brown and white sugar, and mix them together. Add the margarine and shortening, and mix them in well. Add the blue cornmeal, white flour, baking powder, and milk. Mix the ingredients together. Add the eggs and mix them in.

Pour the batter into greased mini muffin pans. Bake the muffins for 15 minutes, or until the tops begin to brown.

makes approximately 6 dozen muffins

Flour Tortillas

2	cups flour
1	teaspoon salt
3	teaspoons baking powder
2	tablespoons canola oil
1	cup water *(or as needed)*, **very hot**

In a medium bowl place the flour, salt, and baking powder. Mix the ingredients together so that they are well blended.

Add the oil and mix it in well. Add enough of the hot water and mix it in so that a soft *(but not sticky)* dough is formed.

Knead the dough 15 times so that a smooth ball is formed. Divide the dough into 10 balls and flatten them.

On a lightly floured surface roll out each ball so that a round, thin tortilla is formed *(see chef's comments on this page)*.

Heat a seasoned griddle or cast iron skillet on medium high until it is hot. Cook each tortilla for 15 to 20 seconds on each side.

makes 10 tortillas

"You can buy fairly good flour tortillas, but I think that the homemade ones are better. Traditional recipes call for lard or shortening. We used to use Crisco, but changed to canola oil. Nobody really knows what Crisco is, except for the people who make it. Look at the list of ingredients on the can.....it is frighteningly long!"

"The hard part in making the tortillas is the rolling out of the dough. It is fairly elastic and you have to relax the gluten. Start from the middle of each ball, and roll it away from you. Rotate the dough a quarter turn after each stroke. Keep doing this until the tortilla is the right shape and thickness."

Peter Raub
Santa Fe School of Cooking

"I have an employee, Oscar Mendez, who is from Mexico, and he has been rolling tortillas since he can first remember. One day he came rushing out of the cooking school to where I was in the store, and told me, 'There are a bunch of gringos in there rolling out tortillas and they all look like a map of the United States.....they are not even close to round!' So now I have Oscar demonstrate how to roll them, and he's wonderful."

Susan Curtis
Santa Fe School of Cooking

Focaccia

1½	**cups warm water**
2	**tablespoons yeast**
2	**teaspoons salt**
2	**tablespoons olive oil**
4	**cups flour** (or as needed)
¼	**cup fresh rosemary**
2	**tablespoons lemon zest** (outer yellow part grated off)
½	**cup white raisins**
3	**tablespoons olive oil**

In a medium bowl place the warm water and yeast. Let the yeast sit for 5 minutes, or until it is dissolved.

Add the salt and the 2 tablespoons of olive oil, and stir them in.

Add half of the flour and mix it in (so that it looks like paste).

Add the rosemary, lemon zest, and white raisins, and mix them in.

Turn the dough onto a floured surface. Knead in the remaining flour (or as needed) so that a soft, silky textured dough is formed.

Place the dough in an oiled bowl and cover it with a towel. Let it sit for 35 to 40 minutes, or until it has doubled in size.

Divide the dough in half. Use a rolling pin to form two 10" rounds that are ¾" to 1" thick.

Place the dough on a greased baking sheet. Brush the tops with some of the 3 tablespoons of olive oil. Cover the dough with a towel and let it sit for 30 minutes.

Preheat the oven to 350°.

Lightly press your fingertips into the top of the loaves to give them some texture (be careful not to collapse them).

Place the loaves on a flat sheet and bake them for 30 minutes, or until they are golden brown, and firm on the top and bottom. Remove the loaves from the oven and brush them with the rest of the olive oil.

makes 2 loaves

"Focaccia is a flavorful, round, flat Italian bread that has lots of uses. You can cut it in wedges and serve it with a meal, or you can slice it horizontally and use it for a sandwich. Spread on your vinegar and oil, garlic mayonnaise, or whatever dressing you are using, and then add your meats, cheeses, and vegetables. Wrap it up tightly with plastic and let it sit for several hours. Then cut it into wedges and serve it either warm or cold. There are herbs that you can add to the dough which add wonderful flavors. Some good combinations that we use at the restaurant are roasted garlic and sun-dried tomatoes, scallions and parsley, crushed black peppercorns and Parmesan cheese, or sage and caramelized onions. Chopped prosciutto or cooked Italian sausage also can be added."

Jane Stacey
Pranzo Italian Grill

"Jane does all of the breads and desserts in the restaurant. I like having her around because she is very talented. I can bounce ideas off her and she gives me good feedback."

Steven Lemon
Pranzo Italian Grill

Beefy Tomato Starter

⅔   cup beef bouillon
1⅔   cups V-8 juice
4   teaspoons lemon juice, freshly squeezed
¼   teaspoon celery salt
2   dashes Worcestershire sauce
2   dashes tabasco sauce
4   celery sticks

In a small saucepan place all of the ingredients (except for the celery sticks) and bring them to a boil over high heat. Reduce the heat to low and simmer the mixture for 1 minute. Pour the liquid into 4 mugs and garnish each one with a celery stick.

serves 4

"Here's a good 'hair of the dog' drink, minus the alcohol. Make it when you have partied too hard the night before, because it's great for putting the nutrients back into your body."

"For some reason, men absolutely love this drink. It tastes very beefy and substantial."

Louise Stewart
Grant Corner Inn

Hot Cranberry Cup

1   cup apple cider
1½   cups cranberry cocktail juice
12   whole cloves
12   whole allspice
4   sticks cinnamon

In a medium saucepan place all of the ingredients (except for the cinnamon sticks) and bring them to a boil on high heat. Reduce the heat to low and simmer the mixture for 20 minutes.

Strain the liquid and then pour it into 4 heated mugs. Garnish each drink with a cinnamon stick.

serves 4

"This is a wonderful winter drink that is perfect to sip by a cozy fire when it's cold and snowy outside. The red color is festive and it's great for the holidays. Kids especially seem to love it."

Louise Stewart
Grant Corner Inn

Piña Colada Cooler

½   **cup fresh pineapple chunks**
2   **teaspoons lime juice, freshly squeezed**
½   **cup pineapple juice, chilled**
3   **teaspoons cream of coconut** (canned)
10   **ice cubes**
4   **pineapple wedges**

In a blender place all of the ingredients (except for the pineapple wedges). Blend them on high speed for 1 minute, or until the mixture is smooth and creamy.

Pour the mixture into 4 frosted goblets and garnish them with the pineapple wedges.

serves 4

"This is an absolutely delicious drink with no alcohol. Of course, some might prefer it with some dark rum! Make sure that you put the goblets in the freezer so that they get really ice-cold and frosty."

Louise Stewart
Grant Corner Inn

Ginger Lemon Tea

1   **gallon water**
1   **cup fresh ginger root, peeled and thinly sliced**
2   **cups honey**
2   **cups lemon juice, freshly squeezed**

In a large stockpot place the water and ginger, and bring them to a boil over high heat. Reduce the heat to low and simmer the ingredients for 30 minutes. Add the honey and lemon juice, and stir them in.

Strain the tea and then chill it overnight. Serve the tea over ice with lemon and orange slices.

makes 5 quarts

"Here is a wonderful drink for those hot summer days. It's an excellent thirst quencher, and the ginger gives it an energizing quality. I like to make teas out of ingredients other than leaves. Tea is an infusion of flavors, and you can make it out of almost anything."

Pete Zimmer
Inn of the Anasazi

Scallop Broth

1	tablespoon olive oil
1½	cups scallops
1	tablespoon olive oil
½	cup celery, chopped
½	cup carrots, chopped
1	cup onions, chopped
4	cups white wine
2	cups water
	salt *(to taste)*
	black pepper *(to taste)*

In a medium sauté pan place the first tablespoon of olive oil and heat it on high until it is hot. Add the scallops and sear them for 45 seconds on each side. Set them aside.

In a medium large stockpot place the other tablespoon of olive oil and heat it on medium high until it is hot. Add the celery, carrots, and onions. Cover the pot with a lid and sweat the vegetables for 5 minutes *(shake the pot so that they don't burn)*.

Add the seared scallops and the white wine. Cover the pot again with the lid and sweat the ingredients for 10 minutes more.

Add the water and simmer the ingredients for 30 minutes.

Strain the broth and then season it with the salt and the black pepper.

Note: This broth may be frozen.

makes approximately 1½ quarts

"This recipe calls for scallops, but you can use any kind of fish to make a good broth. As with all stocks, it can be frozen for future use."

Frank Peña
Ogelvies

"I am not a chef, but I know the restaurant business inside and out. To be a good manager you have to know a lot about preparing food.....everything from cutting meat to washing dishes. Eventually you have to do it all, depending on what unexpected crisis happens. I'm not the type of manager who sits in an office all day.....I'm a working manager, getting my hands dirty, and doing whatever is necessary to have the restaurant run smoothly."

Eric Sanders
Ogelvies

Basic Chicken Stock

1	**gallon water** *(or as needed)*
4	**pounds chicken bones**
2	**large onions, coarsely chopped**
2	**large carrots, coarsely chopped**
1	**bunch fresh parsley**
1	**tablespoon black peppercorns**

In a large stockpot place the water and chicken bones. Bring the liquid to a simmer *(skim off the foam that rises to the surface)*. Add the remaining ingredients and simmer them very slowly for 6 to 8 hours. *(If necessary, add more water so that the ingredients are covered.)*

Strain the liquid through a fine sieve. Refrigerate the stock. Skim off the fat that rises to the top.

Note: This will keep in the refrigerator for 5 days, or in the freezer for 1 month.

makes approximately 4 quarts

"You need a big pot to make this chicken stock. Instead of bones, you can use a whole chicken, and then use the meat for other recipes. A simple way to view making chicken stock is this: put whatever bones or chicken pieces you have in a pot, add your carrots, onions, parsley, and black peppercorns, cover everything with water, and then simmer it. A good rule of thumb for the length of time to cook different stocks is 2 hours for vegetable stock, 8 hours for chicken stock, and 24 hours for veal or beef stock."

Steven Lemon
Pranzo Italian Grill

Blackening Spices

1	cup paprika
1½	teaspoons cayenne pepper
1	teaspoon granulated garlic
1	teaspoon fennel seeds
½	teaspoon onion salt
½	teaspoon dried oregano
½	teaspoon dried thyme
1½	teaspoons salt
½	teaspoon white pepper
½	teaspoon black pepper

In a medium small bowl place all of the ingredients and mix them together well. Store them in a tightly covered jar.

makes approximately 1⅛ *cups*

"There is a story that the original concept of blackened food was a mistake. The Cajun chef who invented it left something on the stove too long and it got black. He tasted it, liked it.....and a whole new way of cooking was born!"

Isaac Modivah
Ore House

New Orleans Spice Mix

1	tablespoon cayenne pepper
2	tablespoons garlic powder
2	tablespoons dried thyme
2	tablespoons dried basil
3	tablespoons paprika
9	tablespoons salt
2	tablespoons black pepper
1	tablespoon white pepper

Place all of the ingredients in a jar with a tight lid. Shake the spices together so that they are well mixed.

Store the spice mix in the refrigerator.

makes approximately 1 cup

"This spice mix is a typical New Orleans' taste. You can use it to season any food that you want. The spices used are in balanced proportions so that the completed mixture does not overwhelm what you are cooking. It's a wonderful seasoning for enhancing the flavor of food."

Skip Kirkland
Pontchartrain

Magic Spice Mix

½   **cup Spanish paprika**
½   **cup sugar**
½   **cup cayenne pepper**
⅔   **cup coriander seeds, crushed**
½   **cup cinnamon**
½   **cup salt**

Place all of the ingredients in a tightly covered container. Shake them together so that they are well mixed.

makes 3¼ cups

"This is the most exceptional spice mix I have ever tasted. If you put it on meat, poultry, or fish before you grill it, you will not believe how outstanding the flavor is. Use it and you will get a reputation for being a very talented cook!"

Pete Zimmer
Inn of the Anasazi

Hot Desert Seasonings Mix

1   **cup salt**
¼   **cup cayenne pepper**
¼   **cup white pepper**

Place the ingredients in a jar with a tight lid. Shake them together so that they are well blended.

makes 1½ cups

"This recipe is so simple that it's embarrassing, and yet it has all of the necessary components for a correct seasoning. The salt develops the flavor, the white pepper gives you heat, and the cayenne pepper gives you a nutty, more aromatic heat on the back of your palate. Use this mix whenever salt and pepper are called for."

Pete Zimmer
Inn of the Anasazi

Basic Crêpes

¾	**cup flour**
1	**cup milk**
3	**eggs, lightly beaten**
1	**tablespoon sugar**
1	**tablespoon vegetable oil**
1	**lemon, zested** *(outer yellow part grated off)*
1	**orange, zested** *(outer orange part grated off)*

In a medium bowl place the flour and milk, and mix them together so that they are smooth.

Add the eggs, sugar, vegetable oil, lemon zest, and orange zest. Mix them together so that they are well blended.

Let the batter sit for 5 minutes.

Heat a 6" nonstick sauté pan on medium until it is hot.

Lightly wipe the inside of the pan with a paper towel dipped in oil *(or spray it with Pam)*.

Pour approximately ¼ cup of the batter into the pan. Tilt the pan in all directions so that the batter completely covers the bottom. Cook it for 30 to 60 seconds, or until the edges start to color. Turn the crêpe over and cook the other side for 10 seconds. Flip the crêpe out onto a towel and let it cool.

Repeat this process until all of the batter is used. Stack the crêpes and cover them with another towel *(the crêpes must be cool before they are stacked)*.

Note: The crêpes may be frozen.

makes 12 to 15 crêpes

"I make millions of crêpes, so I have the technique down pat. There is some skill required, but if you use a nonstick pan, you should get the hang of it pretty quickly. Put as little of the batter in the pan as possible.....just enough so that it thinly covers the bottom. Also, when you add the milk to the flour, just dump it in all at once. If you add it slowly, then the batter will be lumpy."

"I learned to cook as a little boy when I was in the Boy Scouts in Switzerland. When we camped out in the woods I always volunteered to make the meals. I cooked over an open fire and put everything in one pot, because my theory was the fewer pots you use, the fewer pots you wash. To this day my favorite way of cooking is to make a complete meal in one pan."

Ernie Bolleter
Inn at Loretto

Pizza Dough

"This is a fairly standard pizza dough recipe that even a non-baker can successfully make at home. The only different thing about this recipe is the addition of the honey, which gives the dough a nice, subtle flavor. I think that it's fun to make your own crust, and people always appreciate your effort. Actually, you can use any kind of a bread dough recipe that you have, and it will work just fine. One neat thing to do is to roll out the dough in cornmeal, instead of flour, so that you get some texture on the bottom of the crust."

1¼	cups warm water
1	tablespoon yeast
1	tablespoon honey
2	tablespoons olive oil
2	teaspoons salt
1½	cups semolina flour
3	cups white flour (or as needed)

In a small bowl place the warm water. Sprinkle in the yeast so that it dissolves.

In a medium large bowl place the dissolved yeast, honey, olive oil, and salt. Stir the ingredients together.

Add the semolina flour and stir it in.

Add 2 cups of the white flour and mix it in so that the dough forms a mass.

Place the dough on a flat, floured surface. Knead in enough of the remaining flour so that a stiff, smooth dough is formed.

Place the dough in an oiled bowl and cover it. Let the dough rise for 1 hour, or until it has doubled in size.

Divide the dough into 3 sections. Roll out each section of the dough into a very thin, 12" round.

makes 3 to 4 pizzas

"There is something primeval about baking your own bread.....it is satisfying on a very deep level. To work the dough with your hands and to have them understand what to do without having your mind involved is very therapeutic. I love the ways the loaves are shaped and the way they smell when they are baking in the oven."

Jane Stacey
Pranzo Italian Grill

Tart Crust

2¼ **cups flour**
½ **pound butter**
¼ **cup water** *(cold)*
1½ **tablespoons almonds, finely chopped**

In a medium bowl place the flour and butter. Cut them together so that pieces the size of hazelnuts are formed.

Add the water and mix it in so that a dough is formed. Divide the dough in half. Wrap each piece in plastic and chill them in the refrigerator.

Preheat the oven to 375°.

Butter and flour an 11" tart pan with a removable bottom. Roll out one of the chilled pieces of dough *(freeze the other one until you are ready to use it)*. Line the tart pan with the dough and then prick it with a fork. Sprinkle the chopped almonds on the bottom. Line the tart crust with foil and weight it down with dry beans *(or rice)*.

Bake the shell for 20 minutes, or until it is dry on the bottom. Remove the dry beans and foil.

makes 2 tart crusts

"I don't fuss around with the appearance of a plate as long as the food is hot and well prepared. Other than garnishing the dish with a sprig of fresh herb or parsley and wiping off the edges of the plate, I like to whisk the food out to the customer immediately. To me, food by itself looks pretty good, and doesn't need much done to its natural appearance."

"Food is best when it is served hot. Once I had a girlfriend who would take 60 minutes to finish a plate of food. I couldn't understand what she was doing. 'I'm savoring it', she would say. 'What do you mean you are savoring it?' I'd ask. 'The sauce is congealed and the potatoes are cold!' "

"Years ago I worked at an Italian restaurant, and I never had so much fun in my life. The cooks were just insane.....they would scream in your face one minute, and the next minute they would be slapping you on the back and buying you wine. All day long they would sing and laugh and argue and talk. I loved it!"

Wayne Gustafson
Julian's

Tart Shell

1¼ cups pastry flour
4 ounces unsalted butter *(cold)*, **cut into small pieces**
3 tablespoons sugar
2 tablespoons orange zest *(outer orange part grated off)*
⅛ teaspoon salt
1 egg, lightly beaten

In a food processor place all of the ingredients *(except for the egg)* and blend them so that fine granules are formed.

With the processor running, add the egg in a slow, steady stream. Blend the ingredients until the mixture holds together and begins to form a ball.

Form the dough into a disc. Wrap it up and chill it in the refrigerator.

Preheat the oven to 400°.

Roll the dough into a 13" circle and fit it into an 11" tart tin. Chill it in the refrigerator.

Adjust a rack so that it is in the lower third of the oven. Bake the shell on this rack for 4 minutes, or until it just begins to set. If there is any shrinkage, remove the pan from the oven and press the pastry back into the sides of the tin.

Bake the shell for 5 to 6 minutes more, or until the pastry is set and is beginning to color.

Remove the shell from the oven and let it cool.

makes 1 tart shell

"I have an Italian philosophy of cooking, which means that I work with whatever is fresh in the marketplace. Each part of Italy is dependent upon its regional production of food. What is readily available in the south might be prohibitively expensive in the north. Here in the United States we are very spoiled because we have access to almost any food product all year round."

"My background is in art as well as cooking, and when I first moved to Santa Fe I hoped I might find success as a painter. Eventually I opened this restaurant (my first one) and it has been an exciting, hair-raising experience. From day one I have had a local following, which continues to grow, and for this I am very grateful."

Ken Calascione
La Traviata

LP CALDWELL

Desserts

Blue Corn Chocolate Piñon Torte

½   cup sweet butter
18   ounces semi-sweet chocolate, broken up
2   cups piñon nuts *(pine nuts)*
½   cup blue cornmeal
10   egg yolks
1   cup sugar
1   tablespoon vanilla extract
1   cup whipped cream *(optional)*
1   cup fresh strawberries, stemmed, washed, and cut

Preheat the oven to 350°.

In a simmering double boiler place the butter and chocolate, and slowly melt them together *(stir them occasionally)*.

In a food processor place the piñon nuts and coarsely grind them.

In a medium bowl place the melted chocolate, ground piñon nuts, and blue cornmeal. Stir them together well.

In another medium bowl place the egg yolks, sugar, and vanilla extract. Beat the ingredients together, add them to the chocolate-nut mixture, and stir them in well.

In a greased and floured 9" cake pan place the batter. Bake the torte for 20 minutes.

Cut the torte into thin slices. Serve each one with a dollop of whipped cream and some strawberries.

serves 10 to 12

"When you melt the chocolate in a double boiler make sure that no water gets into it. Water and chocolate are mortal enemies. Trust me on this one.....if any water gets in the chocolate, then the recipe will be messed up."

"This dessert is rich and decadent, but the key is to serve it in tiny pieces. I would recommend making this for a nice dinner party, and then storing the leftovers in the refrigerator. It will last for a week, and anytime you get the need for a chocolate fix you can cut off a thin sliver. You will be so happy that you took the trouble to make it.....it's well worth the effort!"

"To come up with a recipe that is totally unique and original is almost impossible, because everything has been done before. Once a fellow chef and I came to this conclusion: If you put Julius Caesar's chariot driver in the cockpit of the Concord, he would have no idea of what to do. But, if you put him in a modern kitchen of today, he would make you a nice meal!"

Mark Hawrylak
The Evergreen

Margarita Pie

1½	cups pretzels, finely crushed
1⅓	cups sugar
½	cup butter, melted
1	lime, zested *(outer green part grated off)*
½	cup lime juice, freshly squeezed
1	14-ounce can sweetened condensed milk
2	tablespoons gold tequila
2	tablespoons triple sec
1	cup heavy cream, whipped
2	drops green food coloring *(optional)*
½	cup heavy cream, whipped
12	pretzels
12	mint leaves

In a medium bowl place the crushed pretzels, sugar, and melted butter. Mix the ingredients together well and press them into a 9" buttered pie pan. Chill the crust in the refrigerator for 1 hour.

In another medium bowl place the lime zest, lime juice, sweetened condensed milk, tequila, and triple sec. Mix the ingredients together.

Fold in the 1 cup of heavy cream, whipped, and the green food coloring. Pour the mixture into the pie crust. Freeze the pie for 4 hours.

Decorate the pie with the ½ cup of whipped cream, pretzels, and mint leaves.

serves 8 to 10

Natillas

4	egg yolks
¼	cup flour
1	cup milk
½	cup sugar
3	cups milk
½	teaspoon vanilla
⅛	teaspoon salt
4	egg whites, beaten into soft peaks
	cinnamon *(as needed)*

In a medium bowl place the egg yolks and flour. Mix them with an electric beater for 1 minute, or until a smooth paste is formed.

Add the 1 cup of milk and mix it in so that it is well incorporated.

In a medium saucepan place the sugar, the 3 cups of milk, vanilla, and salt. Heat the ingredients on medium heat for 2 to 3 minutes, or until the milk scalds.

Lower the heat to medium low. While stirring constantly, slowly add the egg yolk mixture.

Continue to stir the mixture for 5 to 8 minutes, or until it is thickened *(so that it will coat the back of a spoon)*. Remove the pan from the heat. Chill the custard in the refrigerator.

Add the beaten egg whites and fold them in.

Serve the custard in individual dessert bowls with the cinnamon sprinkled on top.

serves 6 to 8

"This is a type of custard, and it's very popular with traditional New Mexican families. You can make it with skim milk, but you will not get the same result. This is easy to make.....just follow the directions."

"I grew up in the Pennsylvania Dutch country where we had a Mennonite cook. She would show me how to do things in the kitchen and let me help prepare the food. I vividly remember going to her farm on many weekends, and having wonderful, fresh strawberry shortcake and warm milk from the cow. All of the farms were impeccably manicured and very pristine. The lines were stark and there were only two colors..... white and green."

Peter Raub
Santa Fe School of Cooking

Lime Sorbet with Champagne Syrup

Lime Sorbet

3   **limes, zested** *(outer green part grated off)* **and zest blanched**
1   **cup sugar, dissolved in 1 cup hot water**
1   **cup water**
⅓   **cup lime juice, freshly squeezed and strained**
1   **cup water**
      Champagne Syrup *(recipe follows)*
4   **cookies**

In a small saucepan place the lime zest and the sugar water mixture. Simmer the liquid for 10 minutes and then let it cool. Remove the lime zest and pat it dry with paper towels. Set the zest aside.

Add the first cup of water to the cooled syrup.

In an ice cream maker place the cooled syrup, lime juice, and the second 1 cup of water. Start the machine and mix the liquid so that it freezes. In each of 4 well chilled dessert bowls place small scoops of the sorbet. Spoon on the Champagne Syrup. Sprinkle on the lime zest. Serve the sorbet with a cookie.

serves 4

Champagne Syrup

½   **bottle champagne**
1   **cup corn syrup**
      honey *(to taste)*

In a medium saucepan place the champagne. Boil it for 30 minutes, or until it is reduced to ¼ cup.

Add the corn syrup and stir it in.

Add the honey and stir it in. Let the syrup cool.

Makes 1¼ cups

"My husband Wayne and I run the Galisteo Inn by ourselves, and it's a demanding, wonderful experience. We have acres of landscaped grounds, horses, an orchard, a swimming pool, and a duck pond. People like to stay here because they appreciate the authenticity of our 250-year-old building, and it's a nice alternative to the more commercialized Santa Fe."

Joanna Kaufman
Galisteo Inn

"When I first thought of making a champagne syrup I took a whole bottle of champagne, added sugar, and boiled it forever. It never thickened, not even when I put it in the freezer. Finally I thought of using corn syrup, and this saved the day. This is very, very sweet, so you don't want to use very much."

Tom Wright
Galisteo Inn

Chocolate Hazelnut Tart

2	**cups hazelnuts** *(filberts)*
1	**cup sugar**
3	**tablespoons orange zest** *(outer orange part grated off)*
¾	**cup unsalted butter** *(room temperature)*
2	**whole eggs**
3	**egg yolks**
1	**Tart Shell** *(recipe on page 301)*
½	**cup heavy cream**
4	**ounces bittersweet chocolate, broken**

Preheat the oven to 350°.

Spread the hazelnuts on a baking sheet and toast them for 15 minutes. Place the warm nuts in a pillow case and rub them so that the skins are removed. Remove the nuts *(no skins)* and let them cool.

Preheat the oven to 375°.

In a food processor place the nuts, sugar, and orange zest. Chop them so that they are finely ground, but not yet a paste.

In a medium bowl place the butter. Cream it with a mixer so that it is smooth.

With the mixer running on low speed add the nut mixture and blend it in.

One at a time, add the eggs and egg yolks. Blend them for 5 minutes, or until a creamy emulsion has been formed *(do not let the mixture aerate)*.

Pour the mixture into the Tart Shell and bake it for 15 to 20 minutes, or until it is puffed and golden.

In a small saucepan place the heavy cream and bring it to a boil.

In another small saucepan place the pieces of chocolate. Add the boiling cream and stir it so that the chocolate melts and a smooth cream is formed. Strain the sauce through a fine sieve. Let it cool so that it is of a spreadable consistency.

Spread the sauce on top of the tart.

serves 12

"I love hazelnuts, and that's why I developed this recipe. When I am in Italy I eat tons of their chocolate hazelnut ice cream. And, if I ever see a hazelnut cookie, I am always quick to try it."

"This dessert sounds very rich, but it tastes very light. You must remember that each person is served only a thin sliver, so the total amount of butter, cream, sugar, and chocolate consumed is minimal. It tastes almost like candy, and it will keep in the refrigerator for a long time."

"What do I like about cooking? The end result!"

Ken Calascione
La Traviata

Raspberry Pie

1½   cups vanilla wafers, crushed
½   cup toasted almonds, chopped
½   cup margarine, melted
½   cup light cream cheese
1   tablespoon raspberry purée *(see chef's comments on this page)*
2   teaspoons sugar
2   tablespoons heavy cream
½   teaspoon almond extract
1½   pints fresh raspberries
1   cup raspberry purée *(see chef's comments on this page)*
½   cup sugar
1¼   tablespoons cornstarch, mixed with ⅛ cup
     water *(no lumps)*
½   teaspoon almond extract
1   cup heavy cream, whipped *(optional)*

Preheat the oven to 400°.

In a medium bowl place the crushed vanilla wafers, chopped almonds, and melted margarine. Mix the ingredients together so that they are well combined. Press the mixture into a pie pan.

Bake the pie crust for 5 minutes.

In another medium bowl place the light cream cheese, the 1 tablespoon of raspberry purée, the 2 teaspoons of sugar, the 2 tablespoons of heavy cream, and the first ½ teaspoon of almond extract. Blend the ingredients together with an electric mixer until the mixture is smooth and creamy. Spread it in the bottom of the baked pie crust. Place the fresh raspberries on top.

In a medium saucepan place the 1 cup of raspberry purée. Bring it to a simmer on medium low heat. Add the ½ cup of sugar and stir it for 2 minutes, or until it is dissolved.

While stirring constantly, add the cornstarch mixture and cook the glaze for 5 minutes, or until it is thick and clear. Add the second ½ teaspoon of almond extract and stir it in.

Chill the glaze and then spread it on top of the fresh raspberries. Chill the pie for 2 hours before serving it.

Decorate the pie with the whipped cream.

serves 8

"Although this recipe may not qualify for what you call 'lite', it is a wonderful way to splurge if you have room for dessert. When we make the pie at the restaurant it is quite a bit richer than this version, which has been modified for publication in this book. It's a wonderful, beautiful looking pie, and you don't feel heavy when you eat it."

"For the raspberry purée use 20 ounces of frozen raspberries (defrosted). Push them through a fine sieve so that only the juice and pulp go through."

"When I was 12 years old my father got me a job washing dishes through a friend of his who owned a restaurant. I remember looking with awe at the cooks in the back of the kitchen and thinking, 'Boy, that really looks like fun!' Over the years I've worked in quite a few restaurants under a lot of different people, and I've enjoyed every minute. I get satisfaction in seeing that the kitchen runs smoothly night after night, and I enjoy making the customers happy."

Chris Arrison
Steaksmith

Lemon Tart

5	eggs
1	cup sugar
⅓	cup butter, melted
3	tablespoons heavy cream
1	cup lemon juice, freshly squeezed
5	lemons, zested *(outer yellow part grated off)*
1	11-inch Tart Crust *(recipe on page 300)*

Preheat the oven to 375°.

In a medium bowl place the eggs and sugar. Beat them together for 5 minutes, or until the sugar is dissolved.

Add the butter, heavy cream, lemon juice, and lemon zest. Mix the ingredients together.

Pour the filling into the Tart Crust. Bake the tart for 20 to 25 minutes, or until the filling is set.

serves 8 to 12

"We will never be a pretentious restaurant..... in fact, I have fired waitpeople for being pretentious. I don't require a lot of experience in my waitpeople, but I do want good manners and a willingness to ask questions. I always tell my new staff that the only mistake they can make is to assume that they know the answer when they don't. It's okay to ask the same question a hundred times, as long as they get it right and give the correct answer a hundred times."

"Wayne, the chef, approaches cooking the same way he approaches fly fishing. He doesn't just go out and fish while trying different things, hoping that one will work. Rather, he researches what the exact conditions are that day and what the trout are eating. With food, he knows what herbs cancel out other herbs in terms of flavors, and he knows exactly what he is doing. He is a thinking cook, and this quality combined with his intelligence, experience, and talent, make him one of the best in the business."

Lou Gustafson
Julian's

Campfire Cake

2	cups pecans, chopped
1	cup honey
½	cup sugar
½	cup butter
4	pears, peeled, cored, and sliced
4	cups flour
1	tablespoon ground ginger
¼	teaspoon allspice
¼	teaspoon cinnamon
¼	teaspoon black pepper
3	eggs
1¼	cups molasses
1½	cups dark brown sugar
½	cup butter, melted
¼	cup lemon juice, freshly squeezed

Preheat the oven to 350°.

In a medium saucepan place the pecans, honey, sugar, and butter. Heat the ingredients on medium high and cook them for 3 to 5 minutes, or until the mixture is thickened. Pour the glaze into a greased and floured 9" round cake pan. Arrange the pear slices on top.

In a medium bowl place the flour, ginger, allspice, cinnamon, and black pepper. Mix the ingredients together and set them aside.

In another medium bowl place the eggs, molasses, brown sugar, and melted butter. Mix the ingredients together with an electric beater until they are smooth.

Add the flour mixture and fold it in. Mix the batter for 1 minute. Add the lemon juice and mix it in for 3 minutes.

Pour the batter into the cake pan. Bake the cake for 20 to 30 minutes, or until a toothpick inserted comes out dry.

serves 8

"The name of this dish comes from the old days, when cowboys would be out on the trail. They would throw all of the ingredients into a cast iron skillet and cook the cake over their campfire. The recipe is very straightforward, with nothing tricky. You can eliminate the butter in the glaze if you want.....just add ¼ cup water instead."

"Cooking is an incredible art form because its variables are endless. Not only can you see the colors and textures, but food gives you aromas, flavors, sounds, and sustenance. Food also has the ability to evoke powerful emotions and memories. It is something that you can continue to appreciate anew, because each time you eat it and it is gone, you get to make it again."

Pete Zimmer
Inn of the Anasazi

Crêpes Americana

3   cups blueberries
½   cup sugar
1   tablespoon cornstarch mixed with 1 tablespoon cold water
3   cups raspberries, cleaned
½   cup powdered sugar
1   banana, peeled and sliced into ¼" rounds
1   kiwi, peeled and diced into ¼" pieces
1   cup strawberries, stems removed, and diced into ¼" pieces
½   cup blueberries, cleaned
½   cup blackberries, cleaned
½   cup raspberries, cleaned
1   papaya, peeled and seeds removed
1   mango, peeled and meat cut off from around pit
½   cup powdered sugar
1   ounce Myers Rum
12   crêpes *(recipe on page 298)*
4   dollops whipped cream *(optional)*, sweetened

In a small saucepan place the 3 cups of blueberries and the sugar, and mash them together. Simmer the ingredients together for 10 minutes, or until the blueberries fall apart. Add the cornstarch-water mixture and stir it in. Simmer the sauce for 1 minute, and then set it aside to cool.

In a food processor place the 3 cups of raspberries and the first ½ cup of powdered sugar, and purée them. Push the mixture through a fine sieve with a rubber spatula. Set the raspberry sauce aside.

In a medium bowl place the bananas, kiwi, strawberries, the ½ cup each of blueberries, blackberries, and raspberries. Gently mix the fruit together.

In a blender place the papaya, mango, the second ½ cup of powdered sugar, and the Myers rum. Purée the ingredients together. Add the purée to the mixed fruit and gently fold it in.

In the center of each crêpe place the fruit mixture. Roll the crêpe up and place it on a plate, seam side down. Serve 2 crêpes for each person. Pour the blueberry sauce along one side of the crêpes. Pour the raspberry sauce along the other side. Place a dollop of whipped cream on top.

serves 6

"This is a recipe that I came up with for the Fourth of July because it's red, white, and blue. The whipped cream is necessary only for the white color, so you can eliminate it or use a low-cal substitute. Once the crêpes are made, it's quite simple to make."

"Years ago I worked at a restaurant in Switzerland on Lake Geneva. About once a month a fellow chef and I would take a boat across the lake to France, where they had a casino. If one of us would get lucky and have a decent win, then we would treat the other one to dinner. We would go to one of the tiny little restaurants along the waterfront, and the owner would serve us whatever he had in the kitchen that evening. Usually we would be served 4 or 5 courses, and they were always fantastic. These days you would have to be a millionaire to eat like that!"

Ernie Bolleter
Inn at Loretto

Desserts

White Chocolate Mousse with Coconut Crusted Figs

White Chocolate Mousse

1   **egg**
1   **egg yolk**
2   **tablespoons rum**
2   **tablespoons crème de cacao**
1½   **gelatin sheets, softened in water**
6   **ounces white chocolate, melted**
1⅛   **cups whipping cream**
     Coconut Crusted Figs (recipe follows)

In the top of a simmering double boiler place the egg, egg yolk, rum, and crème de cacao. Whip the ingredients for 3 to 5 minutes, or until the eggs are fluffy. Add the gelatin and stir it in. Fold in the white chocolate. Set the mixture aside so that it cools to skin temperature (do not let it get firm).

In a medium bowl place the whipping cream and beat it for 3 to 5 minutes, or until stiff peaks are formed (do not overbeat it or it will turn to butter). Add the whipped cream to the chocolate mixture and fold it in. Chill the mousse in the refrigerator for at least 8 hours.

For each serving place a small scoop of the mousse on an individual dessert plate. Circle the mousse with the Coconut Crusted Figs.

serves 8

Coconut Crusted Figs

8   **figs, cut into rounds ⅛" thick**
2   **eggs, lightly beaten**
¾   **cup shredded coconut** (or as needed)
½   **cup butter**

Dip the figs in the eggs and then coat them with the coconut.

In a medium sauté pan place the butter and heat it on medium high until it is melted and hot. Add the coated fig slices and sauté them for 1 minute on each side. Drain them on paper towels.

"This is a very rich and delicious dessert. I thought about giving a recipe that just used fruit, but decided that it wouldn't be too interesting because anybody can go to the produce market, buy fresh fruit, cut it up, and serve it. This dessert is really something special, and only a small scoop is served to each person. Take tiny bites and savor each one. If you are really watching your diet, then maybe you will take only one bite..... but that bite will be heavenly!"

"To melt the chocolate you should put it in the top of a barely simmering double boiler. It should be melted very slowly and stirred occasionally. When I am making this I don't have much time to watch it, so I set it on a warm spot on my stove (not on a burner) and leave it there for about 1 hour."

"I really love to eat. If it were possible I would sit in a restaurant and eat solidly from noon to midnight every day of my life. I have to exercise and diet to control my weight. If I didn't I would turn into a barrel and you could roll me right down Burro Alley!"

Martin Lackner
The Palace Restaurant

Prickly Pear Mousse

⅓ **cup prickly pear fruit juice, freshly squeezed**
⅓ **cup sugar**
1¼ **teaspoons unflavored gelatin**
¼ **cup water**
2 **teaspoons dry sherry**
½ **lemon, zested** (outer yellow part grated off)
1½ **teaspoons lemon juice, freshly squeezed**
1 **egg white, beaten to soft peaks**
¼ **cup whipping cream, beaten to soft peaks**

In a medium saucepan place the prickly pear juice and the sugar. While stirring constantly, heat them on medium for 5 minutes, or until the sugar is dissolved.

In a small bowl place the gelatin and sprinkle on the water. Let the gelatin sit for 10 minutes and then add it to the prickly pear juice. While stirring constantly, heat the mixture for 1 minute, or until the gelatin is dissolved.

Remove the saucepan from the heat and let the liquid sit for 5 minutes. Add the dry sherry, lemon zest, and lemon juice.

Pour the liquid into a medium bowl. Place it in the refrigerator for 15 to 20 minutes, or until the mixture is thickened, but not set (the consistency should be like honey, or room temperature jelly).

Remove the mixture from the refrigerator and beat it until it is frothy. Gently fold in the beaten egg white and whipped cream.

Place the mousse in the refrigerator and let it chill for 1 hour, or until it is set.

serves 4

"Prickly pears are the fruit of the paddle cactus plant. They have a very delicious, sweet, almost buttery flavor.....like the combination of strawberries and bananas. You should be able to find them in the Southwest, as well as in the larger cities. They can be specially ordered if necessary, and sometimes you can find the juice in a concentrate form. Their flavor is so exquisitely subtle that it is well worth the effort to seek them out. If you can't get them, then substitute pomegranate juice."

"Squeeze the fruit in a juicer to get the juice out. However, be SURE to wear gloves when doing so, because the cactus has very tiny stickers that will get into your skin, and they are impossible to get out!"

"The only tricky part is to make sure that the gelatin is set to the right consistency before the other ingredients are added. Don't let it get sticky and hard. Check it every several minutes."

Rocky Packard
Francisco's

Citrus Compote

2	cups sugar
2	cups water
½	tablespoon vanilla extract
1	lemon, zested *(outer yellow part grated off)*
1	orange, zested *(outer orange part grated off)*
4	oranges, peeled, seeds and membranes removed *(see chef's comments on this page)*, and sectioned
4	lemons, peeled, seeds and membranes removed, and sectioned
4	limes, peeled, seeds and membranes removed, and sectioned
2	grapefruit, peeled, seeds and membranes removed, and sectioned
2	cups melon balls

In a medium saucepan place the sugar, water, vanilla extract, lemon zest, and orange zest. Bring the ingredients to a boil. Strain the zest from the syrup. Place the syrup in the freezer so that it is ice cold.

Add the citrus segments to the cold syrup. Chill the mixture in the refrigerator for 4 to 12 hours.

Serve the compote over the melon balls.

serves 4

Lemon-Hazelnut Biscotti

½   cup sweet butter, room temperature
¾   cup sugar
2   eggs
2   tablespoons Marsala wine
2   tablespoons lemon zest *(outer yellow part grated off)*
2¼   cups flour
¼   teaspoon salt
1½   teaspoons baking powder
¾   cup hazelnuts, chopped
1   teaspoon anise seeds

Preheat the oven to 350°.

In a medium large mixing bowl place the sweet butter and sugar. Cream them together with an electric mixer *(use the paddle attachment)* for 2 minutes, or until the mixture is light and fluffy.

Add the eggs, Marsala, and lemon zest. Mix the ingredients together for 1 minute, or until they are combined.

In another medium bowl place the flour, salt, baking powder, hazelnuts, and anise seeds. Mix the ingredients together. Add them to the butter-egg mixture and mix them on slow speed until they are well combined.

Turn the dough out onto a lightly floured work surface. Form the dough into sausage-like rolls that are 2" in diameter and the length of a baking sheet.

Place the rolled dough pieces on a greased flat sheet and bake them for 15 to 18 minutes, or until they are set and the edges are slightly browned. Remove the rolled pieces from the oven and let them cool for 10 minutes.

Slice the baked dough diagonally into ½" thick pieces. Place the cut pieces back onto the baking sheet and return them to the oven. Bake them for 5 minutes, or until they are golden brown. Store the cookies in an airtight container *(they will keep for weeks)*.

makes approximately 2 dozen cookies

"Biscotti means cookie, and this is a variation of a very traditional Italian recipe. I believe that it came into being because it was a very inexpensive way of making a lot of cookies. You will love this recipe because it is so forgiving.....you can make lots of mistakes, and the cookies will still come out good."

"There is creativity in baking, which many people may not be aware of. The essence of baking is manipulating the same ingredients over and over again, in thousands of different ways.....butter, sugar, eggs, flour. Once you gain the confidence in using these ingredients and you have the knowledge of how they work together, then you are free.....you can do whatever you want!"

"I used to teach baking in New York and there were some people who just couldn't get the hang of it, and others who took to it like a duck takes to water. There is a definite talent that you are born with."

Jane Stacey
Pranzo Italian Grill

Flan

1	cup sugar
1	cup water
4	whole eggs
3	egg yolks
2	cups milk
1	cup half and half
2	tablespoons lemon rind, coarsely cut
¼	cup sugar
1	sprig fresh rosemary
1½	teaspoons vanilla

In a medium saucepan place the 1 cup of sugar and water. Cook them on medium low heat for 10 to 15 minutes, or until the sugar turns brown and there are large bubbles (or a candy thermometer reaches 275°). Pour the caramelized sugar in the bottom of 6 individual ramekins.

Preheat the oven to 350°.

In a medium bowl place the eggs and egg yolks, and beat them together.

In another medium saucepan place the milk, half and half, lemon rind, the ¼ cup of sugar, rosemary, and vanilla. Heat the ingredients so that the milk scalds.

Strain ¼ of the hot milk into the bowl of eggs and whisk it in. While constantly whisking, very slowly strain in the rest of the hot milk. Pour the mixture into the ramekins.

Place the ramekins in a deep baking pan that is half filled with water (the water should go at least half way up the cups). Bake the flan for 1 hour, or until a toothpick inserted into the center comes out dry. Let the flan cool, and then chill it in the refrigerator.

Cut around the edge of each dish of flan with a small knife. Place a small plate on top of each dish and turn it upside down. Shake the flan out with a quick, but firm, downward motion. Lift the dish from the plate. Let the sugar syrup pour on top of the flan.

serves 6

"Flan is a baked custard, and it is what I call the international kids' treat. Every country in the world has its own version, and each mother has her own special way of making it. This recipe is a little different because it has the extra flavorings of the lemon rind and rosemary. Flan purists may object, because traditionally vanilla is the only flavoring used. But I like the subtle quality these 2 ingredients give it, and I think that they elevate it from a kid's dessert to an adult's dessert."

"Some experience might be necessary in making the flan correctly. It would be ideal if you could watch an experienced person make it first. Caramelizing the sugar is especially tricky, and you don't want to burn yourself. Just one small drop of the hot sugar will cause a deep burn that goes right to the bone. But if you've never tried making this, don't worry. The recipe is clearly written, and so you probably will do just fine."

Ned Laventall
El Farol

Lemon Chiffon Pie

¾	ounce gelatin
1	cup lemon juice, freshly squeezed
½	cup water
6	egg yolks
6	tablespoons sugar
6	egg whites
6	tablespoons sugar
2	9-inch pre-baked pie shells
2	lemons, thinly sliced

In a small saucepan place the gelatin, lemon juice, and water. Let the gelatin soften. Gently heat the mixture for 2 minutes, or until the gelatin is dissolved. Remove the pan from the heat and place it in a water bath so that the mixture cools.

In a medium bowl place the egg yolks and the first 6 tablespoons of sugar. Whip them for 5 minutes, or until the yolks are pale yellow. Add the cooled lemon juice mixture and mix it in.

In another medium bowl place the egg whites *(see chef's comments on this page)*. Beat them for 7 to 8 minutes, or until they form peaks. Slowly add the second 6 tablespoons of sugar, and gently beat them in.

Gently fold the egg yolk mixture into the egg white mixture so that it is incorporated.

Pour the mixture into the pie shells and then chill them in the refrigerator. Place the lemon slices on top.

makes 2 pies

"This recipe comes from a restaurant in New York where it was called a 'spa' dessert. Even though it has some calories, it is very light and refreshing."

"When you whip the egg whites there are several things to remember. First, you should start with a very clean bowl made of either stainless steel or glass. The egg whites should also be very clean, with no specks of yolk in them. Start the mixer on a low speed, and then gradually go faster. When the eggs start to look like a very soft meringue, you slowly add the sugar. If you add the sugar too fast, then the egg whites will collapse, unless you are very lucky. You can use a sugar substitute if you want, but don't use too much because the flavor is very concentrated."

"I prefer being a pastry chef as opposed to doing other kinds of cooking. I enjoy the chemistry of it, and I find it to be very creative within the parameters of the ingredients that are used."

Frank Ferrara
Casa Sena

Raspberry Whip

½	**ounce gelatin**
¼	**cup raspberry purée** *(see chef's comments on this page)*
2	**egg yolks**
1	**teaspoon sugar**
2	**egg whites**

In a small saucepan place the gelatin and raspberry purée. Stir the mixture over low heat for 2 minutes, or until the gelatin is dissolved. Remove the pan from the heat and place it in an ice bath so that the mixture cools.

In a small bowl place the egg yolks and sugar. Beat them together for 5 minutes, or until the yolks are pale.

In a medium bowl place the cooled raspberry purée. While beating constantly, slowly add the egg yolk mixture and blend it in.

In another small bowl place the egg whites and beat them for 7 to 8 minutes, or until stiff peaks are formed. Slowly add *(in small amounts at a time)* the egg whites to the egg yolk mixture, and blend them in.

Pipe the Raspberry Whip into dessert glasses. Chill the dessert in the refrigerator.

serves 4

"For the raspberry purée you take fresh raspberries, put them in a blender, purée them, and then strain them through a fine sieve."

"To me, this is very simple to make, and as you can see by the ingredients, it is very light. You don't have to pipe it into the dessert glasses, although this looks the nicest. You can just spoon it or pour it in."

"Because I get to work around 3:30 in the morning I like to think of myself as part vampire in disguise.....I catch a few daylight rays but they don't destroy me! Actually, I love to get to work that early when no one else is around. The solitude is really nice, and I get a lot of work done because I can use all 4 stoves and ovens at once."

"When I bake I do everything from scratch and I take no short cuts. And, when possible, I like to do some fine finish work on my product. You can make desserts look exquisitely beautiful..... much more so than in other kinds of cooking."

Frank Ferrara
Casa Sena

Guiltless Chocolate Cake with Orange Liqueur Icing

Guiltless Chocolate Cake

1	cup flour
⅓	cup cocoa powder
1	teaspoon baking soda
1	teaspoon baking powder
6	large egg whites
1⅓	cups brown sugar, packed
1	cup nonfat vanilla yogurt
1	teaspoon vanilla extract
1	tablespoon hazelnut liqueur
	Orange Liqueur Icing *(recipe follows)*

Preheat the oven to 350°.

In a medium bowl place the flour, cocoa powder, baking soda, and baking powder. Mix the ingredients together and set them aside.

In another medium bowl place the egg whites, brown sugar, vanilla yogurt, vanilla extract, and hazelnut liqueur. Beat them for 2 minutes, or until they are well blended.

Fold the flour mixture into the egg white mixture.

Pour the batter into an oiled and floured 8" springform pan. Bake the cake for 25 to 30 minutes, or until the center is slightly firm to the touch.

Let the cake cool to room temperature. Spread on the Orange Liqueur Icing.

serves 8

Orange Liqueur Icing

3	egg whites
¾	cup sugar
⅛	teaspoon salt
3	tablespoons water
1	teaspoon orange liqueur

(continued on next page)

"My whole family is very concerned about not consuming fat (although to look at me you wouldn't believe it!), and this is a recipe that my sister gave me. I tasted the cake and fell in love with it. It's wonderful because it is decadent, but guiltless. There are hardly any calories and there is no fat to speak of. If you have a loved one who has to be very careful with their diet, this is something that you can serve them and feel good about.....and they will love it. The recipe is straightforward and I don't think that it is possible to mess it up. The cake will be moist. The center should be pretty level, with not much of a dip, and when you shake it there should be a little jiggle."

"My parents were excellent cooks, and our dinners were real family events. After eating, we would stay at the dinner table for hours, talking about politics and all sorts of things. As a family we decided that everyone would be responsible for preparing the evening meal. I was given a specific job, like to make the salad, and I got to invent my own dressing. So at an early age I became familiar with being creative in cooking."

Robert Goodfriend
ek mas

In a small bowl place the egg whites, sugar, salt, and water. Mix the ingredients together well.

Place the mixture in the top of a simmering double boiler and beat it for 3 to 4 minutes, or until it is somewhat stiff, but spreadable (like honey).

Add the orange liqueur and mix it in.

covers 1 cake

Khir Pudding

4	**quarts milk**
1	**cup basmati rice, rinsed**
7	**cardamom pods, shells removed and seeds ground**
½	**cup sugar**
1	**teaspoon rosewater**
7	**saffron hairs**
1	**tablespoon water**
¼	**cup pistachios, shelled and ground**

In a large saucepan place the milk. While stirring constantly, gently boil the milk for 20 minutes (do not let it froth and bubble up).

While stirring constantly, slowly add the rice. Continue to stir and cook the rice for 15 to 20 minutes, or until it is done.

Reduce the heat to low. Add the ground cardamom seeds and sugar, and stir them in. Cook the ingredients for 1½ hours (stir them occasionally). Add the rosewater and stir it in.

In a tiny bowl place the saffron and water. Let them sit for 10 minutes, or until the water is colored.

Place the pudding in individual serving bowls. Sprinkle on the saffron water. Garnish each serving with the ground pistachios.

serves 4 to 6

"Several years ago my father had triple bypass surgery. That made me really think about how I could make good, interesting, full flavored dishes, but not have them kill people. So I started getting away from my classical French background, and looked to other cuisines for ideas."

"I find cooking to be a truly enjoyable experience. I cook on my days off, and when I go out of town I always take my knives with me."

Robert Goodfriend
ek mas

"This is one of the most popular East Indian desserts that is served on holidays and special occasions. It is a rice pudding that has a very heavy, liquid consistency. There is a certain knack in the stirring and cooking of the rice, but if you follow the recipe you should do okay. Don't let the milk foam up and boil over, and don't let the rice stick to the bottom of the pan."

Baldev Singh
India Palace

Fresh Blueberry Kanten

4	cups fresh blueberries, rinsed, sorted, and stems removed
2½	cups apple juice
1½	tablespoons agar agar flakes
2	tablespoons honey

In a small saucepan place ½ cup of the blueberries, the apple juice, and the agar agar flakes. Over high heat bring the ingredients to a boil. Reduce the heat to low and let the mixture simmer for 10 minutes *(stir the mixture occasionally)*.

Remove the pan from the heat and strain the mixture through a fine sieve. Let the juice sit for 5 minutes.

In each of 6 dessert glasses place the remaining blueberries. Pour the juice over the berries, making sure that all of the fruit is covered. Chill the kanten before serving it.

serves 6

"It is difficult to explain what this dessert is like. I think that the most accurate description is to call it a natural fruit jello. It's very fresh and light, with a wonderful blueberry flavor."

"Kanten is another name for agar agar, which is a sea vegetable that is used as a thickening agent. It can be found at natural food stores."

"When people come to my restaurant I want them to be treated graciously, to enjoy a delicious, sensual meal, and to feel happy when they leave."

Lynn Walters
The Natural Cafe

Lime Mousse

1	egg yolk *(optional)*
5	egg whites
½	cup sugar
1	cup lime juice, freshly squeezed
4	cookies

In the top of a simmering double boiler place all of the ingredients *(except for the cookies)*. Whisk and cook them for 4 to 5 minutes, or until they bind together and thicken.

In each of 4 champagne flutes place the mousse. Chill them in the refrigerator. Garnish the dessert with a cookie.

serves 4

"This is a very creative way of making a mousse that is extremely light and healthy. The egg yolk is optional, but it definitely adds a richness."

Karen Woods
Rancho Encantado

Almond Cookies

¾ cup flour
½ cup sugar
6 egg whites
¼ cup milk
¼ teaspoon almond extract

Preheat the oven to 350°.

In a medium bowl place the flour and sugar, and mix them together.

One at a time add the egg whites and mix them in so that they are well incorporated. Add the milk and almond extract, and mix them in.

Place the batter in a pastry bag with a #4 round tip. Onto an oiled cookie sheet squeeze out small amounts of the batter *(the size of a quarter)*. Bake the cookies for 6 to 7 minutes, or until they are lightly brown.

makes approximately 15 cookies

Fried Bananas with Honey and Anise

3 tablespoons sweet butter
4 large bananas, peeled and cut in half lengthwise
⅓ cup honey
1 teaspoon ground anise

In a large sauté pan place the sweet butter and heat it on medium until it is melted and hot. Add the bananas *(flat side down)* and sauté them for 3 to 5 minutes, or until they are golden brown.

Flip the bananas over. Drizzle on the honey and sprinkle on the anise.

serves 4

Orange Chiffon Cake

1	cup cake flour
½	cup sugar
1½	teaspoons baking soda
¼	teaspoon salt
2	egg yolks, room temperature
1	tablespoon orange zest *(outer orange part grated off)*
⅓	cup orange juice, freshly squeezed and strained
2	tablespoons vegetable oil
4	egg whites
¼	teaspoon cream of tartar
1	orange, very thinly sliced and seeds removed

Preheat the oven to 325°.

Sift the flour, sugar, baking soda, and salt together into a medium mixing bowl.

Make a well in the center. To the well add the egg yolks, orange zest, orange juice, and vegetable oil. Mix the ingredients on slow speed for 7 to 8 minutes, or until the ingredients are combined.

In a medium small mixing bowl place the egg whites and cream of tartar. With clean beaters, mix them for 8 to 10 minutes, or until the whites are stiff. Using a rubber spatula, gently fold the egg whites into the batter, ⅓ at a time, so that they are just incorporated.

Pour the batter in a 9" greased and floured tube pan. Bake the cake for 50 minutes, or until a toothpick inserted comes out dry. Remove the pan from the oven, and invert it immediately *(see chef's comments on this page)*. Let the cake cool completely.

Remove the cake and let it sit overnight. Decorate it with the orange slices.

serves 12

"This is what is called a 'spa' recipe from Gurney's Inn in Long Island, New York. The dietician there determined that each slice contains 90 calories, and there is hardly any fat. Gurney's Inn is an international health spa where all sorts of movie stars and big shots stay. When I was working there the rooms (food not included) were $400 a day, and at today's prices who knows what they cost now!"

"When you add the beaten egg whites to the batter, do not overmix them. Just fold them in so that the whites disappear.....otherwise, the cake will fall."

"After you take the cake out of the oven you should immediately turn it upside down on a flat surface. If the cake pan does not have a rim to prevent the top of the cake from touching the surface, then place the center of the tube over the neck of a glass bottle (like a wine bottle)."

"You can dust the cake with some powdered sugar before you add the orange slices. Another nice decorative idea is to use mandarin orange segments."

Frank Ferrara
Casa Sena

Grapefruit and Pink Champagne Sorbet

½   **cup sugar**
½   **cup water**
1   **grapefruit, zested** (outer yellow part grated off) **and zest blanched 1 minute**
1   **cup ruby grapefruit juice, freshly squeezed and strained**
1   **cup pink champagne, simmered until it is reduced to ½ cup honey** (to taste)
4   **cookies**

In a small saucepan place the sugar, water, and grapefruit zest. Simmer the ingredients for 10 minutes and then store them in the refrigerator overnight. Remove the grapefruit zest from the syrup and dry it with paper towels. Set the zest aside.

Place the grapefruit juice and the reduced pink champagne in an ice cream maker. Squirt in the honey to taste. Start the machine and mix the liquid so that it freezes.

In each of 4 well chilled individual dessert bowls place 3 small scoops of the sorbet. Place 1 scoop on top. Sprinkle on the grapefruit zest. Add a cookie to the dish.

serves 4

Sopa

1½	cups sugar
3⅓	cups water
½	cup raisins, covered with sweet wine and soaked
3	tablespoons butter
1½	teaspoons vanilla
12	slices day-old whole wheat bread, torn into bite size pieces and toasted
½	cup pine nuts
½	cup Monterey Jack cheese, grated
8	small scoops frozen yogurt (optional)

In a heavy, medium saucepan place the sugar and heat it on medium. Whisk the sugar for 5 minutes, or until it melts and turns a light caramel color.

Carefully add the water and heat it until it is hot.

Reduce the heat to low. Add the raisins (and any excess sweet wine), butter, and vanilla. Stir the mixture until the butter is melted.

Preheat the oven to 350°.

In a medium bowl place the whole wheat bread and pine nuts. Add the hot syrup mixture and stir it in well. Let the bread sit for 20 minutes, or until it is saturated with the syrup.

Place the soaked bread mixture in a buttered baking dish. Sprinkle the cheese on top. Bake the dessert for 30 minutes, or until it is set. Serve the sopa with a scoop of the frozen yogurt.

serves 8

"This is an old, traditional dessert that is very rich and delicious. It is not low-calorie, so the key is to take just a small amount when you eat it. Sopa means soup in Spanish, and the name comes from the bread floating in the caramel syrup. I have made this recipe less soupy, so it is more firm. It's a great way to use up your stale bread."

"The caramelizing of the sugar takes some care. Be careful when you add the water, because the hot syrup will bubble and splatter. It might solidify, but it will liquify as it reheats."

Peter Raub
Santa Fe School of Cooking

Strawberries and Figs

1	12-ounce package frozen strawberries, thawed
½	cup super-refined sugar
12	fresh imported figs, washed and cut in half
4	dollops whipped cream *(optional)*
4	sprigs fresh mint

In a food processor place the strawberries and sugar, and purée them.

On each of 4 individual dessert plates place 6 fig halves *(open side up)*. Pour the strawberry purée on top. Add a dollop of whipped cream. Place a sprig of mint on top.

serves 4

"I don't know why, but men absolutely love this dessert! It must be the figs, which are a work of art in themselves. Be sure that the figs are fresh. They are expensive, but I think that they are well worth the money."

Sylvia Johnson
Celebrations

Supplemental Information

Listed below are sources that provide mail order sales of Southwestern ingredients. Please call them for a free catalogue.

Coyote Cafe General Store
132 W. Water St., 1st Floor
Santa Fe, NM 87501
(505) 982-2454

Santa Fe Emporium
104 W. San Francisco
Santa Fe, NM 87501
(505) 984-1966

The Chile Shop
109 E. Water St.
Santa Fe, NM 87501
(505) 983-6080

Index

330

COOKBOOK ORDER FORMS

Please send me the book(s) which I have indicated below. For shipping charges I am enclosing $2.75 for the first book, and $1.50 for each additional book.

Quantity	Book Title	Price	Total
_____	Santa Fe Lite & Spicy Recipe	$15.95	_____
_____	* Santa Fe Recipe *(softbound)*	$13.95	_____
_____	** Taos Recipe *(softbound)*	$12.95	_____
_____	*** Southern California Beach Recipe *(hardbound)*	$17.95	_____

☐ Check here if you would like the book(s) autographed by the author.

Shipping Total: _____

TOTAL AMOUNT ENCLOSED: _____

Ship to: _____

Address: _____

City: _____

State: _____ Zip: _____

Make check or money order payable to **Tierra Publications**. Send it to:

Tierra Publications
2801 Rodeo Road, Suite B-612
Santa Fe, New Mexico 87505
(505) 983-6300

(MasterCard and Visa phone orders accepted)

Please send me the book(s) which I have indicated below. For shipping charges I am enclosing $2.75 for the first book, and $1.50 for each additional book.

Quantity	Book Title	Price	Total
_____	Santa Fe Lite & Spicy Recipe	$15.95	_____
_____	* Santa Fe Recipe *(softbound)*	$13.95	_____
_____	** Taos Recipe *(softbound)*	$12.95	_____
_____	*** Southern California Beach Recipe *(hardbound)*	$17.95	_____

☐ Check here if you would like the book(s) autographed by the author.

Shipping Total: _____

TOTAL AMOUNT ENCLOSED: _____

Ship to: _____

Address: _____

City: _____

State: _____ Zip: _____

Make check or money order payable to **Tierra Publications**. Send it to:

Tierra Publications
2801 Rodeo Road, Suite B-612
Santa Fe, New Mexico 87505
(505) 983-6300

(MasterCard and Visa phone orders accepted)

---

* **Santa Fe Recipe** *"A Cookbook of Recipes from Favorite Local Restaurants"* • 300 recipes • 305 pages

** **Taos Recipe** *"A Cookbook of Recipes from Restaurants in Taos, New Mexico"* • 170 recipes • 177 pages

*** **Southern California Beach Recipe** *"Recipes from Favorite Coastal Restaurants"* • 335 recipes • 352 pages

Notes